POLICING

YOUR HEALTH

POLICING YOUR HEALTH

A common sense guide to healthier living for all in the police service

Stewart Calligan &
Allan Charlesworth (eds)

Policing Your Health

This book is not a substitute for medical diagnosis and the reader should always consult a doctor for the specific diagnosis of a personal health matter.

Reference to a particular gender in this book
is not intended to show bias or discrimination.

First edition 1999
The New Police Bookshop

ISBN: 0 9533058 8 0

The New Police Bookshop
East Yorkshire, England, UK
(Law Authentication Work)
PO Box 124, GOOLE
DN14 7FH

The New Police Bookshop
Surrey, England, UK
(Benson Publications)

Cover illustration by Rich King
Text illustrations by Rich King, Mairead Amos
and contributing authors
Cover reproduction by Rainbow Reproductions
London E14 7EQ
Printed and bound in Great Britain by
The Cromwell Press, Trowbridge, Wiltshire
Distributed by The New Police Bookshop (East Yorkshire)

To order
Please write with cheques for (UK)£10 or (USA)$20 per book
(incl p&p) made payable to The New Police Bookshop
and send to: The New Police Bookshop (E Yorks)
PO Box 124, GOOLE DN14 7FH

Contents

6. Controlling over-reaction....................79

*Allergies - identification, prevention and
treatment*

PART THREE: OCCUPATIONAL AND OPERATIONAL HAZARDS

Editors / co-authors

Allan Charlesworth was the Deputy Chief Constable of West Yorkshire Police responsible for all personnel matters including Occupational Health. He is now the Chief Executive of the Institute of Trading Standards UK. Allan has two sons who are healthcare professionals and he has many contacts in the health sphere.

Stewart Calligan (LLB(Hons)) was in charge of Personnel and Training in Humberside Police. He has written manuals and books on police-related subjects for 20 years. Stewart is living proof that there is life beyond retirement if you look after your body.

Between them they have called upon a dentist, a podiatrist, a psychologist, doctors and surgeons to compile a book which will be invaluable as an aid to those who care about their health in an increasingly stressful profession and a world of growing complexity.

They hope the manual will help to address the high cost in suffering, time and money that police illness costs families, friends and taxpayers every day. They are greatly indebted to the following contributors, without whom the book would not have been possible.

Contributors

Dr Bruce Charlesworth MBChB

Peter Charlesworth BSc(Hons), MCOpton

Dr Douglas Duckworth BSc, MPhil, PhD, CPsychol, AFBPsS

Dr Chris Shinn MBChB, BSc(Hons)

Wendy Smith BSc(Hons), SRCh, MChS

Jane Temple BChD

Acknowledgments

Mention must also be made of the sterling work undertake by Greta Charlesworth and Christine Calligan in the research, computing and administration departments, who burned the midnight oil in great quantities to meet impossible deadlines.

Foreword

Specifically designed for all those who work in the police environment, this book is the first of its kind. Although written from a British perspective, it has been designed to assist with the health of police colleagues in the United States of America and throughout the world. Research contained in the book is generally British-based, but has reflected all the important developments world-wide. New editions will be prepared to keep pace with the rapid advances in medical science.

Post second world war headlines in police journals have included:

'Average of seven years on police pension'

'Officers vulnerable to heart attacks'

'Arthritis and Rheumatism problems growing'

'Cancer kills retired officers'

Data available from the United Kingdom Office of Population Censuses and Surveys suggests that police officers suffer among the highest rates of heart disease compared with other occupational groups. Interestingly this is despite being currently below average for cigarette smoking. International research indicates that police officers have higher risks for peptic ulcers, oesophageal cancer and cancer of the lower bowel, and also much higher rates of suicide in comparison to other municipal workers. All of this points to a high risk occupation which requires good health management.

What should we do to prevent illness? The simple answer is to take positive preventative steps to eliminate the causes, both in and out of work. The ways to achieve this are dealt with in the ensuing pages. It is hoped that the new Millennium will herald a more enlightened approach to healthcare and that old attitudes of machoism, invulnerability, and disregard of personal risk will disappear.

My own experience tells me that we can improve greatly on the post war period of police health. Inadequacies of clothing, transport and equipment have all been addressed. And though the demands of duty around-the-clock in all weathers continue to take their toll, improvements in working patterns, healthier eating and exercise facilities have all taken place. There have been dramatic advancements in our knowledge of occupational health issues in recent years and much more effort put into determining how to stop poor health developing in the first place.

The complex facets of a proactive, preventative approach towards maintaining a healthy lifestyle have been simplified in this book. Whether you are a front line officer exposed to the risk of injury, a member of a specialist team concerned about contact with body fluids, a support worker worried about the effects of using VDUs, or a shift worker wishing to know more about how to counteract the debilitating effects of irregular sleep patterns, this manual is for you.

I commend it to you as a common sense approach to living healthier - and longer.

Good health!

Chris Shinn (MBChB BSc(Hons))
November 1998
Wakefield, West Yorkshire, England

Dr Shinn is the Force Medical Officer with West Yorkshire Police and manages the WYP Occupational Health Unit. He has been at the leading edge of OHU developments for over a decade and lectures widely to police audiences on the topic.

Introduction

Putting health in perspective

The main aim of this book is to promote a healthy lifestyle for all police employees. The contributors draw upon up-to-date research and techniques necessary to build and maintain good practice, bearing in mind the special demands and risks particular to the police service.

Background

Historically the police service has had a poor health record. Shift work - giving rise to irregular eating and sleeping patterns - and exposure to the inclement climate - has had a lot to answer for.

What may not be remembered is that prior to the upsurge in the use of vehicles for patrol work during the sixties, there were very few cars in the police service other than a sprinkling of traffic patrol cars. Most policing was done on foot, in all weathers, based on the shift pattern of 0600-1400, 1400-2200 and 2200-0600 hours. But at that time there was no guarantee of straight eight-hour shifts. Many staff had to endure the further pressures of splitting their working day to cover peak periods of activity or extending their shifts as there was little protection for the constables from management whims. This also put pressures on the officers' families. Officers retiring after 25 years of shift working had poor life expectancy beyond their retirement.

One 'benefit' of the pre-1980s system was that many officers were given less physically demanding tasks as they neared retirement. These ranged from telephone work, gaoler, control room, enquiry office, property store, court usher, to other 'inside' nine-to-five jobs. In this way those who could not have continued to undertake gruelling beat duties could continue until they completed their 25 years' pensionable service.

Policing today

It is generally accepted that policing in today's society is one of the most stressful of occupations, both physically and mentally, which can be followed. A number of factors combine to make this so.

The 'light duty' nine-to-five jobs have either been removed to the private sector or have been civilianised over the years. Such jobs are no longer available for the 'burnt out' or injured officer and as a result there has been a rise in ill-health premature retirements.

At the same time we have witnessed an erosion in the respect shown for law and order with increasing attacks on police officers and an upsurge in general lawlessness demanding a more physical style of policing. The drug abuse of the latter part of the 20th century has also contributed to the escalating violence and heightened the requirement for physically fit police officers - a situation which will no doubt continue into the 21st century.

However, the fitness which was a by-product of participating in police sport has also largely disappeared. The previous positive encouragement to take part in sport by granting time-off has been removed in the interests of productivity as police forces have had to contend with growing public demands and in real terms fewer resources. A conscious individual effort, therefore, is now required to keep fit enough to perform the arduous task of policing.

Stress has become more widely recognised in the police service during the last decade. It can be attributed to the slow down in recruiting, the increased work load per officer, the increasing complexities of policing systems and the constant changing and introduction of law and procedures, stress has taken its toll on police health.

Emotionally raw officers who have little if any knowledge and experience of hardship, death, injury and disease witnessed during the world wars have had to cope with large scale human tragedies giving rise to post traumatic stress disorder, the effects of which have at least now become recognised.

Your good health

There can be no dispute that policing is an inherently risky occupation. Improvements have and are being made - as evidenced by the extension to the police service of the Health and Safety at Work legislation. However, as far as general health is concerned, there is a tendency to react too late.

An objective of this book is to concentrate on up-to-date practices in our modern lifestyle which contribute to physical and mental fitness, and to be aware of common problems which may arise due to the nature of the job.

We each have a responsibility to ourselves and our family to keep in good shape. We owe it to our children or other dependents to give the same advice and encouragement to them.

The adoption of just some of the advice mentioned in this book will certainly influence your mental and physical well-being. In it you have at your fingertips state-of-the-art medical opinion and advice about looking after one of your most valuable assets in the world - your body. We hope that the process will lead you towards happier and longer lives.

Good health!

Keith Hellawell
QPM, LLB, MSc
Chief Constable (retired)
Now the United Kingdom
Anti-drugs Co-ordinator

July 1999

PART ONE

OVERVIEW

1. From hiring to retiring

*Medical screening &
occupational health*

1. From hiring to retiring

Medical screening & occupational health

The role of medical practitioners in the police service may appear to many to be restricted to taking blood from drunk drivers, attending murder scenes, and perhaps examining potential recruits to or retirees from the service.

In reality, the varied nature of policing requires its medical staff to have a broad understanding of the many specialities within the service and the issues each carry beyond the work situation. They must have an interest in people, psychology, social factors, organisations, and other paramedical subjects.

There must be a relationship of trust, in which the health professionals balance the needs of the individual with the police services' aim for a healthy workforce.

Fitness for policing

Factors which influence an individual's performance can be broadly grouped into physical, psychological, and social categories. It is important to remember that none of these issues can be separated from the requirements of the police service itself and the political influences upon it.

The medical standards for recruiting are presently being set service-wide, but are often tailored to job-related factors which vary across the country to reflect the type of work officers are called upon to do.

Typically there is no shortage of applicants nowadays and recruitment standards are rigorous. This has not always been the case. One factor observed to have been linked to the very high premature retirement rates of the early nineties, was the very low recruitment standards of the early seventies. It was very difficult to attract people into the organisation at that time.

A subtle but crucial aspect to fitness for duty relates to force culture and in particular that of focus of managers at all levels.

Fluctuating medical retirement rates in one large police force over the last decade can be explained by changing management policy on intervention. As shown in the chart overleaf, during the period 1989/90 medical retirements were actually encouraged by senior management. The rationale was that two new enthusiastic officers could replace an older, sick or demotivated one at no extra cost.

In the period between September 1990 and December 1991 the rate was curtailed by active involvement of senior management who scrutinised each case. However, management intervention then ceased, having been deemed inappropriate interference in medical matters and so the rate soared again until the end of 1992. Finally at the beginning of 1993, at the suggestion of medical staff officers were not allowed to pursue medical retirement without first being interviewed by management.

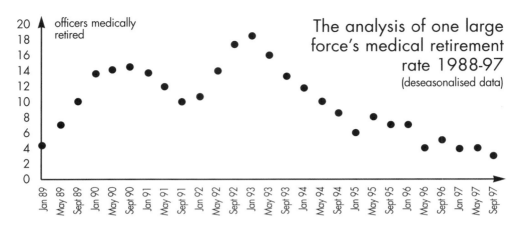

The analysis of one large force's medical retirement rate 1988-97
(deseasonalised data)

Managing behaviour patterns

A key feature of staff culture and management is motivation. Appropriate attention and recognition to those members of the work-force who are doing a professional standard of work is a motivator. If managers simply give the bulk of their attention to those who are under-performing, morale is likely to deteriorate and sickness is likely to become endemic. In short, concentrating upon good behaviour is more productive than emphasising bad behaviour

The following theoretical model illustrates proportions of unwanted behaviour identified in a group.

By then placing a special emphasis on a particular aspect of behaviour it can be seen that the proportion of the group exhibiting that behaviour increases. This is illustrated in the solid columns where particular attention has been given to behaviour type F.

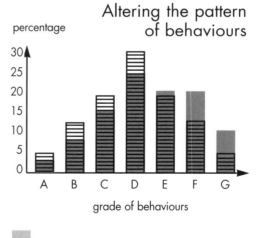

represents altered behaviour pattern

Attention to behaviour F has skewed the distribution of behaviour in the group. The percentage of people displaying behaviours E, F, and G has increased, and behaviours A, B, C, and D have decreased. The cultural pattern of the population has thus been altered.

behavioural distribution within the group

percentage

grade of behaviours

This principle has been used to powerful effect in:

√ reducing smoking in public where **attention has been given to non smokers** by providing smoke free zones;

√ making drink driving **unacceptable through education and awareness**;

√ reducing joy riding by **providing appropriate diversionary activities**;

√ reducing the medical retirement rate of police officers by transferring **attention to rehabilitation**.

In the past attention has been wrongly focused on the negative or unwanted aspects of behaviour:

✗ smoking; ✗ drink driving;

✗ joy riding; ✗ poor attendance;

at great expense and with little benefit.

To successfully manage:

√ recruitment;

√ placement;

√ safety;

√ absence;

√ performance, and

√ control of premature retirement;

quality behaviour must be defined and be given appropriate attention.

On the basis of the principles discussed, if positive behaviour is given this attention, the percentage of those exhibiting this behaviour will then increase and quality performance is likely to follow.

In summary, when considering the health and well-being of police staff - be it in relation to recruiting, placement, or retirement - the requirements of the organisation and the influences of its culture are crucial. They are possibly more influential to an employee's 'fitness for duty' than the factual health information and guidance available from the medical staff.

Recruitment standards for officers

The police service needs fully fit officers able to complete all aspects of front-line policing for a period of 30 years. It cannot afford to recruit anyone who, at the outset, may not be able to give a full period of service. Logically this precludes applicants who have a history of illness or injuries that may result in premature retirement in years to come. It is estimated that a medical retirement - without an 'injury on duty' enhancement - may cost in the region of half a million pounds.

Common reasons for rejection are:

diabetes and epilepsy - cause sudden loss of consciousness;

joint disease - in particular knees, ankles and spine which are vulnerable areas and the cause of a high proportion of retirements;

asthma - uncertain reaction to incapacitant sprays;

history of poor absence record - likely to be recurrent;

history of psychiatric problems - some may recur under pressure

digestive problems - frequently recur with shift working.

> New recruits must have fully intact senses of:
>
> √ hearing;
> √ smell;   *(See relevant chapters*
> √ vision.   *in Part Four)*

A record of hearing on joining the force is also necessary in the event of any future claims that some aspect of police duty caused damage through inappropriate noise exposure. Claims have been successfully made in the past by firearms officers, motor cyclists, machine operators and surveillance officers.

Lung function is recorded for similar reasons. In the event of exposure to damaging fumes at some time during service, the effect on the officer's lungs from this exposure can be more accurately assessed.

These records are for the protection of both the force and the officer concerned should any future claim be necessary.

Medical examination should reveal no evidence of pathology or the taking of illegal substances.

Lifestyle - The recruits' medical also allows time to advise on the importance of maintaining health by living a balanced lifestyle (see Part I). This provides another opportunity to place appropriate emphasis on this aspect of behaviour further influencing police culture in a positive direction.

Immunisation - An important aspect of health education during the medical is a discussion of immunisation status. The new recruit must be immunised against tetanus, polio and tuberculosis - and a course of immunisation against hepatitis B is recommended.

Guidance for recruits

Recruitment evenings

Some forces hold evening events for recruits, their partners and families to cement the importance of these relationships in supporting the officer throughout their careers. The formal proceedings include the recruits' attestation before a magistrate. Brief presentations will cover important aspects of the organisation, both in the care of its staff and its role in the community. The evening also provides opportunity to give an insight into the nature of policing and the breadth of activities it encompasses, of which many are unaware.

Those attending such 'family' events learn that help is available and how it may be accessed.

The evening is concluded by an opportunity for socialising and the discussion of concerns with a cross section of the workforce.

Probationer training

During the first module of probationer training time is set aside for training on welfare, health maintenance and body fluid handling.

Rest and recuperation

The traditional cultural adages of
- a change is as good as a rest
- work hard/play hard
- trust no one - are exposed as
being counter productive.

The importance of appropriate rest periods is given particular emphasis. It takes just as long to rest and recover from activity as it does to take part. Everybody needs in the region of eight hours' sleep a night and a whole day's rest per week to recover from the remainder of the week's activities, be they work or play.

The aim is to instill a professional approach to work and also to achieve a fulfilling lifestyle away from work. There is a recognition that health outcomes are affected by factors both at and away from the workplace.

Confirmation

Probationary constables are confirmed into the force after two years' satisfactory service and a health check. Immediately prior to confirmation, medical and absence records will be checked to ensure, as far as possible, that they still have an excellent chance of successfully completing their service. Their mental health will also be considered.

Some recruits may, by this time, have experienced an injury that may threaten a full 30 years of service. This poses a moral dilemma for management; especially if the injury was received on duty and the officer has recovered. Difficult decisions have to be taken about the long term view.

If a decision is taken that an individual is unfit for whatever reason to be confirmed into the service, it is vitally important that the force provides support and assistance so that person may come to terms with the situation and adopt a positive approach to alternative employment outside the service.

In service support

Individual fitness

Many employees will have had little direct contact with force health professionals during the course of their service - unless a specific injury or health problem has arisen or they are posted to certain specialists units (see following section).

However the availability of free medical examinations to staff who are over, say, 35 years old is good practice and these should be repeated every five years. Such examinations should also be available to any police staff with a specific concern about a health-related issue.

Each examination should take about an hour and cover the following:

√ interview and general advice on lifestyle issues;

√ specific advice on areas of concern;

√ full examination;

√ ECG (electro-cardiogram);

√ lung function test;

√ comprehensive blood screen (including a cholesterol estimation).

On a more informal basis, health professionals should always run local 'drop-in' clinics for health advice and blood pressure checks should be available.

Regular doctors' clinics are a good way of encouraging personnel who are on sick leave into their workplace and to address any other health related problems on site. They are also a good means of avoiding prolonged paper trails.

Free access to a consulting occupational psychologist to provide a confidential counselling service is a good bolt-on facility to health support. Links should be established between the psychologist and the health professionals in terms of learning from each other, but confidential information should not be exchanged in the interests of maintaining credibility.

Access to a free physiotherapy service should also be available, with an emphasis on early treatment for acute injuries. A practical approach in this sphere can often reduce the number and severity of injuries.

A fitness culture

One way in which to promote a proactive approach to health issues is through the establishment of a Fitness Leader post, to provide a role model influencing all aspects of fitness.

Particular attention should be given to:

√ providing appropriate supervised fitness facilities;

√ fitness assessment;

√ providing supervised rehabilitation;

√ assessment of fitness standards for specialist roles;

X discouraging heavy unproductive 'iron bending' workout sessions (sometimes linked to substance abuse in the form of anabolic steroids);

√ ensuring that the correct attitude is taken to the physical aspects of training courses.

Such an appointment has a powerful effect on the culture, placing more emphasis on health-related fitness and avoiding ill health and injury. Funding can be offset against the more reactive facility of physiotherapy services.

▶ The Fitness Leader can capitalise on the opportunities afforded during self defence and other physical training to reinforce health related fitness and sensible lifestyle messages.

▶ The Fitness Leader must be careful to avoid a 'macho culture' in which 'pumping iron' and 'stomach six-packs' become the norm. Mixed gender classes with a concentration on suppleness and stamina are preferable to physically punishing routines

Management training

The emergence of Advisory Teams comprising support staff with personnel skills is of valuable assistance to local personnel managers. Linked to each of these teams should be a Welfare Officer and a Nurse. Health professionals should be available to give presentations on all aspects of health and welfare. Subjects such as first aid, counselling skills and body fluid handling are helpful to police staff.

Policies on Health and Safety, Equal Opportunities and Grievance Handling, with the appointment of the appropriate staff to support them, can also make a significant contribution to making the workplace less hazardous and more conducive to productive work.

On promotion to a higher grade, it is helpful for staff to be briefed on issues of health management as well as on valuing other staff. This encourages a more balanced view of welfare management and discipline handling.

Medical staff may also provide specific inputs to training programmes - typically centring on aspects of pressure and stress, how these problems develop and how they might be avoided. Particular emphasis must be given to the cultural issues already discussed, highlighting the influence supervisors have on all members of the team as well as local management colleagues.

Workshops

Workshops to promote relationships between local personnel managers and health support professionals are an effective way of managing health issues within the work place.

On motivation and performance...

Workshops are also valuable in addressing those factors which directly affect motivation and performance. It is important to consider 'styles' of management and their impact upon personnel as part of health promotion.

Examples do emerge of middle managers who have a preferred style of managing by frustration rather than encouragement, or direction rather than involvement in order to assert their authority. The stress and emotion for supervisor and supervised in such relationships must be identified and hopefully reduced.

A specific example of stressful management would be a supervisor putting two police officers - living together in a permanent relationship - on separate shift patterns/rotas because of minor disciplinary matters. The result is that the couple cannot get reasonable time to see each other away from work, and there is pressure on both to turn to sickness as a way of alleviating the situation. Two embittered officers are created - possibly providing a less than satisfactory service and stirring up bad feeling among colleagues.

At what cost is this to the force? And all to prove who is in control! Such negative behaviour must be redirected. Workshops with input from medical staff can provide a forum to address such issues from an occupational health perspective and emphasise a route to a more positive management style.

The preferred approach would be to advise the officers and then steer them back to professional behaviour through encouragement, avoiding bitterness and confrontation. Again the emphasis should be on the positive rather than concentrating on the negative.

On referral...

Another important issue for workshops revolves around trust, and is often related to referral for medical assessment and confidentiality. Often staff have been referred to in-service health professionals by a manager, without being fully informed of the reason for the referral. The result is suspicion and anxiety.

Open dialogue needs to be encouraged in such situations to create a climate in which:

√ there are no secret agendas;

√ all relevant issues have already been addressed - indeed some will have been resolved;

√ there is no embarrassment at the medical - 'I don't know why I'm here Doc...'.

The doctor's assessment should be copied to all relevant parties ensuring that everyone knows the plan. This open, honest and above-board approach encourages trust among individuals and within the culture. It reduces stress and hopefully encourages a greater focus on the job in hand.

Specialist roles

There are a number of specialist roles in policing where medical advice is a necessary input at the time of appointment and then throughout the officer's service within that role.

Some officers such as those posted to Underwater Search Units must undertake a compulsory medical under HSE (Health and Safety) legislation.

Another obvious example is that of applicants for Firearms Units. These officers must undergo, not only eyesight and hearing test, but blood tests designed to reveal any hidden health problems, including drug and alcohol abuse.

There are also a number of Support Staff roles for which regular medical checks are recommended. These include paint sprayers (compulsory lung function check), communications, paper shredder and baler operators (hearing tests).

Regular medical checks are vital in the interests of the police staff and the force. The police role is physically demanding and mentally challenging and both parties share responsibility. A major benefit for the individual is personal protection. The benefit for the force is insurance against litigation.

There is of course the very important cultural effect of reinforcing good practice and ill-health prevention as opposed to reacting to injury.

Medical retirement

There was a time when medical decisions regarding retirement were very straightforward. The doctor would be asked whether this officer could stand up with a shield in the riot scenario or not. Managers had little concern to motivate unfit officers to come back to work. Colleagues tended to ridicule those not seen to be pulling their weight in the policing role.

Commutation of pension and an invested lump sum was an attractive retirement inducement. It was not until managers began to realise the long terms costs that the situation changed.

Weighing up the options

Nowadays the medical role is not only to diagnose the medical condition but also to define what an ill or injured officer is able to do, if and when recovery can be anticipated. In those cases in which a return to full policing duty is less than certain it is imperative that the doctor provides a prognosis of recovery.

The role of police managers

It is important to remember that the doctor is an advisor. The responsibility lies with managers to consider the formal retirement questions with advice from the medical practitioner. Generally the doctor will have considered all redeployment possibilities before the following questions are raised:

? Does the condition prevent the officer from performing the normal duties of a police officer?

? Is the condition permanent?

? Is the condition linked to an injury on duty?

There is, of course, the possibility that officers are ill because they no longer wish to serve in the force. For a member of the support staff the problem can be resolved simply by resignation and a change of employment. For officers no longer in sympathy with the policing role it is different. Classically such disaffected personnel suffer from psychological problems, high blood pressure or gastric disturbances such as a peptic ulcer.

If the problem is identified as job mis-match it is appropriate to assist the officer to leave the service as painlessly as possible and to make counselling available.

Recognition of the situation is the first step towards a successful resolution. There is much to be done to encourage the officer to come to terms with his or her predicament and to approach alternative employment positively. The Force Welfare Officer will probably be instrumental in giving practical advice regarding fitness and job opportunities as well as providing support to family members

Some officers in the past reached the point of no longer wishing to serve because of the way they had been treated by the organisation or their colleagues.

Fortunately such cases are now rare but they do still occur. It is the duty of police managers to distinguish between those who are genuinely affected and those who are 'playing the system'. The aid of the Police Federation and health professionals can provide the opportunity to get to the heart of the issue

There is evidence that successful grievance procedures reduce the number of officers seeking to use medical retirement inappropriately as an exit route from the organisation due to mismanagement.

The culture of medical retirement

The more enlightened approach of managers has led to a change of culture. In the early nineties it was not uncommon for three or four officers seeking medical retirement to appear at an afternoon clinic. The officers would eagerly describe what they could not do, or how they could no longer cope. There was simply no management commitment to work with these officers by discovering their problems and restoring their motivation. There was no appreciation at all of the financial and human cost of medical retirement. The emphasis was on instigating the retirement process - a 'get rid' approach being seen as the simplest of solutions.

With so much focus on this approach it should have been obvious that the problem would grow. Until there was an appreciation of the cultural change model described at the beginning of the chapter, little changed.

> Today the emphasis is on what an officer can still offer the force. Premature retirement is viewed as a last resort when all other employment avenues have been explored.

Medical retirement procedures

If medical retirement is the only option it is very important to have in place a fair and transparent system for calculating the degree of enhancement that an officer should receive. Ideally the system should have been derived in consultation with Staff Associations and should be robust enough to withstand scrutiny. The essential approach is:

1. The Force Medical Officer should first decide whether or not a permanent disability exists as a result of an injury on duty.
2. The nature of that disability should then be defined in terms of what the officer is still able to do by way of work.
3. This definition must then be compared with job descriptions of staff posts in the organisation and/or on the open employment market.
4. A potential earnings capacity in terms of an annual salary can then be determined as a basis for making the calculation for disability enhancement.

The use of this type of calculation (example show overleaf) can greatly reduce the number of appeals against awards and, provided it is fair in its operation and application, it can save anxiety and unnecessary expense by all parties.

Example - calculating disability enhancement

1. salary at retirement
   eg £25,000 pa   £25,000 pa

2. Minus potential earnings
   capacity eg £10,000   £25,000
                          - £10,000 pa
                          = £15,000

3. Divide by salary at
   retirement   £15,000
                          /£25,000
                          =   0.6

4. multiply by 100 = %   60% IOD

This figure may be reduced by a further percentage if, in the doctor's opinion, the injury is not wholly responsible for the disability - there may have been, for example, a pre-existing problem with arthritis.

5. Injury 80% responsible
   for disability   60%
                          x 80%
                          = 48% IOD

Conclusion

Occupational health is a relatively recent but growing practice within the police service

It is a contract between the police service and their employees to concentrate upon selecting and releasing all who have failed physically and/or mentally to cope with the rigours of policing by fairness, awareness and support.

There is a requirement for openness - on both sides - to ensure both parties enter the contract from a standpoint of mutual trust.

Systems will only work when both parties understand that the return of the huge investment made in recruiting and training staff can only be realised through enlightened management. It is as much about understanding behaviour as it is about health promotion.

PART TWO

LIFESTYLE

2. Fit to be healthy?

Making the connection between fitness and health

Exercise has come into fashion during the last 20 years. Presidents, film stars and the girl next door either jog, attend aerobic classes or otherwise 'work-out'. The police service generally has stricter fitness testing than ever before. Television, society's big hitter in the field of fads and fashions, promotes sport and beautiful fit bodies.

Most large companies and organisations have now realised the benefits of having a fit workforce and, if only from TV and media propaganda, most people should realise the benefits of exercise. It is surprising, therefore, that in a recent survey in the UK, 80 per cent of the population is not active at a sufficient level to benefit their health.

There is always a tendency to wait for problems to arise before dealing with them but a proactive regime is suggested here to prevent the problems ever arising.

Making exercise work for you

Your health depends on your environment, your genetic make up, your lifestyle and your outlook on life.

You have no control over inherited health factors, probably little control over your environment, but you have full control over your lifestyle and attitude of mind. It is possible to maintain a very healthy lifestyle in today's Western world but the converse is also true. We have the choice of whether we use leisure centres, swimming, squash, football, aerobics - or sit at home as 'couch potatoes', watching television or videos, or playing with computers.

The majority of the world's population does not have such a wide range of choice and indeed does not have the long life expectancy which we enjoy. As police forces go, throughout the world, our Western forces are relatively safe, living in comparatively stable democratic societies.

The choice is ours. Today is the first day of the rest of our lives and now is the time to take stock.

We all have a fairly clear idea of what is good for us and what is not. Exercise is usually neglected through pressure of work, laziness, family pressures or some other de-motivating factor. Now is the time to decide on your lifestyle, both physical and mental and to set out your exercise plan for the rest of your life. One of the truer sayings where the body is concerned is:

'Use it or lose it.'

Regular exercise is essential for good health. It helps to keep the muscles, the bones and joints, the circulatory system, the respiratory system and the mind all in good working order.

Varying degrees of exercise may be appropriate, depending on who you are and what you want from the exercise. If an elderly person takes a brisk walk and performs a bit of housework or gardening, that may be sufficient for their daily needs.

If the 20, 30, 40 or 50-something police officer wants to keep fit then more has to be done than driving to work, driving police vehicles and relaxing behind the personal computer or TV when off duty. Time has to be put aside for some type of exercise.

Exercise caution

A word of warning is necessary at this stage, especially for those who have not exercised for some time. If at any time during exercise you feel pain in the chest, neck or arms, or experience severe breathlessness, palpitations or faintness then stop exercising and see your doctor for advice.

From the force's mouth...

Force doctors have commented:

'A lot of officers are overweight and unfit - exercise to help keep your weight and fitness in order.'

'I wish police officer's backs were stronger - don't neglect back strengthening exercises.'

'Ill health retirements are headed by bad backs and stress-related illness such as heart disease.'

'Officers push themselves too hard - be gentle with yourself and realise your capabilities as you get older.'

?

Many new officers and civilian police staff ask:

? Is there anything forces do to help with physical education and the promotion of a healthy lifestyle?

? What facilities do forces offer and how can new recruits discover how to make best use of these?

? Are there, or could there be, fitness routines designed specifically for officers or with shift work in mind?

The answer to these questions is a regrettable: 'It is very much "hit and miss".' Some forces employ physical training experts but they obviously will not be available around the clock for shift workers. While most police staff will have access to a gymnasium on police premises, the use of such facilities is up to the individual to organise.

Selecting the best exercise

When selecting the type of exercise best suited to you, consider your present physical condition, your time available for exercise, what facilities are available in your area - and how much money you want to spend on exercise. Will you be content to keep a low profile or are you the high profile wearer of flashy designer gear?

You must seriously consider what function you want the exercise to fulfil. Some exercises are good for the circulatory and respiratory systems, some for the muscles, joints, ligaments and flexibility, some for strength and some for stamina (see File 2.1 'Exercise Options' at the end of the chapter).

It is always a good idea to initially consult a physical training expert either within the service or outside to help determine your precise exercise needs. Particularly if you are unused to sport or exercise it could be money well spent to seek out a local health or leisure centre for some professional advice.

If you are unsure about what you want to achieve, a starting point could be to look in the mirror. Strip and find a full length mirror (not necessarily in that order). What you see should tell you what kind of routine you need. Start at the face and neck - would exercise help? Shoulders, chest, arms - are you happy? Stomach, hips and thighs - do they need any correction? Legs - seem too big, too small or all right?

The most common concern will be about being overweight coupled with not being fit. The next will simply be about being unfit. There will be a few wishing to put weight on or build up the body.

The same exercises can be used to remedy all the above desires. The secret lies in the effort you put into them. The harder you work the greater the muscle definition; the more gentle you are while working for longer periods the more muscle fat and flab is removed.

A common fault is rushing into exercise routines which do not deal with the problem, or do not give all round fitness. This will result in frustration and lack of motivation which is why it is worth consulting an expert first if you don't know exactly what you are doing.

If you are really out of condition, or haven't had exercise for a long time, a visit to your doctor to discuss your decision to exercise, get into shape, lose weight etc will soon reveal whether you need a 'medical'. If you have any health problems, such as recovering from a heart attack, a fitness check is essential - while even

for those who have a good physique and no apparent problems, a test is advisable.

A test will include height and weight measurement, the level of body fat, the blood pressure and pulse, and also urine and blood samples. Your heart will be further tested by physical exertion on a rolling road, exercise bike or similar, while the heart's efficiency at pumping blood is measured. Your resting pulse will be taken, then the pulse rate immediately after a workout - then further pulse readings are taken to measure the recovery to normal.

You must then be guided by your doctor's advice. In 90% of the cases all will be well, but the doctor could advise further tests, a gentle introduction to exercise, or even specialised physiotherapy for those for example with joint, muscle or back problems.

Give yourself at least six months of a fitness programme to see any benefit and it should be this benefit that spurs you on to include exercise in your lifestyle as a permanent feature.

Do...

√ seek medical advice if you have any doubts as to your health, or experience any of the following while exercising - dizziness, faintness, severe breathlessness, palpitations, back pain or pains in the neck, chest or arms;

√ after a meal, wait two hours before exercising;

√ wear comfortable, loose-fitting clothes - of cotton material where possible as it is more absorbent than man-made fabric;

√ wear warm clothing if exercising in cold conditions;

√ seek ways of keeping fit in everyday life - cycling or walking instead of taking the car or bus, climb the stairs instead of the lift, if you do take the bus get off a stop or two earlier and walk;

√ seek a doctor's or a physiotherapist's advice if you have continuing joint or muscle pains while exercising.

Don't...

x push yourself too hard or it could produce more stress than it relieves;

x exercise more than 20 minutes for the first few sessions - build up gradually;

x exercise when you are ill, or excessively tired;

x exercise without a proper warm-up period;

x wear tight, thin-soled trainers - buy the correct size with cushioned soles, especially if you intend to do any running as part of your programme;

x take part in competitive sports if you are susceptible to stress.

The effect of exercise on the body

The short term effect of exercising is a feeling of well being when the muscles, ligaments and joints are well stretched, 'on top of their job' and working in harmony. The longer term effect is to keep the heart in good condition, which is the body's most important muscle.

The heart

The best way to prevent heart disease is to couple an aerobic exercise routine with a healthy diet (see File 2.1 'Exercise Options' at the end of the chapter). Particularly in the Western world, we risk the health of our hearts and associated blood systems by ill-considered diet (see Chapt 3: A Fitting Diet). The biggest killer in the West is heart disease, when the heart's function is impaired with a build up of fatty deposits in its own arteries.

Stopping smoking and being sensible with alcohol and caffeine will also help to keep the heart healthy (see Chapt 5: Drugs of First Choice). The exercise itself will help a person to stop smoking and heavy smokers should notice an improvement after only a few days.

Burning up fat

Besides the fatty deposits within arteries, people who are out of condition have fat deposits within and around their muscles. Exercise helps to reduce this fat. The sooner you get into an exercise routine with which you (and your body) are happy, the sooner your routine will start to burn off any excess fat. The 'basal metabolic rate' (BMR) is the amount of energy the body needs to maintain its functions, such as breathing, circulation, body temperature etc. BMR increases as we exercise, worry, become frightened or stressed and so on.

Most people function somewhere midway between the extremes of BMR. However, while some can eat what they want without putting on weight, others will increase their weight by storing food as fat even when making drastic cut-backs in their consumption of food and drink.

BMR is generally under the influence of hormones which dictate the rate at which the body's cells process chemicals. The rate of processing the chemicals varies considerably according to age, sex, size and shape.

Usually it is the young, fit male who has the highest BMR. The older, unfit female would tend to store excess food in the form of fat. It is said that a good way to burn off fat is to use the 'long slow distance' type of exercise when you work at a third of your maximum effort.

The muscles

Most people who simply want to achieve and maintain general fitness should choose an all round exercise routine and not dwell on a particular kind of exercise.

Muscles work by contracting after stimulation from nerve impulses. Bundles of muscle fibres contract or relax depending on what job they do in the body. Skeletal muscle is under the voluntary control of the brain and enables us to run, walk, talk etc. We have over 600 skeletal muscles.

Two other muscle functions are the involuntary or automatic movement of internal organs such as the bladder and intestines by smooth muscle, and the heart beat - the cardiac muscle. Exercise is not only good for the more obvious skeletal muscles but also for the smooth muscle and cardiac muscle.

To understand the effects on the muscles of particular types of exercise (again see File 2.1

'Exercise Options') the muscles themselves need to be understood. Exercise will increase the size of the muscles, but it is said that the type of muscles you have is decided genetically.

There are two types of muscle - fast-twitch and slow-twitch. This makes the difference between the sprinter and marathon runner, but unless it is obvious to you that you are a much better sprinter than a long distance runner, the only way to know which of these types you have the most of is by biopsy.

(A small piece of muscle tissue is taken for electronic stimulation. The sprinter's muscle should twitch faster than the long distance runner's muscle.)

The fast-twitch muscles use fuel and not oxygen - ie there is the oxygen debt to repay after the sprint is over - and are therefore anaerobic. Slow twitch muscles need glucose and oxygen for their energy and are aerobic. The build-up of lactic acid (the painful muscle inhibitor) is slower in the slow-twitch muscle, allowing the long distance runner to exercise for longer periods.

The isometric and isokinetic types of exercise are the best for improving the fast twitch muscle fibres. Isometric, fartleck and interval training are the best for slow-twitch muscle fibres. (Again see File 2.1 'Exercise Options'.)

Spin-offs from exercise

Apart from healthier muscles - including the heart - and weight loss, there are other advantages to be gained from exercising.

Helping to stop smoking

If the exercise is a precision sport - such as squash, golf, or badminton - players have felt smoking takes the edge off their game. They may be more likely to miss the vital shots or lack energy at a vital time.

Improved sex life
This is a result of the general feeling of well being and extra energy.

Improved performance
An improvement in health, stamina and concentration results in a better overall performance - at work and at home.

Improved sleeping patterns
After exercise it is usual to go to bed physically fatigued, but with less worries or depression.

Reductions in pain
Exercise improves the overall function and well-being of the body and can greatly reduce problems such as period pain or back pain.

The potential risks of exercise

There is a down-side to everything we do, but adverse effects of exercise are minimal and can be reduced by taking simple precautions.

Heart attacks
Always precede a new exercise routine with a medical check up if you are in any doubt. Stop exercising immediately if chest, neck or arm pains, dizziness, faintness, palpitations or acute breathlessness occur and seek medical advice before exercising again.

Addiction to exercise
For general health, three sessions of 20 to 30 minute periods per week of aerobic type exercise will be sufficient. Addiction to the 'buzz' from exercise can become a problem for some people and it is important to recognise if this is happening to you.

Injuries from physical sports
Take care, especially with contact sports. Even when doing static exercise, muscles and/or joints can be damaged without the correct warm-up.

We frequently hear of a pulled, torn or strained muscle. Such injuries cause bleeding within the muscle tissue and, as they heal, a scar forms shortening the muscle slightly from its natural length.

Muscles can go into spasm as a reaction to pain from muscle strains or slipped discs (this can also be a result of poor posture or stress). Muscle-relaxant drugs could be used to relieve the muscle spasm. These block the nerve signals from the brain that tell the muscle to contract. However, be aware of possible side effects of drowsiness and/or weakness in the muscles.

If there is a lack of blood supply to a muscle, cramp may occur or, if nerve impulses have been disturbed, 'pins and needles' may be experienced as when sleeping with an arm bent under the body.

Muscles can also become infected, for example with gangrene and tetanus.

Preparing for and ending exercise

Warming up

It is important for all body types to warm up and cool down. The muscles take several minutes before a good flow of blood is achieved.

You should always start with a little light exercise such as jogging or cycling; or static exercises such as neck stretching, shoulder shrugs, rotating arms, waist stretches, hamstring stretches, hugging knees to chest and so on. Once the circulation has been stepped up, a selection of limbering or stretching exercises can be done. These will not help the heart or circulation much, but will help the body's joints and ligaments to deal better with the ensuing exercise, thereby reducing the risk of injury.

If you are warming up and stretching at home, be careful not to overdo it at the beginning. The warming up exercises should only slightly increase your pulse rate. Take it easy if your pulse rate is getting near double its normal rate.

A rough guide for calculating your maximum safe pulse rate is to subtract your age from 200 - for example, if you are 40 years of age then 160 beats per minute is your maximum.

The stretching exercises should not put too much strain on your joints, ligaments and muscles. Stretch the particular part of the body until you know you are near its limit and then stop to prevent injury. As time goes on you will find the stretching and general flexibility will become easier and that your range of movement will increase.

'Maintenance' and 'building' exercise

The main exercise period can now begin. 'Maintenance' exercises can be varied to suit your individual requirements, but generally addresses your health and endurance needs.

Anaerobic (the short burst of movement using no oxygen), aerobic (the slower oxygen using movements), and the other forms of exercises can now be used singly or combined for 20 to 30 minutes.

NB: If you wish to include body building exercise of the isometric type (muscles working against a static resistance) within your routine these should not usually be undertaken on the same day as aerobic exercise.

Cooling down

After all exercise it is important to end with cooling down exercises. This prevents loss of flexibility and stiffness, as muscles tend to shorten during maintenance and building exercise and also after an anaerobic or aerobic session. Also blood is still being pumped to the warmed-up muscles at the end of a session. If there is no cooling down exercise period, this blood may gather in the larger muscles at the expense of other areas of the body and cause fainting or dizziness.

After a hard exercise session, slow down gradually to allow the circulation to return to nearly normal. Light exercise with some gentle stretching exercises is suggested such as, squats, knee hugging either standing up or lying down and hamstring stretches. Runners would benefit from stretching exercises for hamstrings and achilles tendons, which should prevent them shortening and so prevent stiffness.

In summary... a general exercise routine would be a warm up and stretch routine with either an aerobic session or a body building session to follow. For general good health an aerobic routine at least three times per week consisting of 20 to 30 minute sessions should suffice. Body building could be done on alternate days or under the supervision of a trainer. But after every session cooling-down exercises are a must.

File 2.1: Exercise options

Aerobic

This exercise allows the muscles to work at such a speed that the body can keep up with the muscles' demand for oxygenated blood.

The body's energy stores of fat, sugars and glycogen (a starchy material) need oxygen to allow them to release the energy in a usable form. As the muscles receive the correct levels of oxygen, aerobics can be sustained for quite some time. The muscles burn up fatty acid for their energy as opposed to glucose and give off water and carbon dioxide.

Aerobic exercise will improve the efficiency of the oxygen-delivery system to meet the requirements of the muscles. Aerobic exercise is the kind of exercise which causes you to breath faster - which in turn puts more oxygen into the lungs for onward transmission to the muscle fibres.

It is one of the best exercises for strengthening the cardiovascular system. It also helps with muscle strength and flexibility and is most effective when performed just below your best level for longer periods. In other words it is better to go nice and steady for 30 minutes rather than at peak performance for five minutes.

The popular keep-fit classes, in which exercise is accompanied by music, use a lot of aerobic movement. Aerobic exercise runs contrary to the saying 'no gain without pain', as the idea is not to exercise through the pain barrier for each muscle, but to gently increase the work rate of the heart and lungs.

This form of exercise should be enjoyed and if performed along with others in a gymnasium, club or adult education centre, the added social element is a bonus. Many people experience a mental and spiritual improvement from this different pass-time as well as the physical improvement.

Brisk walking jogging, cycling, rowing and swimming are other good examples. The advantage of walking, jogging or cycling is that they can be fitted into a busy day and do not need much preparation. A jogging or cycling route can be chosen to give you 10, 20 or 30 minutes' exercise - or longer if your breaks can be variable. Even in city centres a 'scenic' route can be chosen, including a park or riverside. If a force or divisional gymnasium is available then rowing or cycling machines are excellent substitutes. Rolling roads or running machines are also excellent as these machines take away the dangers of the road traffic and exhaust emissions and are unaffected by the uncertainties of the weather.

Sports which are classed as aerobic include soccer, rugby, hockey, basketball, baseball, swimming and tennis. Bear in mind that some sports are better than others for keeping fit and some are only seasonal. An all year round activity is needed - swimming is the best of these for all round exercise. The cardiovascular system, suppleness and muscle strength can all be well developed this way.

The benefits of aerobic exercise are an increase in endurance and stamina, but they must be done for at least 20 minutes three times a week or more. The large trunk and limb muscles must be involved. Other benefits to health are improved flow of blood to cells, improvement in the cells' ability to use oxygen and in the amount of oxygen the muscles can use in a set time. The heart muscle will become stronger and will not have to beat as often to supply the body with the required amount of blood.

Isometric

This is exercise which does not entail any movement. A group of muscles work against a static resistance - such as a desk or wall - or against another set of muscles; for example, pushing the heels of the hands together across the chest to develop the pectoral muscles. Isometric exercise was hailed as the 'white collar workers' saviour' and called dynamic tension. Exercises were developed to perform when sitting at an office desk. A selection of such exercises is as follows.

√ Hands under the desk, either back or palms upwards would help develop the biceps when you tried to lift the desk.

√ Putting both knees under the desk and trying to lift would exercise the rectos femoris muscles, that is, the one attaching the patella (knee-cap) to the hip bone.

√ Hands on the top of the desk pressing down would develop the triceps running from the elbow to the back of the shoulder.

√ Putting the hands on the chair at either side of your hips while sitting on the chair and taking your weight on your hands would exercise most of the muscles in the shoulders.

Isometric exercise is designed to increase muscle strength, but not to improve stamina or cardiovascular system, ie it does not help in the aerobic area. In a small number of people isometric exercise may increase blood pressure, so take care. All the exercises can be held for a count of five, 10, 15 etc before relaxing and repeating for several times.

Other similar exercises that could be done at the office desk, preferably when no one is watching - depending on your level of extroversion - are face exercises.

√ Forehead muscles can be exercised by placing fingers above the eyebrows and raising the eyebrows against slight pressure from the fingers

√ To increase the cheek-bone muscles, place two fingers above each cheek bone and, exerting a slight downward pressure, smile to tighten and raise the cheek bone muscles against the finger pressure.

√ Exercise lip muscles by smiling and knotting the muscles at either side of the mouth

√ Neck muscles in the 'double-chin' area can be helped by forming an 'O' shape with the mouth and then smiling until you feel the neck muscles at the front begin to tighten.

All such exercises help prevent 'sagging faces' and should be held until the muscles begin to ache and then repeated after a few seconds' relaxing.

Isotonic

This type of exercise is a moving exercise in which the tension on the muscles remains constant, with the body working against its own weight or external weights. The movement then takes the muscles through their range of movement; for example, press-ups or push-ups, squat-thrusts, sit-ups. Some aerobic exercise can be described as isotonic, such as swimming or running.

Ten to 20 sit-ups - push-ups, knee bends for leg muscles, lying on the stomach and arching the back for the back muscles - per day helps the overall fitness. Any combination of exercises to suit you will be all right, provided you try to cover most parts of the body.

A word of advice to avoid a round-shouldered tendency is to balance pectoral exercise with suitable back exercises. Too many trainers neglect the back muscles and do too many chest exercises, resulting in the round-shouldered look.

Isokinetic

This is a combination of the isometric and isotonic exercises. By using the specialist gymnasium equipment of the 'multigym', reasonably heavy weights can be moved while putting the muscles through their complete range of movement. The weights can be adjusted to suit individual strength and needs.

Strength training is mixed with aerobic exercise, but isokinetic exertion is usually confined to the health farm, leisure centre or well equipped health club. Many of the larger hotel chains offer such facilities to non-residents.

The resident trainer will normally give you a pulse and blood pressure check, a body fat reading and a suggested programme to suit your level of existing fitness. The programme will be progressive, using machines for biceps, triceps, pectoral, back, legs and stomach.

Callisthenics

These are repetitious rhythmic exercises. They are similar to isotonic exercise as they are done in one place and help to build up muscle strength and stamina.

You probably did callisthenic exercises at school such as jumping jacks and sit-ups. To use such exercises now you will need to persevere for longer periods than in those school days to receive any benefit. As callisthenic exercise doesn't use equipment, the external resistance is low. You only have the weight of your body to exercise against. However, with rhythm and repetition the body weight works well if you are out of shape.

For officers who are already in good physical condition callisthenics will not raise your strength dramatically, but will help with your co-ordination and stamina.

Interval training

This consists of short bursts of movement requiring a high level of exertion, alternated with periods of rest or low level exertion.

Another type of interval training is called 'fartlek' which means 'speed play'. This is a less structured form of interval training which takes place over rough ground on varying gradients. It is a useful form of exercise to train for marathons, half marathons or other distance running.

Long slow distance

This form of training entails exercising over a long distance using a low level of exertion. Muscle fat is encouraged to burn up with this type of exercise. It is not confined to running, but can be used on all aerobic exercise. The object is to persevere over time with a low energy output.

Pilates' exercise

This was devised by a German, Joseph Pilates, around the beginning of the 1900s. His idea was to bring about the complete harmonisation of the body, mind and spirit by working with the muscles and not on or against them.

Pilates set up a studio in New York in the 1920s and further developed his technique especially in the field of dance. Dancers liked the way the Pilates' system gently limbered, strengthened, stretched and toned their bodies reducing the risk of pulled muscles etc. The emphasis is on soothing gradual controlled exercise and not the aggressive, competitive behaviour of some exercise routines.

The Pilates' system is normally used and based at a fitness centre where one-to-one tuition is available.

The Nautilus system

Devised by the American weight lifter, Arthur Jones, the Nautilus system is almost the opposite of the quiet calm of the Pilates routine. Jones designed machines to help with body-building by working the muscles equally hard throughout all their range. The Nautilus studio can reach muscles that others can't, or can't as easily. One machine, for example, is designed solely to exercise the inner thighs. Some machines are designed for male body building only.

Such machines are mainly housed at fitness centres or studios and should only be used under expert supervision in the initial stages. The gymnasium supervisor should work with you to come to an agreement as to what programme you need. Machines can help with general fitness and stamina as well as body building and if you are just starting training a more varied programme would be advisable, rather than just one area.

3. A fitting diet

The importance of diet to overall health

Background

Our eating habits have developed in response to varied and increasing demands upon our time. Today's lifestyle dictates that the demands we make upon our bodies are very different from the days of hunter-gathering

These change raise some particular considerations about the Western diet.

?

? Why don't we eat more unprocessed foods?

? Why do we add fat, salt and sugar etc to our food?

? What are the effects of adding colouring and artificial flavours to our food?

? Why do we over-eat?

? Why do we crave for sugar and fats in sweets, candy, cakes, gateau, biscuits, cream and cheeses?

Most of these habits can be related to social conditioning - pressures from our own environment and those handed on from previous generations. Many can be traced through the influence of family and friends.

Considering Britain as a case in point, it was probably the last world war which helped to mould an attitude to food that is only now beginning to change. When food like butter, meat and sugar had been rationed, it seemed only natural to over-indulge on such foods when they became plentiful in the post war period.

Old habits die hard and the habit of overeating on fatty foods and sweet sugary foods still persists. Sweets, candy, confectionery etc are still regarded as a treat for children.

Other habits have been handed down. Adding salt and sugar to make food more 'tasty', or colouring it to make it more attractive to the buyer are all questions of inherited 'taste' which are more psychological than physical in both cause and effect.

Finance and the media of course play an ongoing role in the pressure of advertising.

The media and large food corporations have played, and are still playing, a part in promoting the consumption of unhealthy food and drink.

There are however promising signs that certain sections of society are becoming more aware of the necessity of healthy eating for themselves and their children and that TV and other media adverts could be curtailed concerning their wondrous claims for various food and drink.

Together with the ongoing debate on genetically modified (GM) food and the scares of BSE (mad cow disease), e-coli and salmonella, the whole food picture is very blurred and confusing for the consumer. This chapter aims to help readers make a more educated choice regarding diet for themselves and their families.

Modern living

On the one hand, the speed of life and the desire for convenience has led to more and more processed food being used. On the other, a perceived need to cook and prepare food to achieve gastronomic extravaganzas perhaps comes hand in glove with a sophisticated society. After a hard day, we have the urge to treat or spoil ourselves with food and drink that looks good, tastes good, but nutritionally may be of little good at all.

The police professional's busy lifestyle leaves officers particularly vulnerable to both the need for convenience food and the feeling that, if they have the time, they 'deserve' whatever they wish to eat. It goes without saying that this sometimes leads to neglect of a properly balanced diet.

All that is required, however, to restore the balance, is to spend a little time and effort to include foods which will supply most of the bodily needs without causing weight loss or gain. Account has to be taken of course of shopping and preparation time but healthy eating does not necessarily require a vast amount of either - it is often more a case of educating eating habits around quick changeover shifts and the inevitable late finish.

Unsocial hours and diet must be planned for, taking into account the nutritional information contained in this chapter. Modern living should be tempered with a mild dietary discipline and not used as an excuse for fattening takeaways and junk food.

A strategy for healthy eating and drinking

'We are what we eat...'

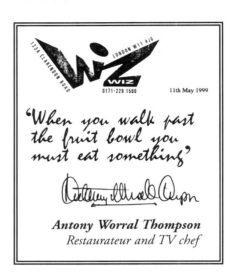

Antony Worral Thompson
Restaurateur and TV chef

Diet is probably the most important area in which we can influence our health. We have power over the fuel for life. If the wrong fuel, or shortages of certain types of fuel occur, the fire can begin to flicker, die down or even go out. By contrast over-fuelling can cause obesity and disease.

Many people in Western society frequently eat more than they need of the wrong kinds of food - and police officers are no exception. We tend to consume too much alcohol, fat, sugar, salt and refined processed food. It has now been proved that such diets can cause cancer, heart disease, liver problems, joint problems, diabetes and tooth decay.

You may say:

'I'm not depriving myself. I work hard and I deserve a couple of beers / bottle of wine / my favourite meal / chocolate / night cap etc.'

Or you may say:

'OK, I'll keep a bit fitter, but I'm not eating bran, fibre, apples, pulses, or drinking more water. I need my fried breakfast, beef burgers, fish and chips, fizzy drinks and coffee.'

However, what is today considered to be a healthy eating strategy is based upon cumulative knowledge of nutrition and disease, built up since records began.

Your diet needs to provide the nutrients to grow, repair your body and perform the necessary chemical processes. It needs to give you sufficient energy for your daily activities, bearing in mind that we are all different in this respect.

To make informed choices about our eating strategy we need at least a working knowledge of our body's requirements and the foods which best suits those requirements - and and at the same time suit us and our lifestyle.

Whatever you say you know that a healthy diet makes sense. The choice is yours!

The importance of water

Water is vital for the body's survival. Over half of the body is made of water - actually around 60 per cent. It is essential for metabolism and the movement of chemicals around the body. Water leaves the body as urine, sweat, other bodily fluids, or in the faeces. It needs to be replaced daily.

Although much of our food contains water it is recommended that you drink several glasses of plain water per day.

Water facts on tap...

1. Drinking water with meals or at any other time will not put permanent weight on.

2. Water is calorie-free.

3. Dieting by reducing the liquid in your body will not give any permanent weight loss.

4. The average sized adult should drink one to one and half litres (one-and-three-quarters to two-and-a-half pints) of plain water a day. Do not wait until you feel thirsty but spread the consumption evenly.

5. Water may be lost from the body by drinking too much tea, coffee, or cola as the caffeine content is a diuretic (something which excites the discharge of urine). Alcohol is also a cause of dehydration as it takes water from the body to metabolise or break down the alcohol at the ratio of about four of water to one of alcohol.

6. Water loss via sweat increases dramatically if you suddenly move to a hot climate (eg flying to the tropics) or during vigorous prolonged exercise - and your water intake should be increased accordingly.

7. The correct balance of water in the body is normally taken care of by the kidneys and your thirst mechanisms.

8. Water content of the body varies from time to time, eg a woman may retain fluid just before menstruation.

Twenty points towards a 'Healthy Eating Strategy'

One

Vary your diet as much as possible. When choosing fruit don't just eat apples - eat pears, orange, bananas, red and white grapes, pineapples, grapefruit and so on. Also try some of the 'exotic' fruits now available. Along the same lines, meat, fish and vegetables should be varied as should cereals, bread and other carbohydrates - rice, pasta, potatoes and crepes/ pancakes.

Two

Eat a variety of proteins, combining them as explained under 'Proteins' (post).

Three

Avoid or cut down on processed foods by preparing your own whenever possible (even pre-packed salads or lettuce maybe washed in preservatives or contain preserving gas). Always buy fresh rather than pre-packed fruit, salad, vegetable, meat and fish etc.

More and more questions are being asked about proven or suspected dangers from food packaging or processing. For example chemicals leeched into food via plastic lining or wrapping has been linked to a falling sperm count in the Western world. It may be wise to use glass containers until this debate is resolved - think of the drinks sold in plastic bottles, or plastic-lined cartons or cans; the plastic-wrapped cheese, meat and fish, and the plastic trays for takeaway food. Avoid microwaving food in plastic wrapping or containers.

The above also applies to food storage and preparation for babies and toddlers. (Attention has focused recently on links between cancer and pliable plastic products, particularly toys for young babies.)

Processing is thought to remove too much fibre from food and add too many debatable chemicals, fats, sugars and salts. Get to know what goes into pies and sausage or stick to plain meat.

We must get our priorities right when it comes to food and its preparation. We all find time to watch TV and/or play computer games but do not have time to maintain our most prized possession - our health. Cultivate an interest in food and its preparation for your own sake.

Four

Eat fresh food. Don't buy your vegetables to last the week as the vitamins will deteriorate, even in the fridge.

Given the convenience of the weekly trip to the superstore, coupled with the inconvenience of unsocial hours, it is appreciated that daily shopping sprees will be few and far between. However it may be possible to pass a market, even after a night shift, with only a little detour, or a partner may be able to shop at lunchtimes or in the evening if working regular hours.

It is also well worth investigating the possibility of buying from a local organic producer, and, better still, one offering a delivery service in your area.

Five

Eat whole foods, for example whole wheat or grains as opposed to refined wheat or grains. A bowl of porridge made from oats has far fewer additives than a bowel of cornflakes. Muesli-type cereals are less 'processed' than those which bear no resemblance to their original form.

Six

Eat raw foods, for example raw carrots, celery, lettuce, tomatoes, peppers.

Seven

Avoid one large meal a day - eat three or four small meals a day instead.

On early start most officers eat their main meal in the evening, but try to avoid a large meal within two hours of going to bed. It's is better to eat alone at four or five in the afternoon than to wait for a partner coming home from work late, then eating a large meal at 8pm and going to bed at 9.30.

On night shift it is usual to have the main meal around 6 or 7 in the evening before leaving for work at 9pm. This is fine - but avoid rich food and take or buy a light easily digestible meal for the middle of the night. Meals that can be eaten cold or a flask of hot soup are the most versatile as there can be an urgent call just as your are sitting down to your 'meat and two veg'.

Eight

On rest days or when working regular hours try to eat your main meal at lunch time - allow time to digest food before going to bed.

Nine

Drink fresh water as opposed to drinks containing caffeine.

Ten

Avoid fizzy soft drinks - that is, those that are high in sugar or additives.

Eleven

Avoid full-fat milk and dishes containing high-fat concentrations.

Twelve

Don't rely solely on dairy produce (for example, milk, butter, cheese, eggs) for your protein.

Thirteen

Drink skimmed milk, herbal or weak teas, fruit juice and decaffeinated coffee.

Fourteen

Eat five or more helpings of fruit and vegetables per day. A pear (banana or apple) with a slice of unbuttered bread is a good start to the day. Consider another piece of fruit as a mid morning snack, salad for lunch, and vegetables for the main meal (or *vice versa*) and this is our 'five-a-day' ruling.

Fifteen

Drink bottled water in preference to tap water, which may contain lead or other contaminants - or at least filter tap water before drinking. Beware of ice in drinks which may have been frozen from contaminated water, particularly on holidays abroad.

Sixteen

Eat more fish and poultry, as opposed to red meat. Worries have surfaced regarding the antibodies fed or injected into animals reared for human consumption. Links have been made between cancer and heart disease, and red meat eaters - white meat and fish are a more healthy alternative. However, remember that farmed fish including salmon, trout, durade and loup (sea bass) are fed pellets as opposed to 'free ranging'. It is suggested to opt for 'wild' fish until the long-term effects of fish farming have been examined - for example cod, haddock, herring, plaice, monkfish, mackerel, sardines and tuna.

Seventeen

Eat an 'oily' fish once or twice a week (see 'Unsaturated fat' post)

Eighteen

Avoid losing vitamins and minerals by over-boiling vegetables.

Nineteen

Avoid or cut down on sauces, creams, custards, salad dressings and butter mixed with vegetables. If you must, then use the 'light' or low fat varieties.

Twenty

Get to know the calories that your food contains. Men need about 2,500 per day and women about 2,000. Check the chart at the end of the chapter as a brief guide.

What is food all about and how does the body use it?

Carbohydrates

Carbohydrates provide the body with energy and are divided into two main groups - starches and sugars.

It is probably because of the association of starch and sugar with gaining weight that carbohydrates have had a bad press. However they are not fattening in themselves. Only when they are eaten in excess and along with oil or butter do weight problems occur.

Carbohydrates are necessary for metabolism within the body cells - ie the chemical process of producing energy from glucose. The body breaks down carbohydrates into glucose which can be used immediately, but can also be stored in the muscles and liver. When there is a long term excess of glucose it is made into fat.

These days we tend to get most of our carbohydrates from refined sugar (cane and beet) and this is digested more quickly than starch, leading to the danger of eating too much sugar. Sugar or honey should only be consumed in small quantities because of the potential for causing weight gain and also the associated tooth decay problems.

Our sugar intake is obtained from neat sugar, honey, some fruits, jams, cakes, sweets, candies, chocolate, sweet drinks etc.

All the starches come from vegetable (as opposed to animal) sources. Our starches intake can be from for example potatoes, pasta, bread, flour, rice, oats, peas and beans.

Try to get most of your daily carbohydrates from starches as opposed to sugars. These foods should be in their natural form as far as possible - ie potatoes with jackets on, whole-meal bread and wholegrain cereals. (NB it has only recently been recognised that the fibre part of vegetables is necessary in our diets - see later. As the unrefined vegetables and cereals have all the fibre left in them, these are the ones we should eat.)

The recommended daily allowance of carbo-hydrates is about 10 ounces (280 grams).

Remember that sugar excess is a cause of obesity.

Fat content of food

Fats form an important part of the body's cells. All diets must contain some fat and slimmers should bear in mind that it would be danger-ous to try to cut out fat altogether.

There are two types of fat:
 1. unsaturated; and
 2. saturated.

Unsaturated fat

The majority of unsaturated fats are extracted from vegetables and are in liquid form. Unsaturated oils (which help to prevent cho-lesterol) are found in soya, corn and sunflower oil and also in some fish and in poultry. Oily fish include herring, trout, salmon, mackerel and tuna.

Other oils which are mainly unsaturated include, olive, walnut, grapeseed, sesame seed and sunflower oil. This type of oil can be used for salad dressings. (The expensive ones, but those with the most flavour, are sesame and walnut oil.) Olive oil is a good substitute, but like all oils it should be 'cold-pressed' or 'vir-gin' - others may have been collected by using heat or chemicals which can make them into saturates.

Try to reduce or stop frying food, but if you have to fry then use olive, sunflower or corn oil. (The two latter are better for deep frying at high temperatures.)

Butter substitutes are generally unsaturated but may have been produced via a heat or chemical process. As mentioned above this could alter the molecular structure of, or leave chemical deposits within, the substitute. Most will contain preservatives and other additives so it is recommended that butter is generally used, but not in great quantities.

Even though butter is a 'saturated fat', it is a 'natural' fat as opposed to a manufactured one and therefore has few or no additives.

(The habit of spreading bread with fat seems to be a UK and US practice. The French don't spread their baguettes with fat. They merely cut the bread and serve in a bowl without a butter dish being in sight!)

In a diet which contains only a moderate amount of unsaturated fat a little saturated fat such as butter, bacon and egg, biscuits and cake should do no harm.

Saturated fat

Saturated fat is usually derived from animal sources, comes in a solid form and is thought to encourage the body to over-produce choles-terol (the culprit in the blockage of arteries and heart disease).

Saturated fat is found in most red meat (but very little in game, ie rabbit, venison and pheasant), whole milk, cream, butter, cheese, eggs, hard margarines, peanuts, peanut butter, coconut oil and palm oil. Take-away foods - Indian, Chinese and fast-food, including fish and chips and pizzas, all contain varying amounts of fat.

Reducing fat intake

Ways of reducing fat intake should always be borne in mind, especially if you know you have a problem with weight, high blood pressure or a family history of associated health problems.

√ Establish the fat content of takeaway food - or try to eat fewer takeaways - and always check labels for fat content.

√ Avoid the apparently innocent biscuit or piece of cake when you can - it has a high fat content. Also most pastries have butter, margarine or lard (beef fat) in them.

√ Try to eat more fish and poultry rather than red meat.

√ Cut the fat off the fatty meats such as pork, bacon, lamb or mutton and beef.

√ Have the occasional vegetarian dish, and include raw vegetables in your diet

√ Change from frying food - whether shallow or deep frying - to grilling and boiling.

√ Use natural yogurt as a substitute for cream and use semi- or fully-skimmed milk.

Generally, fat should only be eaten in small quantities because it is the most concentrated form of energy. We all need a little fat for cell building and repair, to insulate our bodies and organs such as kidneys and to assist the fat-soluble vitamins to be absorbed by the body.

We only need a daily allowance of fat of around three ounces (84 grams).

Remember that obesity is caused by too much fat.

Proteins

Proteins form the basic structure of the body - the bones, muscles, tendons and other tissues. Protein intake is required at regular intervals for the growth, repair and replacement of body cells which make up the bones and tissue.

In the living world there are 24 types of amino acid, each containing nitrogen. The human body spends a lot of its time extracting these acids from food. A chemical process in the body changes these acids into a new protein for the growth and repair of cells. The molecules in protein contain carbon, hydrogen, oxygen and nitrogen atoms - and sometimes phosphorus and sulphur atoms as well.

Police canteens have been guilty of serving too many fatty meals, although there are signs of improvement. Some in fact are trail blazers, but in the absence of national standards or guidelines in England and Wales, others may benefit from a little pressure from the police representative bodies

After digesting the protein the body builds up amino acids into a chain (or chains). If there is spare protein not needed for amino acid conversion, the body will change it to glucose for energy or, more problematically, store it as fat.

There are many sources of protein - all meats, white and oily fish, peas, beans, rice, cereals, bread, nuts, eggs, cheese, yogurt and milk. The importance of variety when eating food containing protein cannot be overemphasised. The body needs the amino acids from protein to be in particular permutations before it can chemically process them. In other words it needs a mix of vegetable protein (from pulses such as peas or lentils) along with a small amount of protein derived from animals, together with bread and cheese or rice and fish.

Vegetarianism

The body will survive without meat or animal products provided sufficiently varied plant -based alternatives are consumed to supply the essential nutrients. A grain and pulse mix is recommended as a vegetarian permutation of protein. For example baked beans on toast or a vegetable curry with pulses and rice would suit Vegans:

Vegetarians fall into three main groups:

1. vegans who do not consume any meat, fish or animal products - which excludes milk and milk products from their diet;
2. vegetarians who allow themselves milk and milk products but no eggs;
3. vegetarians who have milk and milk products and eggs.

(There is also a category who are 'vegetarian' in not eating meat and meat products, but who will eat fish.)

In terms of a healthy diet, the pros and cons of true vegetarianism are as follows:

For:

√ lower blood pressure;

√ diet high in fibre;

√ low in fats;

√ less sodium (salt) and more potassium (good for nervous system, circulation and kidneys); less chance of kidney stones, cancer and heart disease.

Against:

▶ without careful planning protein or iron deficiency pose a risk;

▶ milk is a very rich source of calcium and when excluded from the diet the body's calcium must be obtained from the less rich sources of nuts, grains, dark green leafy vegetables, seeds etc;

▶ a likelihood of Vitamin B12 deficiency means supplements are necessary.

(See vitamin and mineral charts (post) for more information)

One-and-a-half to two-and-a-quarter ounces (40 to 60 grams) of protein is required a day by the average adult.

Remember - excess protein may be stored as fat.

The fibre content of the diet

Fibre or roughage is the indigestible part of plants. The recommended daily target is one ounce (28 grams) and this should help prevent constipation, and reduces the risk of bowel cancer and other large intestine diseases.

Fibre is also thought to absorb toxins as it passes through the body and to lower the blood cholesterol. The fibre adds bulk to meals, causes us to chew food more thoroughly, makes us feel fuller and encourages the waste products to pass through the body faster. It makes the stools larger and softer and may - if you are not used to eating fibre - cause flatulence in the first instance, but this should settle down in four or five weeks.

The best sources of fibre include bran (the outer part of the wheat grains), unprocessed grains such as oats, pulses like peas, lentils and beans, wholemeal bread, unprocessed fresh vegetables, and fresh or dried fruit. If you eat plenty of fresh fruit and vegetables each day you need not supplement your diet with uninteresting special 'added fibre' foods.

Vitamins and minerals

Vitamins and minerals are needed for the body's chemical processes. Vitamins can act as a catalyst in these processes, and minerals form part of our hormone and enzyme systems and help the muscles and nerves to work correctly.

Some vitamins and minerals are water soluble and can be washed out or cooked out of food. Rice should not be washed before cooking and it is better to steam, stir fry or bake vegetables than to boil them. Add raw vegetables to casseroles shortly before serving.

These alternatives preserve the vitamins and minerals in the vegetables better than boiling. If you want to boil vegetables then leave them as 'crisp' or 'al dente', as possible and use the water you have boiled them in for soups or stocks.

Many vegetables, salads and fruit can be eaten raw. In this way you receive their maximum vitamin and mineral content.

The chart overleaf gives an outline of the key vitamins and minerals the body needs.

Vitamin and mineral supplements

If you are in good health and eat a varied diet, vitamin or mineral supplements should not be necessary. Supplements are no substitute for the whole foods. Having said this, there is a growing school of thought that vitamin C supplements are good for preventing or curing the common cold. It is accepted that vitamin C has anti viral and antibacterial properties and is an antioxidant. Also, as shown in the chart, vitamin E is thought to help reduce the risk of heart attacks and slow down the aging process.

Note - salt

The sodium in salt (sodium chloride) can raise the blood pressure of many people, so health experts recommend limiting the total daily intake of salt to six grams or less. This is roughly one and a quarter teaspoons of salt. The British Nutrition Foundation advises that adults need only four grams. Most adults consume nine grams per day. Bear in mind that only about 20 per cent of the salt in the British diet is added during cooking or at the table - the rest is already in the processed foods we buy.

Parents should be aware of the (potentially fatal) dangers of too much salt in young babies' diets. Avoid adding salt to babies' food or feeding them 'adult' food if it already contains or has added salt.

Vitamin chart

A
Good for...
eye health, the body membranes, lung linings and the digestive system.

Found in...
carrots, liver, milk, eggs, broccoli, spinach.

fat soluble.

B₂ (Riboflavin)
Good for...
eye, skin, hair and nail health - aids repair, growth and reproduction.

Found in...
whole grains, cereals, mushrooms, milk, eggs, cheese, poultry, liver.

water soluble.

B₆ (Pyridoxine)
Good for...
the production of red blood cells, antibodies and protein making - helps the nerves to function properly, the body to use fats and may help with pre-menstrual tension.

Found in...
whole grains, cereals, avocado pears, green beans, bananas, nuts, potatoes, liver, lean meat, eggs, milk.

water soluble.

B₁ (Thiamin)
Helps with...
burning energy from carbohydrates, mental and nerve processes, and growth.

Found in...
pork, whole grains, pulses, pasta, bread, nuts, most vegetables.

water soluble.

B₃ (Niacin)
Helps maintain...
the correct cholesterol and blood sugar levels - and with the production of energy in cells.

Found in...
eggs, avocado pears, yeast, dried beans and peas, nuts, whole grains and cereals.

water soluble.

B₁₂
Good for...
the nervous system, red blood cell production, iron metabolism.

Found in...
eggs, meat, dairy products, yeast extract and fermented foods. NB Vegans may be deficient as they do not eat animal products. Supplements made from certain types of yeast are now available.

water soluble.

Vitamin chart (cont...)

C (Ascorbic acid)
Good for...
bones, teeth and tissue - helps with the healing of cuts and wounds, the resistance of disease and the absorption of iron - it is accepted that vitamin C has antioxidant, antiviral and antibacterial qualities.

Found in...
citrus fruits, tomatoes, raw cabbage, potatoes, strawberries.

water soluble.

D
Helps maintain...
blood calcium and phosphorus levels for the growth of bones and teeth.

Good for...
children and pregnant women.

Found in...
oily fish, fish liver oils eg cod liver oil, dairy produce, eggs - and sunlight on the skin.

fat soluble.

E
Used by the body for...
tissue handling of fatty substances - it is a part of all cell membranes, protecting the circulatory system cells, is thought to help prevent heart attacks and slow down the aging process.

Found in...
vegetable oils, dark green vegetables, eggs, nuts, wheat germ and whole grains.

fat soluble.

Folic acid
Needed for...
healthy cell life and in the prevention of anaemia.

Good for...
pregnant women.

Found in...
fresh vegetables such as avocado pears, leafy vegetables, carrots, pumpkins and in apricots, whole grains and egg yolks.

water soluble.

K
Good for...
the liver to make an agent for blood-clotting.

Found in...
leafy vegetables, egg yolks, cheese, pork, liver, yogurt and also made by intestinal bacteria.

fat soluble.

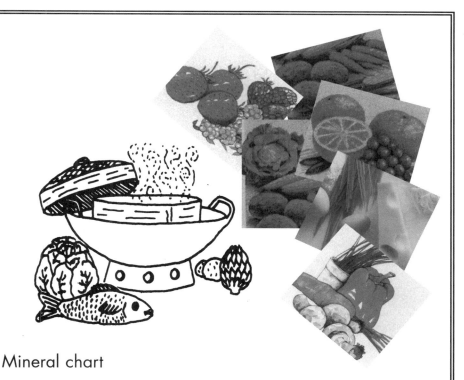

Mineral chart

Calcium

Used by the body for...
blood-clotting, bone and teeth growth, the functioning of nerves and other tissues activated by electricity

Found in...
dairy products like milk and cheese, green vegetables.

Phosphorus

Good for...
heart, kidneys, bone structure

Found in...
meat, dairy products, seeds, nuts, whole grains, eggs, soya, cereals.

Magnesium

Needed for...
the good working of muscles, nerves and cells

Found in...
pulses, nuts, cereals, leafy green vegetables.

Iodine

Used by...
the thyroid gland and in the production of haemoglobin (oxygen carrying compound in the blood)

Found in...
seafood, liver, meat, eggs, enriched cereals.

Mineral chart (cont...)

Potassium

Good for...
the heart muscles, kidneys, blood circulation, the nervous system

Helps to...
balance the fluid in the body

Found in...
fresh and dried fruits, avocado pears, bananas, apricots, potatoes, vegetables, legumes, milk etc.

Sodium
(Sodium chloride - table salt and sodium bicarbonate - baking soda.)

Helps to...
regulate the body's water balance, the heart rhythm, the nerve impulses and the muscle functions

Found in...
salt and baking soda - a natural ingredient of most vegetables - added to processed foods such as butter, cheese, bread, cereals, and cured, pickled or smoked fish and meat.

Iron

Needed to...
make haemoglobin (the oxygen carrying pigment in red blood cells), and myoglobin (the oxygen-carrying pigment in the muscle cells) - also important for the formation of some enzymes, the proteins that help the body's chemical reactions

Found in...
liver, meat, whole grain cereals, fish, green leafy vegetables, nuts, beans.

Fluorine

Helps to...
prevent tooth decay and may also reduce the ability of plaque to make acid which attacks the teeth

Found in...
some toothpastes and in tap water when fluoride has been added -(excess fluoride may lead to a brown discolouration of the tooth enamel when teeth are forming, or to brittle bones in old people).

Zinc

Needed for...
normal growth, the reproductive organs, the prostrate gland, the healing of wounds for cell enzymes and for cells to make proteins and nucleic acids

Found in...
lean meats, wholemeal bread, whole grains, dried beans, seafood, eggs, milk and cheese.

Calories

Calories are a unit of energy - whether derived from carbohydrates, fats, or excess proteins.

For those of you who want to keep a check on your weight, you need to take in no more (or fewer) calories per day than your body burns up on its daily activities.

▶ An adult male between 25 and 45 years of age will burn up about 2,500 to 3,500 calories per day depending on weight, fitness and lifestyle.

▶ A female between 25 and 45 years will burn up slightly less than the male - about 2,250 to 2,750 calories per day.

To lose 450 grams of fat (one pound) you will need to eat 3,000 less calories.

It is relatively simple to make up a diet chart to take account of your likes and dislikes using information in the chart.

For those wishing to lose or check their weight note that 1,000 calories per day is suggested as the safe lowest intake. But choose this 1,000 wisely!

Calorie counting - choose your 1,000 wisely

200 grams of milk chocolate would give you:

1,180 calories

as opposed to:

2 slices bread	140
10 gms butter	80
2 apples	100
100 gms oatmeal porridge	45
100 gms rice	120
100 gms roast chicken	190
100 gms steamed cod	80
50 gms carrots	10
50 gms peas	25
100 gms salad (eg lettuce, cucumber, celery, mushrooms (raw), tomato)	10
50 gms dates	125
50 gms pineapple	23
50 gms plums	20
100 gms milk	65
Water	0
Total:	**1,033 calories**

Calorie chart (Approximate calories per 100g (2 oz))

Meat
Bacon, fried 600
Beef sirloin, lean and
   fat roast 390
Beef steak, grilled 300
Chicken, roast 190
Ham, lean and fat
   boiled 430
Lamb chop (lean and fat)
   grilled 500
Lamb leg, roast 290
Pork leg, roast 320
Pork chops (lean and fat)
   grilled 540
Venison, roast 200

Fish
Cod, steamed 80
Cod, fried 140
Halibut, steamed 130
Lemon sole, steamed 90
Lemon sole, fried 220
Plaice, steamed 90
Plaice, fried 235
Prawns, boiled 105
Salmon, steamed 200
Sardines, in tin of oil 300
Whitebait, fried 540

Dairy produce
(plus alternatives)

Eggs, fried 240
Eggs, poached 160
Cheese, Cheddar 425
Cheese, cream 800
Cheese, Edam 315
Yogurt, low fat 55
Milk 65
Butter 795
Olive oil 930
Margarine 800

Vegetables
Beans, broad, boiled 45
Beans, French, boiled 10
Beetroot, boiled 45
Brussel sprouts, boiled 15
Cabbage, spring,
   boiled 10
Carrots, boiled 20
Cauliflower, boiled 10
Celery, raw 10
Cucumber, raw 10
Leeks, boiled 10
Lentils, boiled 100
Lettuce, raw 10
Mushrooms, raw 10
Mushrooms, fried 215
Onions, boiled 15
Onions, fried 350
Parsnips, boiled 55
Peas, fresh, boiled 50
Potatoes, new, boiled 75
Potatoes, old, chips 240
Spinach, boiled 25
Tomatoes, raw 15
Tomatoes, fried 17

Cereals, bread & flour
Bran (Kellogg's All-Bran)
  310
Cornflakes (Kellogg's 370
Oatmeal porridge 45
Rice Krispies 350
Weetabix 351
Bread, wholemeal 230
Bread, white 245
Ryvita 345
Biscuits, digestive 480
Flour, white household
  350
Macaroni, boiled 115
Rice, polished boiled 120

Desserts
Chocolate, milk 590
Chocolate, plain 540
Honey 290
Ice cream 200
Jam 260
Pastry flaky 590
Cake, plain fruit 380
Scones 370
Sugar, white and
   brown 390
Toffee 435

Fruit and nuts
Almonds 600
Apples 45
Avocado pears 90
Bananas 75
Brazil nuts 645
Cherries, fresh 45
Dates 250
Fruit salad in syrup 95
Grapes 60
Grapefruit 20
Melon 25
Olives in brine 105
Oranges 35
Peaches 35
Peanut 600
Pears 40
Pineapple 45
Plums 40
Prunes, stewed
   (no sugar) 80
Raspberries, fresh 25
Rhubarb, stewed
   (no sugar) 5
Strawberries, fresh
   s(no sugar) 25
Sultanas 250
Walnuts 550

4. Gnawing away at cancer

Cancer prevention through diet

Diet and cancer - the critical link

In the 1950s scientists discovered a link between diet and coronary heart disease, the nation's number one killer. It is now increasingly apparent to scientists that there is also a relationship between diet and cancer, the nation's second leading cause of death.

The scientific evidence that the food we eat can affect whether or not we develop cancer is growing steadily. In the United States the American National Academy of Sciences found this evidence so persuasive that in their landmark report of 1982, *Diet, Nutrition and Cancer*, they urged Americans to begin changing their diets to increase their chances of avoiding cancer.

These recommendations have been supported by later reports from all over the world, including the European Community and the World Health Organisation itself.

Basically, the message is ever the same - eat more fresh fruit and vegetables, wholemeal bread and cereal, and cut down on fat, processed foods and alcohol. We all know that we should eat a more healthy diet. However, understanding the specific reasons for it can be very persuasive - to again quote the old saying, 'we are what we eat' or an updated version 'we are what we extract from our food'.

Based on these reports, the World Cancer Research Fund (WCRF) has devised four dietary guidelines which could help lower the risk of developing cancer.

1. Eat more vegetables, fruits, wholegrain bread and cereals.
2. Cut down the amount of saturated and unsaturated fat in your diet from the current average of approximately 41 per cent to a level of 30 per cent of total calories.
3. Consume salt-cured, salt-pickled and smoked foods in moderation.
4. Drink alcohol in moderation, if at all.

Understanding cancer

To assist in a better understanding of the concept of 'cancer prevention through diet' it will be helpful to answer a few common questions about cancer itself.

What is cancer?

Cancer is a very complex disease which can affect virtually all parts of the body. One thing cancers seem to have in common is that they start out as a single damaged body cell which begins to divide at an uncontrolled rate.

In most cancers the resulting group of abnormal cells forms a lump or swelling - a tumour. This may invade surrounding health tissues. Cancerous cells may eventually break away from the original tumour and spread through the bloodstream to other parts of the body. This is known as metastasis. New tumours formed as a result of this process are called metastases or 'secondaries'.

However, not all cancerous cells form tumours. In cancers of the blood, such as leukaemia, usually no solid tumour develops.

Are all lumps cancerous?

Most lumps or swellings do not invade or spread to other body tissues and are said to be benign (non cancerous). A wart is an example of a benign lump. Doctors often refer to non-cancerous lumps as benign tumours. Generally benign tumours are not harmful, although they can sometimes cause damage by putting pressure on surrounding tissues.

Is cancer inherited?

Cancer is very common. In Britain one in three people currently develop cancer at some time in their lives. This means that many people have relatives who have had the disease, but this does not necessarily prove an inherited tendency.

While most cancers start because of a damaged gene inside a body cell the scientific evidence suggests that in the majority of cases this damage is not inherited. When more than one member of a family develops cancer it is most likely due to chance, or to a similar lifestyle family members share. However, a small number of people are born with a faulty gene inherited from their parents. Some very rare cancers can be passed down from generation to generation,

and it is estimated that between five and 10 per cent of the more common cancers may also have a genetic family link.

Scientists have identified genes (known as 'tumour suppresser genes') that evidently help to stop the formation of tumours. If these genes are faulty, cancer may be more likely to develop. Faulty tumour suppresser genes can be inherited, making an individual more susceptible to cancer.

However, even in these cases, cancer development depends on many other factors and is far from being a certainty. Whether or not an individual actually develops the disease is still likely to be determined by aspects of lifestyle - such as smoking and dietary habits.

How does cancer develop?

In most cases the cancer process starts when one or more of the genes related to cell division becomes faulty. This may occur by chance or because a cancer-causing substance - a carcinogen - has been introduced into, or is produced by, the body.

We are exposed to would-be carcinogens all the time and many of them occur naturally in the air we breathe, the water we drink or the food we eat. They also occur in tobacco, in industrial compounds, or as viruses. Even the rays from the sun can be carcinogenic.

Our bodies are designed to deal with carcinogens - to eliminate them before they can do any harm or repair any damage done by them before it becomes permanent.

But sometimes the body's defences fail. A carcinogen becomes activated inside a body cell and permanently damages its DNA - the genetic information every cell contains. Once damaged in this way, the cell can no longer function properly. It may grow and multiply abnormally and, as it divides, the flawed information it contains may be passed on.

At this stage a damaged cell is not fully-fledged cancer. In fact, the disease may never develop at all.

To become cancer, abnormal cells must reproduce to such an extent that they start to occupy the space of normal cells, or threaten the function of healthy cells or organs. For some cancers that might take a long time, perhaps 10 to 20 years or more.

During this time, other factors are thought to affect how rapidly the damaged cells divide. This process may speed up, slow down or even be stopped altogether before cancer develops.

Some factors - called inhibitors - are believed to slow the process down. Other factors - called promoters - may speed up the rate at which the damaged cells multiply and so encourage the development of cancer.

Hundreds of scientific studies have, for example, consistently found a link between high fat diets and the promotion of some cancers. Hundreds of other studies have shown that certain vitamins, minerals and other nutrients found in fruits and vegetables evidently inhibit the start and growth of cancer.

It is because this development process may be influenced so much by things we can control, like our diet, that we have a chance of actually preventing cancer.

Being aware of the factors that may encourage or discourage cancer cell growth, and taking action accordingly, should reduce our risk of developing the disease.

What role does lifestyle play?

The sequence of events that leads to cancer is complex and varied. A combination of genetic, behavioural, environmental and lifestyle factors are involved in turning a normal cell into an abnormal cell, and an abnormal cell into cancer.

The genetic changes that start the cancer process are often referred to as 'initiation' and the following stages - the events which allow an abnormal cell to divide and grow - as 'promotion'.

The promotion of most cancers is thought to be linked very strongly to lifestyle factors.

Just about everybody knows that cigarettes cause lung cancer.

However, there is a common misconception that the other main cancer-causing culprits are factors like pollution, chemicals, and additives in foods. In fact, many of the things that worry people probably cause only a very small percentage of cancer deaths. That's not to say that we shouldn't be at all concerned about them (after all, it would be unwise to expose ourselves needlessly to things that could cause harm) but it does mean that there are far more significant cancer risk factors for us to take into account.

Much current evidence points to elements of the diet being involved in the promotion of several common types of cancer. It is also highly probable that other dietary elements can hinder - or inhibit - the promotion of tumour growth, and so protect us against cancer.

The following chart shows the percentage of cancer deaths estimated to result from various environmental and lifestyle factors.

Environmental and lifestyle factors contributing to cancer deaths

Food additives 1%

Pollution 2%

Alcohol 3%

Occupation 4%

Viruses 5%

Tobacco 30%

Diet 35%

As you can see, the evidence is that diet and tobacco use account for far more cancer deaths than all the other likely factors combined. It follows that healthy eating habits could reduce total cancer deaths by as much as 35 per cent - more than a third. In the UK that would mean 50,000 lives saved each year.

i. Tobacco

The use of tobacco is the single most preventable cause of death and disease in this country and, as shown in the chart, is responsible for an estimated 30% of all cancer deaths. It is also a major cause of coronary heart disease.

However, a combination of alcohol and cigarettes seems to be more likely to cause cancer than just drinking or just smoking alone. Evidence is also continuing to accumulate to show that passive smoking can increase the risk of lung cancer.

ii. Diet and weight

Women who are overweight or obese appear to have a greater chance of developing cancers of the breast and uterus than women who are not

overweight. Population studies of men also suggest that obese men may be at greater risk of colon (bowel) and prostate cancer. Numerous studies suggest that if we lower our calorie consumption, we may lower our risk of cancer and other diseases.

Maintaining a desirable body weight is a matter of balancing calorie intake with physical activity.

Practical steps towards cancer prevention

Cancer is such a complex disease that no one can be offered guarantees against it, but - because cancer is so often linked to lifestyle - there are plenty of positive steps you can take to lower your own likelihood of developing the disease.

How can what we eat influence cancer development?

A cancer does not just suddenly appear. It develops very slowly through different stages, some of which are reversible. And the food we eat can affect many, or perhaps all of these stages; from the first exposure to a cancer-causing substance, to the long, gradual development of a tumour.

Firstly, foods known to contain significant levels of carcinogens should be avoided when possible or should be eaten only in moderation. Salt-cured and salt-pickled foods contain substances called nitrates that can be changed into carcinogens in the stomach. Smoked foods also contain carcinogens.

Secondly some foods contain nutrients and other compounds which seem to help the body's natural defences destroy carcinogens before they can cause serious damage to cells. They also may halt or reverse steps in the cancer development process. These nutrients and compounds are found in fruit, vegetables and whole grain cereals so eating more of these foods is recommended.

Thirdly, certain types of food, if consumed regularly over long periods of time, seem to provide the kind of environment a cancer cell needs to grow, multiply and spread. These foods should be avoided or eaten only in moderation. The main offenders here are foods high in fat. Some of these include fatty meat and meat products, cakes and biscuits, fried foods and high-fat dairy products.

The fact that the food we eat can have such powerful effects on so many of the steps in the development of a cancer is good news! It offers many potential opportunities for interfering with this process and preventing it from happening.

As scientists estimate that over a third of cancer deaths may be linked to the foods we eat, developing healthier eating habits by following WCRF's dietary guidelines may be one of the most significant steps you can take.

Make the right food choices

> The WCRF Dietary Guidelines to Lower Your Cancer Risk are a good starting point. They:
>
> √ encourage eating low-calorie, nutrient rich foods such as fruit and vegetables;
>
> √ encourage eating satisfying, wholesome foods such as whole grain cereals and pulses which are not high in calories;
>
> x discourage eating high-calorie items such as high-fat foods and alcohol.

1. Eat more vegetables, fruits, wholegrain bread and cereals

Some of the substances found in fruit, vegetables, whole grain cereals and pulses that are thought to help prevent cancer are beta-carotene (vitamin A), vitamin C, vitamin E, selenium, and dietary fibre (see previous chapter for further detail).

Ideally, most people should be able to obtain all the nutrients they need for good health from a well-balanced diet. There is no need to fill up your medicine cabinet with bottles of expensive nutrient supplements. Taking nutrient as pills is not a substitute for eating them naturally as part of food. (Vitamin A, for example, can be toxic when taken in pill form well in excess of recommended amounts and should not be taken except under medical supervision.)

In human beings, there is no compelling evidence that taking nutrient supplements can reduce the risk of developing cancer.

There is however growing evidence that foods rich in dietary fibre may help reduce the risk of developing cancer of the colon, or large intestine. British adults consume about 20 grams of fibre a day. Health experts generally recommend at least 30 grams a day, with an upper limit around 40 grams a day. This dietary fibre should come from a variety of fruits, vegetables, whole grain cereals and pulses (lentils, beans and peas).

By following the dietary guidelines to eat more fruit, vegetables, whole grain cereals and pulses we naturally increase our intake of nutritious complex carbohydrates (ie starches). Foods containing mainly simple carbohydrates, such as sweets and sugary drinks, usually contain only small amounts of the nutrients important for good health and for preventing cancer.

> The WCRF recommends even more specifically that each day we should eat:
>
> √ five or more helpings of fruit and vegetables, particularly green and yellow vegetables and citrus fruit;
>
> √ at least half of our daily calories from bread, cereals and other starchy foods such as rice and pasta.

2. Cut down the amount of saturated and unsaturated fat in your diet

The more you substitute the above recommended foods for those high in fat the more you will reduce your overall fat intake - remembering of course the importance of balance in the diet and that some fat is necessary (see Chapt 3: A Fitting Diet).

Scientists are studying how saturated fats in our diets might promote tumour development and how lower amounts of saturated fat might reduce cancer risk. (Eating less saturated fat is also the main dietary recommendation to lower your risk of coronary heart disease, so you can kill two birds with one stone!.)

The WCRF *Dietary Guidelines to Lower Your Cancer Risk* state that you should reduce the amount of fat you eat to 30 per cent of your total calorie intake and that about one third of this - that is 10 per cent or less of your total calories - should come from saturated fat

3. Consume salt-cured, salt-pickled and smoked foods in moderation

Preserving food by curing it, pickling it with salt or smoking it has been practiced for thousands of years. Unfortunately, in some countries, eating large amounts of salt-cured, salt-pickled and smoked foods has been linked to cancer of the oesophagus. The smoke from curing appears to create carcinogens in the food, while salt-cured and salt-pickled foods contain nitrates which can be transformed into carcinogens in the foods or in the stomach.

Grilling food over open flames can also create cancer-causing substances on the surface of foods. Charred foods, particularly charred fatty foods, contain a high concentration of carcinogens, so it is best to cook with less intense heat or cook food a greater distance from the flame to avoid charring.

Note: In Britain this dietary guideline should not be a major cause for concern - it is intended for peoples who consume *excessive quantities* of these types of foods.

4. Drink alcohol in moderation - if at all

Drinking alcohol appears to increase the chances of developing certain forms of cancer. In moderate amounts, alcohol seems to be linked to greater risks for developing cancer of the breast, rectum, and pancreas. In excessive amounts, especially combined with cigarette smoking, alcohol may increase the chances of developing cancers of the mouth, oesophagus and larynx. And in alcohol abusers who have developed cirrhosis of the liver, alcohol increases the risk of developing liver cancer.

In addition to the harmful effects that alcohol itself can have on the body, drinking large amounts can also interfere with eating a healthy diet. That is because alcohol contains calories, but few (if any) nutrients, and it can displace from the diet healthier foods (or drinks) containing nutrients important for preventing certain types of cancer.

In summary...

Can you really lower your chances of getting cancer by eating a healthy diet?

There is evidence to suggest you can do so by following the four dietary guidelines of the World Cancer Research Fund. And, at the same time, you can lower your risk of coronary heart disease, diabetes and obesity. These dietary guidelines are based on the conclusions of the world's leading experts who have carefully reviewed the latest scientific evidence on the influence of diet and nutrition on the development of cancer.

The World Cancer Research Fund is dedicated to seeing that this research continues and to providing the public with the latest, most reliable information available on nutrition and cancer.

To keep informed about what you can do to prevent cancer in your life and the lives of your family, stay in touch with the WCRF. You will find that healthy eating is a highly enjoyable step towards cancer prevention, simply because it is such a pleasure.

If you would like to find out more about healthy eating, the dietary guidelines to lower cancer risk, or general information about cancer prevention write to:

World Cancer Research Fund
105, Park Street, London W1Y 3FB

The information in this chapter is based on current research recommendations from scientists throughout the world, including reports from the United States' National Academy of Sciences, the European Community's Europe Against Cancer Programme and the World Health Organisation.

File 4.1   Other precautionary measures

In addition to making the right food choices, the following practical preventive steps echo the advice of the European Code Against Cancer: A Code for Living. The more of them you follow, the lower your overall cancer risk is likely to be.

Do not smoke - smokers should try to stop as quickly as possible.

At least 90 per cent of lung cancers - and an estimated 30 per cent of all cancers - are due to smoking, which is also a major cause of coronary heart disease. The combination of alcohol and cigarettes is much more likely to cause cancer than drinking alone. Furthermore, passive smoking increases the risk of lung cancer. The longer someone smokes the more dangerous it becomes, but the good news is that the risk begins to fall as soon as you stop.

Take regular exercise

Some cancers are associated with extreme overweight. Regular exercise, combined with a sensible diet, can help maintain a healthy weight as well as improve general health. Try to work up towards 20-30 minutes of exercise two to three times a week. If you don't exercise at the moment, take it one step at a time. For those over 50, or who have a history of poor health, it is wise to consult a doctor first.

Take care in the sun

Too much sun can cause skin cancer, so remember to protect your skin especially in strong sunlight - tan slowly. Avoid burning and use high factor sunscreens, especially during holidays abroad in hot countries. You should be particularly careful if you are fair-haired or have skin which burns easily.

Be aware of the incidence of cancer in your family

The great majority of cancers are not inherited, however a small percentage of common cancers evidently have some genetic family link. Age can sometimes be a clue to any family tendency. Most cancers usually occur later in life, but the small number of cancers with a genetic link generally occur at a younger age. If several close family members have developed colon (bowel), breast or ovarian cancer at a young age (under 45) it may increase your possibility of developing the same type of cancer. To be on the safe side you should talk to your doctor about the options you may have for special screening.

Females...

i. Be breast aware

Examine your breasts regularly. Get to know how they look and feel at various times of the month. If you notice any lumps, a dimple or puckering or any other unusual changes, don't panic (eight out of 10 lumps are not cancer) but do see your doctor as quickly as possible. Breast cancer is more common in later life, so for women over 50, regular screening (called mammography) is advisable. *(See Chapt 14: Checking Your Change.)*

ii Have a cervical smear test every three - five years

The smear test can detect abnormal changes in the cells of the neck of the womb before cancer has actually developed and when it is possible to prevent it from starting. If cervical cancer has already developed and yet is treated at an early stage, it too is curable. If you have not had a smear test within the last five years, it makes sense to go to your doctor or family planning clinic and ask for one now.

File 4.2 Cancer diagnosis, treatments and cures

How is cancer diagnosed?

When a patient has symptoms that might be caused by cancer, a doctor will first carry out a physical examination, along with blood and urine tests. These tests often show that the symptoms are related to another, less serious, condition. If this is not the case, and cancer is still suspected, the patient will generally be referred to a specialist. If a tumour is present, a small sample of tissue may be removed for examination under a microscope. This biopsy - usually a very minor procedure that can be performed in an outpatients clinic - assesses whether the tumour is malignant (cancerous) or benign (non-cancerous). If a tumour is cancerous, x-ray or scanning techniques may be used to find out more about the cancer and assess and advise the patient of the best form of treatment.

How is cancer treated?

The following treatments may be used alone or in combination, depending on the type of cancer and whether or not the disease has spread:

Surgery - may be used to remove a whole tumour or an affected organ.

Radiotherapy - uses carefully controlled doses of radiation on a highly specific area of the body to kill cancer cells and shrink a tumour. Cancer cells are move vulnerable to radiotherapy than normal cells and any normal cells that are affected repair themselves after treatment.

Chemotherapy - uses anti-cancer drugs to kill cancer cells throughout the body or to stop them from multiplying. As well as attacking the main tumour, the drugs circulate around the body in the bloodstream, destroying cancer cells that may have spread elsewhere.

Hormone therapy - may be used to treat certain cancers known to be affected by the level of hormones in the body. The level of the relevant hormone may be reduced or increased or its action may be blocked. Breast cancer development, for example, is often affected by the hormone oestrogen. New hormone therapy treatments which block the action of oestrogen are producing promising results.

Biological therapies - are also new types of treatment which use natural substances made by the immune system to stimulate the body's defences to work harder against cancer cells. Most biological therapies are still undergoing clinical trials and their affects are not yet known.

Complementary therapies - such as acupuncture, meditation, relaxation, and homeopathy are increasingly being used to supplement conventional medical treatment. While there is no conclusive evidence that such therapies can control or cure cancer, many people find that they bring great physical and psychological benefits. Those considering such therapy should first discuss their intentions with their GP or specialist to ensure that the chosen method is safe and doesn't interfere with conventional medical treatments.

Can cancer be cured?

Cancers in some parts of the body often respond very well to treatment - particularly if they are diagnosed at an early stage. Other types of cancer, and cancers diagnosed at later stages of development, are far more difficult to treat successfully. However, a significant number of people who have experienced cancer are cured and go on to live long, healthy lives.

The real hope for cancer lies in prevention. By making certain choices about the way we live, we can take significant control of our own cancer risk. Making those choices can't guarantee that you won't develop cancer, but it can almost certainly guarantee a lower cancer risk.

5. Drugs of first choice

The facts about tobacco, alcohol and caffeine

Reference illegal substances... see the update at the end of the chapter and the 'force policy on alcohol and drugs'

Social trends and acceptance

This chapter examines the effects of drugs which have been part of Western society for many years tobacco, alcohol and caffeine.

It is said that Sir Walter Raleigh introduced tobacco to Queen Elizabeth I - along with the potato. However, promoted by the media and burgeoning tobacco companies, smoking was given a more glamourous role, reinforced by film and television icons. Particularly during the thirties, movies and their stars - Betty Davies springs immediately to mind - glamourised the cigarette smoking image.

During both world wars and in war movies, the cigarette was portrayed as friend and ally. The question of cigarette rations for the troops to maintain morale was high on the war cabinet's agenda.

However many second world war veterans returned home to a suffer a new epidemic - lung cancer. The resulting research commissioned in the UK in the fifties led to the discovery by the then research scientist, Richard Doll, of the link between smoking and lung cancer and heart disease.

Medical science began to point the finger at tobacco as being dangerous to health, and to its resulting drain on health care funds. This was completely contrary to contemporary thinking which held pollution to be a more likely cause and cigarettes to be entirely beneficial - most doctors smoked! Controversy over the issue - fuelled by the social and financial influence of tobacco in society - meant that political and social thinking was generally slow to respond.

When subsequent anti-smoking legislation was implemented, it required that the public be warned of the dangers of smoking and that all cigarette packets and advertising carry a health warning. TV advertising has been banned in the UK and sport sponsorship by cigarette manufacturers widely curtailed.

Generally the use of cigarettes began to fall in both the UK and the US. Since 1970 the number of deaths from heart disease in the US has decreased and this is thought to be because of the reduction in the number of smokers. In the UK, life expectancy, particularly for men, has increased over the last decade by up to five years, and giving up smoking is cited as a contributory factor.

However, a disturbing trend is the use of cigarettes by the younger members of society and an increased use by females. Females are now smoking more than males in percentage terms.

Encouragingly, police officers in the UK smoke less than the average. But, discouragingly, TV programmes still tend to portray the culture of the macho hard-drinking, hard-smoking police officer.

The issue of compensation for smokers is still wide open, particularly since US courts have found against the tobacco companies and in favour of the smoker. Compensation could be a possibility even in the UK.

The stance of governments is always likely to be ambivalent due to the income they receive via taxation. They have a legitimate reason for increasing taxation to make smoking less popular, but may be trapped themselves by the dependence of their economies on revenue raised from tobacco - and from alcohol.

Extremes of legislation governing alcohol consumption have varied between the American prohibition to the all-day drinking in parts of continental Europe. Certain groups are pressing for the more relaxed continental system to be adopted in the UK but as yet there are no signs of further extensions to the UK licensing hours.

Apart from caffeine it is today probably the most socially acceptable drug in the Western World. (Mention must be made here to distinguish societies and religions which do not allow the use of alcohol - notably some Middle Eastern countries and the Mormon religion.)

However, in its many forms, alcohol is integral to the Western way of life. It has long been part of birthdays, weddings and funerals.

A similar ritual to smoking has attached itself to drinking - people feel naked unless they have a glass in their hand at many social occasions, whether formal or informal. The shapes of the bottle and glasses, whether to have ice or lemon etc; the names of the drinks, the advertising hype - all identify types of people with types of drink.

Alcohol users are following long social traditions of drinking. Children show off by imitating parents and later to impress their peers. Pressures include the macho image of beer drinkers and the subtle help from other social and work influences.

Over the years the police culture has tacitly encouraged drinking in a somewhat macho manner. Recently there are signs that this is altering for the better. Several forces have issued policy statements regarding alcohol dangers.

Police staff need an understanding of the dangers of over drinking both for themselves and for the public they serve. The issue of alcohol is doubly relevant to the police service - as an employer, and as a law enforcer. Alcohol has the potential to affect officers in their personal lives, and in dealing with its social and law and order repercussions - such as drink driving, disorder, domestic problems and child abuse.

Caffeine must be the most commonly used drug in the developed world. However, its widespread use in the West has raised some cause for concern and most health advice now ranges from a sensible caffeine intake down to non at all.

Police staff are exposed to caffeine domestically, at work both in the police office and when in contact with the public and, finally, in their social lives. They need to know what contains caffeine and what are the danger levels of consumption.

These 'social' drugs should be used sensibly, if at all. In the police service the culture lends itself to the use of and sometimes encouragement in the use of all three. Peer group pressure, the still-macho image and the very nature of the often stressful job of policing can, and quite often does, get an officer or member of the support staff addicted to at least one of them.

Tobacco

Why do we use tobacco?

Tobacco is a 'social' drug purported to be used for social, relaxation and pleasure purposes.

The common reasons for starting to smoke include peer group pressure, emulating role models, curiosity, and as a means of impressing others. Young people particularly think it is 'cool' to smoke - sometimes viewing it as a status symbol.

Reasons why smokers continue include:

to reduce stress and tension - in the workplace, or when driving;

for stimulation - especially when concentration is needed;

for the ritual of smoking - many smokers say they would not know what to do with their hands if they stopped;

habit - 'I always have one after a meal or between courses';

relaxation - as a source of comfort, perhaps when watching television.

image - emulating famous people who have used smoking as a trademark.

Many 'police' films and TV police characters are portrayed as smoking - or against the background of a smoking culture. How many shining examples of health can you think of from police films and soaps? Whose example would you follow? Bear in mind that it is now the norm for police officers to smoke less than the national average.

The harmful effects of tobacco smoking

Smokers should all be clear about the addictive quality of nicotine and the numerous areas of our lives that smoking damages. They need to know the many ways available to cut down or stop smoking and not to be misled by the apparently 'safer' alternative of low tar cigarettes, pipe smoking or cigars.

'Tipped' cigarettes usually contain the same strength of tobacco, but the tar is regulated through minute laser holes in the tips to give different strengths. Tipped cigarette are advertised as 'low tar' and are claimed by the manufacturers to be 'safer' than 'medium' or 'high tar' cigarettes.

However, as all smoking deprives the blood and other body organs of oxygen due to the carbon monoxide intake, it is difficult to prove any benefits from low tar cigarettes. The image of the 'safer cigarette' is counter productive - it encourages the smoker into a false sense of security. Also people who use these cigarettes are likely to smoke more to maintain their blood nicotine levels.

It is said that the risk of lung cancer is not as great for pipe and cigars smokers as most do not inhale. However, the risk of lip, mouth, throat and oesophagus cancer is just the same as for cigarette smokers and the risk of lung cancer is much greater than for non smokers.

Most people nowadays associate tobacco use with lung cancer.

An interesting fact is that the risk of developing lung cancer begins to fade as soon as smoking is stopped.

However there are many other complaints associated with smoking.

Other cancers - cancers of the bladder, kidneys and pancreas, cancers of the mouth, pharynx, larynx, oesophagus, and other less common head and neck cancers.

Bronchitis and emphysema - are directly linked to smoking. (Emphysema is a disease where the lungs' air sacs become damaged causing shortness of breath, respiratory failure or heart failure.)

Coronary artery disease - in which there is damage to or a malfunction of the heart caused by the narrowing or blockage of the arteries supplying blood to the heart muscle, is also linked to smoking. Cigarette smoke contains poisons such as cyanide which could damage heart muscle.

Peripheral vascular disease - is a related disease in which blood flow is restricted in the legs or arms due to spasm as well as narrowing by blockage. In severe cases amputation is necessary.

Strokes - smoking is also a cause of strokes ie when the brain is damaged through a burst blood vessel or because of a blockage of the blood supply to a part of the brain.

Immunity - Smokers' immune systems are less effective than those of non-smokers. Common complaints such as colds or flu can be caught more easily and the smoker may take longer to recover.

Effect on pregnancy - It is now widely accepted that smoking during pregnancy can be detrimental to the baby. The unborn baby of a smoking mother can be damaged and may be born smaller than average, with a greater risk of mortality than babies of a non-smoking mother. Children of parents who smoke have a greater risk of being asthmatic or succumbing to other respiratory diseases and complaints. Smoking is also said to adversely affect the fertility of both males and females.

Other parts of the body affected by tobacco include:

the brain - lack of oxygen due to carbon monoxide in the blood may cause excess narrowing of the blood vessels, making headaches likely;

the heart - will beat faster and therefore have to work harder - this organ will also suffer from reduced oxygen because of the carbon monoxide in the blood - as nicotine causes the blood to clot more easily, this increases the chance of a heart attack;

stomach - problems such as ulcers and diarrhoea can be caused by smoking;

the circulation - can be adversely affected as nicotine raises the blood pressure, carbon monoxide encourages cholesterol to develop and this can lead to heart attacks, strokes and amputations.

Tobacco smoke affects the passive smoker as well as the tobacco user. It has been estimated that the passive smoker has about a third of the risk of the actual smoker. This is more so with younger children.

There is evidence to show that the non-smoking partner of a smoker is open to a higher risk of cancer compared with living in a smoke-free environment, and is likely to have a shorter life span.

The damaging components of tobacco

The three most damaging components of tobacco are nicotine, tar and carbon monoxide.

Nicotine

Nicotine acts as a stimulant and is responsible for smokers' addiction. Some of its components are used in pesticides, but nicotine itself has no medical use.

Once smoke is inhaled into the lungs, the nicotine, along with the necessary oxygen, is quickly taken up in the bloodstream, affecting the central nervous system until it is broken down in the liver to leave the body via urine.

Nicotine stimulates the central nervous system which is why a cigarette helps you feel less tired and more alert. It also stimulates the release of adrenaline into the blood - which can cause raised blood pressure - and acts on the autonomic nervous system which regulates the involuntary functions of the body such as the heartbeat. Depending on how long you have smoked, the heartbeat can be decreased or increased by nicotine. Seasoned smokers regulate their dose of nicotine automatically by smoking more or less according to their needs.

Taken in sufficient quantity, nicotine can cause vomiting, seizures, and sometimes death.

Tar

Tar is the by-product of burning tobacco and is a carcinogenic substance linked to cancers of the mouth, oesophagus, pharynx, larynx and lungs. Lung cancer is the most common of cancers in the UK, causing 35,000 deaths in England and Wales in 1986. The risk of cancer increases proportionally with the number of cigarettes smoked and also with the younger a person was when the habit started.

Carbon monoxide

Carbon monoxide in the tobacco smoke passes from the lungs into the blood. It combines with haemoglobin (the oxygen-carrying pigment found in red blood cells) in competition with oxygen.

It therefore interferes with the passing of oxygen to the body tissues. It is this interference which eventually leads to hardening of the arteries and possibly coronary thrombosis, (the narrowing or blockage by a blood clot of one of the arteries which supply blood to the heart muscle).

How can I stop smoking?

The first things to realise is that it is never too late to stop smoking and that it is better to be overweight a little than to continue with the risk of smoking.

As smoking quickens some functions of the body, such as the metabolic rate - ie the rate at which the body 'burns up' its food, an increase in weight may occur as the metabolic rate returns to normal. Also, eating more food as a 'comfort' or 'treat' to replace smoking, could be a reason for weight gain. These reasons should be short lived and with a little more self discipline the weight you desire can be achieved. The body has the ability to recover from years of smoking and your life expectancy will improve.

*The important thing to realise is that giving up smoking is a question of mind over matter. It is something that **you can alter** as opposed to a condition that cannot be altered, such as a diabetic needing insulin.*

To stop smoking the first move is to decide:
'I want to stop smoking absolutely.'

Giving up

Approach the task with military planning and precision. Think the matter over. Firstly, decide why you have smoked for so long; secondly, why you want to give up and thirdly, how you are going to give up.

First -

List the reasons for smoking which apply to you, for example:

1. Peer group pressure - all or most of my circle of friends smoke;

2. I think it is 'cool' to smoke - I like the image of smoking and the ritual surrounding it, the box of matches, the lighter, the packet of cigarettes on the table when out socially, the communal feeling of accepting or giving a light;

3. I like the lift a cigarette gives me when tired or frustrated.

Second -

List the reasons why you want to give up, for example:

1. because of the obvious danger to my health;

2. my new partner doesn't smoke and doesn't want me to continue;

3. I spend £1,000 (or $1,500) a year on smoking;

4. I am tired of my breath smelling of cigarettes, my teeth being yellow and of the attitude society now has to smokers.

Finally -

List all the options you have heard of to help to stop - as the following examples - then positively decide which options you will take.

1. nicotine patches;
2. acupuncture;
3. hypnotism;
4. chewing gum or other sweets;
5. bribery by a partner, such as a holiday, or a new car;
6. will power to stop immediately;
7. stop gradually by cutting out the least 'needed' cigarettes each day;
8. replacing the buzz from smoking with a healthy alternative - some form of exercise or maybe yoga;
9. devise other rituals to replace the cigarette ritual and keep your hands occupied - keep a pen or pencil in your hands - exercise your fingers, use a 'stress soother';
10. change your routine to help break the habit - avoid the regular situations in which you reach for a cigarette, eg replace the first of the day with a drink or something to eat; don't light up at briefings or meetings - take a drink (ideally water) instead;
11. enlist support of friends and family to actively encourage you to stop.

Case study

Jane S.
Sgt
Age: 33 yrs
Married
One 7-year-old child

1. *I smoke because its a habit now – I do enjoy it and it helps me through the day*

2. *I know its bad for me – I know its bad for those around me and I can find much better uses for the money.*

3.

√ will power to stop immediately;

Yes, otherwise I know I'll slip back to where I started – I haven't thrown the last packet away but they're in the garage – I plan to have a party in a few weeks to throw them away – a ritual burning.

√ changing routine to break the habit and reduce the 'need' for a cigarette;

√ replacing the buzz from smoking with a healthy alternative;

Yes I must alter my routine, for example instead of lighting up in front of the telly after my evening meal, I will keep busy for half an hour to get over this 'need a cigarette' time. I am planning lots of 'treats' for myself – new clothes and a massage – I know I will start to feel better in a few weeks' time. Also I know I'm getting out of shape and I need to be fitter for the job – I used to swim a lot and I used to play the saxophone – I want to get back to that.

√ substitute the nicotine by chewing gum or other sweets;

√ replacing the cigarette ritual by doing other things with your hands

I'll try and use water and 'tic tacs' for my substitute and will probably always have a pen in my hand.

? nicotine patches;

I'm saying no now, but am prepared to use them if I need to – certainly if the only alternative seems to be to have a cigarette. I'll keep the patches closer than the garage.

χ acupuncture;

χ hypnotism;   *– I'm determined it won't have to come to this*

... bribery by a partner, such as a holiday, or a new car

worth a try! – but now I will be able to afford this myself.

Overcoming dependence

The nicotine content of tobacco develops both a physical and a psychological dependence on the drug. The physical stimulants of the drug - enhancing alertness, reducing fatigue and improving concentration - are reversed when trying to stop smoking and withdrawal symptoms include, tiredness, drowsiness, headaches and concentration difficulties.

As the addiction is also psychological, it is often difficult to positively want to give up and many excuses are put forward.

> ## Common excuses mooted...
>
> *'It's one of my few enjoyments. At least I'll die happy'*
>
> *'Fred has smoked full strength for 50 years and he's OK'*
>
> *'If I stop I'll put weight on'*
>
> *'I've gone onto the low-tar. I'll be all right now...'*

Many things act on the mind of the smoker trying to stop and the craving is particularly acute at the time of a routine cigarette, for example while driving, after a meal, when in other smokers' company or when having a social drink with friends. This is why it is so important to change routines whenever possible to help break the habit.

If there is peer group pressure to continue it is easy to put off trying to give up and believe that the nasty diseases will happen to others. Also realise that if you live or work with someone who is continuing to smoke in your presence your task of stopping will be all the more difficult. Supervisors who smoke should set an example by stopping themselves or not smoking openly in the workplace.

The difficulties of overcoming a dependence should not be dismissed lightly and if undertaking this task you deserve the support and acclaim of all those around you. But to succeed you need the will power and determination that only you can command. Without this every strategy is useless (but help yourself as much as possible by having particular treats to hand).

Have a fall-back action planned should you make the mistake of having 'just one' cigarette such as analysing why it happened and taking positive steps to prevent it happening again. And if, having 'given up', you do start again, this is not the end of the world and is certainly not a reason for not trying again. It will be easier next time! You have to want to stop, and keeping a positive frame of mind is most important.

Alcohol
Why do we use alcohol?

The vast majority of alcohol users drink moderately in company with others. They take advantage of the feeling of euphoria, reduced anxiety and inhibitions. Their social confidence increases and mixing and meeting friends is that much easier.

Other reasons why we drink can be more subtlety dangerous.

Beware of using alcohol regularly to:

✗ unwind after a hard day at work or after domestic pressures;

✗ help forget a bad experience or to drown sorrows;

✗ use as a night cap to help sleep;

✗ help remove feelings of anxiety or depression;

✗ relieve boredom;

✗ compensate for lack of self confidence;

✗ deal with a low self esteem and a self punishing personality.

The harmful effects of alcohol

In the UK, over 1,000 children under 15 years of age go to hospital every year with alcoholic poisoning. There is also evidence to suggest that alcohol directly or indirectly causes 25,000 deaths per annum in the UK. It can cause long term damage to body tissues with main areas of concern as follows:

Reproductive organs - Alcohol can increase sexual confidence (and also contribute to failing to have 'safe' sex) but it can cause impotence.

The brain and nervous system - Alcohol depresses the central nervous system - heavy drinking over the years permanently impairs the brain and functions of the nervous system.

Liver - Alcohol in the blood is broken down in the liver. Permanent damage can be caused by heavy drinking in the form of cirrhosis, liver cancer, hepatitis and fatty liver. Cirrhosis is bands of scar tissue - formed as a result of excess alcohol - impairing the liver's efficiency.

Skin - Heavy drinkers can be seen with red facial flushes which eventually become permanent. The widening of the small blood vessels of the skin also causes loss of body heat.

The heart and circulation - Habitual alcohol abuse can cause coronary heart disease, hypertension (abnormally high blood pressure), heart failure and strokes.

Urinary tract and system - Alcohol is a diuretic, ie it encourages the passing of urine, and prolonged alcohol abuse can cause renal failure. Heavy drinking causes dehydration, thirst and a dry tongue.

Digestive system - Ulcers and gastritis can result from irritation caused by alcohol.

In pregnancy - Women who are pregnant or trying to conceive should avoid alcohol entirely to be safe. We do not know how large or small a 'harmless amount' of alcohol is during pregnancy. Drinking more than two units of alcohol a day or the occasional binge certainly increases the risk of damage to the foetus. Abnormalities may include facial malformation such as a cleft lip and palate, heart defects, lower than average intelligence, and abnormal limb development. Also the risk of miscarriage is increased. Small amounts of alcohol can cause developmental problems such as a low birth weight.

Alcoholic poisoning - Acute poisoning can occur from drinking a lot of alcohol over a short space of time. The central nervous system will be severely depressed and lead to lack of mental or physical control, unconsciousness and possibly death. The effect that the alcohol has is relative to age, body size and any alcohol tolerance. Poisoning is common in young children who raid their parents' spirits cabinet.

Behavioural and social problems

Mentally, alcohol can be very damaging. Behavioural signs include reduced intellect or memory, depression, nervous breakdowns and thoughts of suicide. These problems spill over into the domestic and work life. Relationships can become strained or dissolved because of alcohol-related behaviour such as violence to others or to the partner, promiscuity, child abuse or neglect, intolerance, illogical mood swings, jealousy, uncontrolled anger, and selfishness.

At work the heavy drinkers can display some of the behavioural problems as above, become unreliable, 'fall off' in enthusiasm and workrate and have an above average rate of absenteeism.

Most forces have a policy on alcohol (which will usually include other drugs). A typical policy is summarised at the end of the chapter.

'Safe' limits

Two people with very different drinking habits may both claim to be moderate drinkers, so what exactly do we mean by 'moderation'? According to the Royal College of Physicians this is a maximum of 21 units of alcohol a week for a man and 14 units for a woman.

Most health experts agree that these suggested figures are 'sensible'. But it is important to note that the Royal College of Physicians' report also says that the amount of alcohol that can be consumed without harm varies considerably from person to person.

The World Cancer Research Fund (WCRF) recommends that you are cautious and stay below the danger levels given in the chart.

The absolute limit!

Suggested maximum weekly amount:

Men	21 units with one or two alcohol-free days.
Women	14 units - with one or two alcohol-free days.
Pregnant women	preferably none - 4 units at most consumed as 1 or 2 units twice a week.

Note that it can be dangerous to 'binge' drink, that is to subject the body to an entire weekly limit in one or two nights. It is far better to spread drinks out over the week, with at least one or two alcohol-free nights.

Do you know how much you are drinking?

If you're really not sure how much you're drinking at the moment it might be illuminating to find out.

Even if you don't think you drink up to the limit, why not try keeping a diary - a record of what you drink, when and where you drink it - over the course of a week or so? An example of a diary to assess your level of alcohol consumption each week is included in File 5.2 at the end of the chapter. You may be surprised to see how occasional drinks add up.

In order to realistically measure your units per week, you need first of all to get to grips with the alcohol content of your favourite drinks. Remember that the alcohol content of beers, ciders and wines varies greatly (some extra strength lagers, for example, contain three times as much alcohol as others).

Levels of consumption - the effects and the danger signs

mg alcohol per 100 ml blood	**observable effects**	
	on the light drinker	**on the seasoned drinker**
30 - 50 mg	Those who are not habitual drinkers will become more relaxed and talkative - social confidence will increase.	Experienced drinkers will not show any signs of being affected.
50 -100mg	Will become irresponsible in behaviour and conversation - display mood swings, and judgement and physical co-ordination may be impaired.	This level again may not have an affect on seasoned drinkers that is readily apparent.

(80mg is the legal limit for drivers in the UK and 100mg for the US.)

100-200mg	Brings confusion in physical and social control - unsteady on their feet and speech begins to slur - ie begin to display signs of drunkenness.	The habitual drinker shows less signs.
200-300mg	Causes increasing signs of drunkenness at this stage - aggression, vomiting, crying unpredictable emotions, double vision and so on.	The heavy drinker will probably need 300mg to 500mg to show such signs.
300-400mg	This dangerous stage for light drinkers will range from acute confusion, to drowsiness, difficulty standing, unconsciousness but rousable coma - then unrousable coma and the possibility of death.	Again the heavy drinker may consume enough alcohol to reach 700mg before displaying these symptoms

Over 400mg for light drinkers (700mg for heavy drinkers) increases the risk of death through the arrest of breathing. However, death may be caused by asphyxia due to the inhalation of vomit at an earlier stage, as has occurred with persons in police custody.

Quick unit count

Guide to units of alcohol (pub measures)

Beers, lager and cider		
3-4% ABV	1 pint	2 units
5-6% ABV	"	3 units
8-10% ABV	"	5 units
Wine		
8-11% ABV	125ml glass (6 to a bottle)	1 unit
	1 bottle	6 units
12-13% ABV	125ml glass (6 to a bottle)	1.5 units
	1 bottle	9 units
Fortified wines eg sherry, port 16% ABV	50ml glass	1 unit
Spirits 40% ABV	25ml glass	1 unit

ABV = alcohol by volume

To really be in control of the amount of alcohol you drink, you need to know how the strength of different drinks is measured.

The strength of beers, lagers, ciders and wines is measured by calculating the amount of alcohol in 100ml of the drink. This is called 'alcohol by volume' or 'ABV'. The percentage alcohol by volume is displayed on the label of a bottle of wine, on the side of a can of beer, or on the pump in a pub - ask if you can't find it.

For example, a beer might be labelled '5% Vol' (or 5% ABV) and a regular beer drinker will know that this is a moderately strong brew. However, what 5% ABV means exactly is that the beer has 5ml of alcohol in every 100ml - a unit is equivalent to 10ml of pure alcohol. So, in this example, a half litre of beer (500ml) contains 25ml of alcohol, or two and a half units.

A pint measure is in excess of a half litre (568ml) so using the same example a pint of 5% ABV beer contains almost three units (to be exact 28.4ml of alcohol = 2.84 units). Obviously it is unnecessary to calculate this exactly, but keep a check on the strength of your drink and use the 'Quick unit count' chart as a guide.

Alcohol dependence - alcoholism

The more a person drinks the more alcohol his or her body needs to experience the same effect. A drinker's problems start well before the bottom of the slippery slope to alcoholism. We all think we know how alcohol affects us, (though the 'Effects and the Danger Signs' chart (ante) may have been enlightening).

The light-hearted face of alcohol invokes anticipation of pleasure and the party mood.

Then come the pressure... 'drinking each other under the table', putting pressure on the young or weak willed to 'get some down your neck', 'have a pint instead of a half', 'have a double' and then 'look he or she can't take their drink!'. This is when alcohol reveals its serious face though drinkers may not realise how close to death they come by drinking themselves unconscious.

On a world-wide basis alcoholism has been on the increase for many years and in the UK it is estimated that over one in 50 of the population are alcoholics.

Measuring up - do you have a drink problem?

- ❏ Have you developed a tolerance to drink?

- ❏ Do you need a drink after work?

- ❏ Do you drink when you have problems?

- ❏ Are you a secret drinker - behind your partner's back, or your host's back at a party?

- ❏ Do your friends say you can take your drink?

- ❏ Do you forget what happened during a drinking bout?

- ❏ Do you feel ashamed of what you did or said when drinking?

- ❏ Do you ever need a drink the morning after?

- ❏ Have you ever tried to stop drinking and failed to do so?

- ❏ When in the company of friends are you the last to stop drinking?

- ❏ Do you ever get feelings of persecution or guilt about your drinking?

- ❏ Do you keep promising others or yourself to give up drinking?

- ❏ Have you ever changed your job -eg major crime or surveillance work - or circle of friends to give up drinking?

- ❏ Have you changed from beer to spirits?

- ❏ Have you neglected eating or your appearance because of drink?

- ❏ Do you like to drink in new places or with people you don't know?

- ❏ Have you ever been intoxicated for more than one day?

The following physical symptoms may indicate you have a problem:

- ❏ Shaking, convulsions or hallucinations after a break from drinking?

- ❏ Vomiting, nausea or shaking the morning after?

- ❏ A loss of memory of drinking?

- ❏ Incontinence or urinating in strange places such as bedroom drawers or wardrobes?

- ❏ Stomach pain or cramps?

- ❏ A tingling sensation or numbness?

- ❏ Damaged capillaries in the face?

- ❏ Unsteadiness or confusion?

- ❏ A heartbeat that is irregular?

- ❏ A feeling of weakness in the limbs?

An answer in the affirmative to any of the above could indicate you have a problem. If several describe you or your behaviour you will need to take immediate action to either control your drinking, stop drinking, or seek help.

Alcohol dependence develops over an average of 10 years based on the personality of the drinker. People who like to drink generally gravitate to circles of friends where drinking is the norm and this could be the first rung of the ladder to dependence. Interest and pastimes should be introduced which do not involve alcohol.

The danger signs to be aware of start with becoming tolerant to alcohol. This is where your friends start saying, 'You can hold your drink' and you know that over the years it takes double or more times the amount of drink to experience the usual effects.

The next signs are not being able to remember what has happened during the drinking bouts and loosing control over the alcohol, ie not being certain of stopping drinking when you want to. At this stage you are almost fully dependent and will indulge in longer and longer drinking bouts. Your physical and mental well being will both deteriorate.

How do I stop drinking?

Alcohol addiction is similar to tobacco dependence in as much as the drinker must try to create the right frame of mind to stop. Recognising that you may have a problem is the first positive step. If you feel you are unable to stop, and that cutting your intake to the 'safe' levels is not possible, then it is imperative that you seek help. (Your force policy should give information and advice on where you can best go for help - see File 5.1 'Typical Force Policy' at the end of the chapter).

If you are able to be open and forthright with friends and relatives they may be able to give support. To try and understand the underlying problems or reasons for abusing alcohol would help them and you to tackle the root problems as effectively as possible.

Alcoholics Anonymous (AA)

AA is an international organisation which fights alcoholism and whose members help each other. There is no enrolling fee and as the name implies there is a strict confidentiality code. Members do not reveal the identity of their fellow members and no record of membership is kept. This is an important point for police officers who may feel embarrassed or that it may damage their careers to seek help within their force. (Most occupational health units within forces practice a policy of confidentiality in sensitive areas such as alcohol-related, sexual or psychiatric problems etc.)

The telephone number of your nearest AA group can be found in the telephone directory. Other such organisations may be operating in your areas and the telephone directory may list their contact numbers, eg a department of your local authority, the Samaritans and detoxification centres.

How do I cut down?

If the issue is simply one of 'cutting down', consider how to limit the number of units you drink, whether out socialising or at home.

Drinking at home

Tips for the social drinker...

When you're enjoying yourself at a party or relaxing in the pub, try remembering the following guidelines to help you keep control of your alcohol intake.

√ Eat before you drink
Alcohol on an empty stomach is absorbed into the bloodstream more quickly, so without food you'll get drunk faster. However, while food can slow down the effect of alcohol, it can't limit its overall effect.

√ Drink slowly
Sip your drinks and put your glass down between sips.

√ Mixers
Go for drinks you can stretch with a mixer - like a small gin with a large tonic or a spritzer - wine with sparkling or soda water and ice.

√ Alternate
 alcoholic with non-alcoholic drinks.

√ Make your own decisions
Don't be persuaded by others to have 'just one more'.

√ Quench your thirst
If you're really thirsty quench your thirst first with water or a soft drink.

√ 'Low' and 'no' alcohol
Take advantage of the new - and ever improving - range of 'low' and 'no' alcohol drinks on the market.

√ Judge by amount
Never measure alcohol consumption by how you 'feel'. Remember that tolerance to the effects of alcohol varies with continued drinking. Judge your intake by one standard only - the amount you have drunk.

√ Time limits
Decide on a leaving time at a party etc and stick to it.

√ Drinking companions
Don't end up with heavy drinkers at a party. This will put pressure on you to keep drinking. Keep circulating and if necessary go for some more food.

√ Tea and coffee
If, at the end of a party, you are offered tea or coffee, take it as opposed to asking for more alcohol.

√ Water not wine
Practice ordering water instead of wine in a restaurant.

√ Saying 'No'
Practise a whole range of excuses to make saying 'No' easier (see overleaf), or, if you find it easy, just say 'No thank you'.

Excuses for saying 'no' to 'just one more'

As the social stigma of drink and driving has become stronger it is now the norm to hear:

'No thanks. I'm driving.'

However, if this is obviously not the case...

When friends or acquaintances have had a drink, it is usually pointless saying you have spent your quota on drink or you've run out of money etc. Invariably they will insist on buying you another. Usually the only way is to say you've had enough or don't want a drink (of alcohol, that is) for whatever reason.

▶ 'I had too much yesterday. I'm having an alcohol free day.'

▶ 'No thanks, I still have some work to do later. I need a clear head.'

▶ 'No thanks, I've had enough as I've a difficult court case (or whatever) tomorrow.'

▶ 'No thanks. I've got an important fixture tomorrow (football, rugby, squash, tennis, badminton etc).'

▶ 'I'm on antibiotics (or other such drug) and can't drink.'

▶ 'No thank you. I've got the beginnings of an ulcer.'

▶ 'No thanks, I'm on a diet.'

When you're drinking at home it's all too easy to pour out more generous measures without even realising it. Here's a couple of tips that should help...

If you drink spirits you might like to invest in your own single spirit measure, holding 25ml - equal to one unit of alcohol. You should be able to buy a measure from a department store or kitchen shop.

As wine glasses vary greatly in size, an easy way to keep a count of units of alcohol from wine is to establish how many glasses you can fill with one bottle. (You don't actually need to drink the wine to do this - an empty bottle refilled with water will do the job!)

Most bottles of wine contain between six and nine units of alcohol. So, if you find there are six glass-fulls in a bottle, each glass contains between one and one-and-a-half units depending on the strength of the wine.

The low-down on 'low alcohol'

The important point to remember is that even alcohol 'free' drinks are legally allowed to contain a small amount of alcohol and 'low' alcohol products can be up to 1.2% alcohol by volume. That's about a third of the strength of many ordinary beers.

You would have to drink a large amount very quickly to get drunk on low alcohol products, but it can happen. And it's certainly possible to find yourself over the legal limit for driving.

So do check the alcohol content on the label carefully. Exercise particular caution when drinks claim to be 'lower' in alcohol, but not 'low' alcohol - some lower or reduced alcohol wines are up to half the strength of ordinary table wine.

Caffeine

Caffeine is an addictive drug which occurs naturally in tea and coffee. It is contained in the tea leaves, the coffee beans and also in cocoa beans and cola nuts used in some drinks. It is a stimulant drug and is related to uric acid, as is the similar compound, theobromine, the stimulant in chocolate.

The effects

Caffeine is a nervous system stimulant. It acts on cells by affecting their chemical reactions and by causing the release of more adrenaline and noradrenaline which in turn stimulates cell activity.

In moderate doses, the drug helps to prevent drowsiness and fatigue, reducing the need for sleep. Larger doses can interfere with performance and co-ordination of movement.

The heart rate and breathing rates can be increased - as can blood pressure. Stomach acidity may also show an increase. Agitation and tremors may also be experienced by heavy users or people who are very sensitive to such drugs.

Like alcohol, a tolerance to caffeine may develop with continued use. This means the user will need a bigger does to experience the same effects.

The various parts of the body are affected by caffeine as follows:

The heart - will beat faster after small amounts of caffeine, pumping blood round the body faster and also raising the blood pressure a little. With large amounts the heart could be over stimulated and palpitations (a rapid and unusually forceful heartbeat) may result.

The brain cells - are stimulated with small amounts of caffeine and tiredness is reduced, concentration improved and reactions quickened. Heavy caffeine use may cause anxiety, irritability, dizziness, breathlessness and insomnia.

Muscles - may be given an enhanced performance initially, but twitching may occur with heavy use.

Kidneys - are encouraged to increase the flow of urine.

Stomach - acidity, nausea and abdominal pains may be caused if large quantities are taken, although small quantities may be beneficial to the digestion of food.

Content and consumption

The strength or concentration of caffeine varies with the type of drink or food containing the drug.

Example	
average cup of...	**average caffeine content**
brewed coffee	115mg
percolated coffee	80mg
instant coffee	65mg
tea	60mg
average can or bottle of...	
soft drink	30 - 75mg

For an adult of average health, age and size (without a built up tolerance of caffeine) consumption of 500 to 600mg a day can cause problems such as anxiety, dizziness etc.

One gram of coffee at one sitting can cause ringing in the ears, flashing before the eyes, insomnia, muscle tremor, abnormal heart beat and breathing, intestinal problems such as nausea, vomiting and diarrhoea. To drink more than 100 cups of coffee in a short period could prove fatal.

Caffeine has to be treated with respect. If you are drinking more than five cups a day, you may be damaging your health. (See Case File 8.5 in chapt 8 'Mind Out'.)

Don't forget to add up your daily intake of caffeine from the many different sources, that is, coffee, tea, chocolate, cocoa, some soft drinks and some headache pills.

If you decide to cut down on or stop using caffeine, withdrawal symptoms may be experienced. If you do have symptoms of irritability, drowsiness and headache, a gradual reduction of caffeine may be more acceptable. Heavy users can experience such withdrawal symptoms by going without caffeine for just a few hours.

Medicinally, caffeine is used in combination with painkillers and in drugs to combat migraine.

Update on illegal substances...

It goes without saying that police staff should be 'whiter than white' where dangerous drugs and other illegal substances are concerned. Recruits are checked for traces of illegal substances and random testing is being considered for officers especially those in specialist departments such as firearms, road traffic and drug squads.

Officers should never be tempted to use illegal muscle-building drugs and should seek professional advice in this area.

The following 'typical force policy' deals with drugs and other illegal substances. Police staff should make themselves familiar with the policy and keep up-to-date with any amendments on this fast-moving issue.

In summary...

Officers who do overuse these drugs and have taken the time to read this chapter cannot fail to understand the harm they are doing to their bodies and minds.

However, we very much hope that they will have also gained useful advice and the enthusiasm to stop or cut down as necessary - and appreciate they are not alone if they need help in so doing.

File 5.1: A typical force policy on alcohol and drugs

5.1: 1 The Policy

5.1: 1.i

In order to encourage a climate within Newshire Police which avoids contributing to alcohol/drug related problems, the organisation has adopted a Policy for its staff with the following aims:

a   to encourage and assist all staff who suspect or know that they have a problem to seek help at an early stage;

b   to help any member of staff who has a problem to gain easy access to the most appropriate agency;

c   to provide all staff with the information which will enable them to make sensible decisions regarding drugs and alcohol.

5.1: 1.ii

The following information is provided to all staff to facilitate an understanding of alcohol/drug related problems.

5.1: 2 The concern over alcohol

One unit of alcohol is equivalent to half a pint of beer, lager or cider, or one glass of wine, or one measure of spirits. [For a more in-depth explanation see earlier in the chapter.]

Alcohol consumption was identified as a risk factor by the Health of the Nation White Paper 1995. Excessive consumption of alcohol contributes to raised blood pressure - one of the main risk factors for coronary heart disease and stroke. It is also associated with accidents, crime and a variety of social problems. Overall, men are more likely than women to drink in excess of the recommended sensible levels, and younger men are more likely than older men to exceed these levels regularly. Having said this, while the level of men's drinking has remained relatively stable over the past 10 years, women in Britain are drinking more than ever before. Thirteen per cent of women admitted to exceeding the recommended sensible levels and full-time working women are almost twice as likely to exceed the levels than part-timers or housewives.

5.1: 3 The problems at work

Problems with alcohol can affect an individual at work and this applies at all levels of seniority in any occupation. Heavy drinkers are far more likely to take time off work than their colleagues. In this country alcohol misuse in 1990 cost industry at large £964.37 million in sickness absence and £870.76 million in premature death. The cost to the National Health Services of alcohol misuse was £149.35 million. It is also recognised that drinking to any degree is an important contributory cause of accidents at work which can endanger the health and safety of all staff and have catastrophic consequences.

5.1: 4 Problem drinking

Problem drinking can be defined as the intermittent or continuous consumption of alcohol which leads to a disruption in physical, mental or social well being. In 1992, 27% of men (six million) and 11% of women (2.5 million) in the UK drank above the recommended levels of alcohol.

5.1: 5 Do you know how much you drink?

Use the guide below to see how many units of alcohol you drink each week.

5.1: 5.i
What is a unit of alcohol? [See earlier for a more in-depth explanation.]

-   half a pint of ordinary lager, beer or cider; or
-   quarter of a pint of strong lager, beer or cider; or
-   one single pub measure of spirits; or
-   one small glass of table wine; or
-   one small glass of sherry or fortified wine.

This guide applies to 'pub' measures. Home measures and home brews could be much larger or stronger so take extra care. Eight pints of beer contain the same amount of alcohol as half a bottle of spirits.

Even if your units don't add up to much, remember to spread your drinks out. Don't give your body too much to cope with at once.

5.1: 5.ii
What is sensible drinking?

Opinions vary, but generally up to 21 units of alcohol a week for a man (one - two pints per day of average strength beer or lager) and 14 units for a woman (two half-pints of average strength beer/lager per day are the sensible limits). Women's bodies are usually smaller than men's and they contain more fat and less water, so alcohol stays in a woman's body longer, and becomes more concentrated. Therefore women are more susceptible to physical harm from alcohol. The young and elderly are more at risk and should drink much less. Drinking amounts in excess of these sensible levels may not appear to be immediately harmful, but over a period of time may have an effect on health, family and work.

Please don't forget - if driving, using equipment, pregnant, or taking medication, one drink may be too many.

5.1: 6 Roles and responsibilities

Successful implementation of the policy depends on the co-operation and the understanding of all the parties involved. It is essential therefore that each individual or group is aware of their role relating to the policy.

5.1: 6.i
Role of the individual:

- to be familiar with the policy and procedures;
- to be aware of the effects of alcohol/drugs on his or her health;
- to be aware of the effects of alcohol/drugs on his or her work;
- to set a good example through his or her own sensible use of alcohol;
- to seek help, if concerned about their own drinking;
- to urge colleagues to seek help if they have a problem - covering up or colluding with colleagues does not help the individual concerned.

5.1: 6.ii
Role of the force:

- to provide, through information, a general climate of awareness of sensible drinking, the nature and dangers of abuse of alcohol and use of drugs;

- also through information, to help staff understand the rationale and procedure of the policy;
- to consult with local agencies to ensure their co-operation in implementing the policy.

5.1: 6.iii

Role of the manager:

- to be familiar with the policy and procedures;
- to set a good example through his or her own sensible use of alcohol;
- to ensure that staff understand what is expected of them with regard to attendance, work performance, behaviour and safety;
- to provide opportunities for new staff members to receive education and training concerning the policy;
- to act promptly where there are signs of a problem;
- to adopt a non-judgmental attitude to staff who may have a problem;
- to advise staff to seek assistance where appropriate;
- to use disciplinary measures only when appropriate to do so.

5.1: 6.iv

Role of occupational health:

- to promote awareness of sensible drinking and the dangers of abuse of alcohol or use of drugs, and to encourage early recognition of an individual's need for help;
- to provide advice and guidance on how best to help an individual who has a problem with behaviour or work performance which might be related to the above;
- to provide assessment of the needs of individuals who refer themselves or who are referred for help and to offer a recovery programme with a specialist agency where appropriate;
- to provide effective communication between the employee and all those concerned with recovery - this may include the GP and specialist agencies where appropriate;
- to ensure that the subject of alcohol and drugs together with their related problems is included on all training programmes undertaken by the staff of the Occupational Health Unit;
- to be available for confidential advice to any member of staff who may have a concern regarding drug, alcohol or substance use.

5.1: 6.v

Individual responsibilities:

- to be aware of the hazards involved with drugs, alcohol and substances, these include solvents, steroids and performance enhancing agents;
- to ensure that their own health and safety, or that of others, is not placed at risk by their acts or omissions while at work.

5.1: 7 Prescribed medication

When taking medication, the responsibility rests with the individual to discuss the possible adverse side effects with the prescribing doctor or chemist. When prescribed medication carries such a side effect and the individual is involved in work of a hazardous nature (eg driving, handling machinery or firearms) the matter should be discussed with the individual's line manager so that work of a non-hazardous nature may be arranged.

5.1: 8 Non-prescribed medication

When self medication is obtained 'over the counter' the individual should discuss with the dispensing chemist any possible adverse side effects (for example, certain anti-histamines may impair ability, some cough medication can cause drowsiness). If side effects are an issue, the matter should be discussed with the line manager as above.

Advice may be sought from the Occupational Health Unit.

5.1: 9 Steroid misuse

Various types of medication, illegal or otherwise, are increasingly being used to enhance performance in sport. Commonly misused substances are anabolic steroids. These affect growth, damage sexual organs, increase the risk of liver cancer and may also produce irreversible 'masculinising' changes. One side effect particularly undesirable in the police service is that of increased aggression. The result of the use of these substances to increase performance could literally be 'dying to win'.

5.1: 10 Solvent abuse

This action causes disordered mental and physical function and is therefore strongly discouraged by Newshire Police.

5.1: 11 Getting help

5.1: 11.i

Is your use causing you problems at home, at work, or with your health?

Recognising you may have a problem is the first positive step.

If you are unable to reduce your intake yourself, SEEK HELP!

5.1: 11.ii

You may be able to obtain support or advice from a friend, family member, work colleague or someone in the church. Sometimes just talking about your concerns is the first step in resolving them. Your family doctor can provide general health advice and treatment. Other confidential services are available, ranging from advice over the telephone to counselling and medical help.

5.1: 11.iii

The following local services are there to help you.

(Here a list of local organisations and telephone numbers will normally be given by the Force concerned.)

For example

Alcoholics Anonymous
Samaritans
Local authority counselling services
Drugs help lines

File 5.2: Examples of a diary to help assess your level of alcohol consumption per week.

Week One	Drink	Measure and ABV	Function	Units	Running total
Mon 6/6	beer	2 pts 5%	pub evening	6 (approx)	6
	whisky	single	"	1	7
Wed 8/6	wine	half b 12%	home dinner	4.5	11.5
Thurs 9/6	wine	half b 12%	"	4.5	16
Fri 10/6	beer	1 pt 5%	restaurant	3 (approx)	19
	alcopop	1 b 5%	club	1.5	20.5
	"	"	"	1.5	22
	"	"	"	1.5	23.5
	"	"	"	1.5	25
Sat 11/6	beer	2 pts 5%	pub lunch	6 (approx)	31
Sun 12/6	"	2 pts 5%	pub drink	6 (approx)	37

Week One - 'Safe limit' exceeded for men by 16 units, for women by 23 units.

Week Two	Drink	Measure and ABV	Function	Units	Running total
Mon 13/6	beer	2 pts 5%	squash club	6 (approx)	6
Tues 14/6	wine	1 bottle 12%	birthday	9 (approx)	15
Fri 17/6	beer	1 pt 5%	restaurant	3 (approx)	18
	wine	half b 12%	"	4.5	22.5
Sat 18/6	beer	4 pts 5%	rugby club	12 (approx)	34.5
	alcopop	1 bottle 5%	"	1.5	36

Week Two - 'Safe limit' for men exceeded by 15 units and for women by 22 units.

So the diary goes on... If the diary gives this kind of message then drastic action is required to reduce your weekly alcohol intake.

NB absolute limits = men 21 units; women 14 units

6. Controlling over-reaction

Allergies - their identification, prevention and treatment

The body's over-reaction to the things around us has given rise to an unprecedented growth in allergies. The cause of respiratory problems, skin irritations, food intolerances, to say nothing of reactions to chemicals and man-made materials, allergies have become the scourge of the modern world.

It has been calculated that one in six people in Britain now has an allergy of one sort or another. And allergic reactions are growing daily - especially among children. We are told that soon half the British population will be affected.

What is happening in this world of ours to sensitise our bodies into producing these immune responses which can take many forms from minor irritation to major inflammation? Is medical science facing its final frontier - a battle with the environment itself?

Some experts suggest allergies are a disease of affluence, pointing to the growth of the condition in rapidly developing nations such as China as evidence of that fact. It must be noted that affluence comes hand in hand with polutants, chemicals and additives.

Others contend that, in our modern sterile world in which fewer diseases are life threatening, allergies have in effect become the modern plague. Their contention runs that the more we seal ourselves in our double-glazed, antiseptic, centrally-heated homes, the more we become ready prey to house dust mites which breed unseen in their billions in our beds.

In the sphere of allergies, theories abound as to the causes of over-reaction to things around us.

Pollen has been a popular focus for blame, but comparative country by country studies have tended to remove the spotlight from this popular culprit. Could there then be a reaction between pollen and that other focus of the 'greens' - diesel fumes? Or should passive smoking carry the blame for increased sensitisation?

Has the suppression of childhood illnesses through injections or the increased use of antibiotics anything to do with it? Or is it simply the fall in the number of mothers breast feeding their babies which has resulted in inadequate immune systems? Have smaller families limited the exposure of children to infections which would previously have strengthened their immune system? Or is it our pre-occupation with cleanliness (once thought second only to Godliness) which is to blame?

Whatever the cause of allergies the effects are there for all to see - and for many to suffer.

The big four...

The four most common allergic conditions are:

1. hay fever,
2. allergic rhinitis,
3. asthma,

all of which affect the respiratory system; and

4. eczema,

which affects the skin.

Other potentially serious allergies...

1. allergy to food,
2. latex allergy, and
3. allergy to insect stings,

can trigger the potentially fatal medical emergency Anaphylaxis (inflammatory reaction) which is covered at the end of the chapter.

Allergic reactions tend to run in families. Good news if your family is not so affected but bad news if it is.

More bad news is that if you suffer from one of these conditions, you are more liable to develop others. Statistically speaking, about 50 per cent of people who have eczema will also develop asthma or hay fever.

But there are treatments available and, more importantly, a range of things which can be done to prevent their onset.

Hay fever
(seasonal allergic rhinitis)

Hay fever is the most common allergy in the UK, affecting 20 per cent of all allergy sufferers. Symptoms are often worst in teenagers and young adults, peaking between the ages of 20 and 30. They include frequent sneezing (often in bursts); runny eyes or nose; itchy eyes, nose or throat; a blocked nose not unblocked by blowing. Sensitivity to light, disturbed sleep, headache, sinusitis and an impaired sense of smell may also be experienced.

Triggers are known to be seasonal:

▶ Tree pollen (eg oak, elm, ash, birch, hazel), February - late May.
▶ Grass pollen (eg rye grass, timothy grass), May - September.
▶ Mould spores, May - October.

Hayfever treatments

Antihistamine pills eg terfenadine (Triludan, Seldane, now on prescription only), loratadine (Clarityn) - can relieve sneezing, itchy, runny nose and sore eyes.

Steroid nasal sprays eg beclomethasone dipropionate (Beconase Hayfever) or flunisolide (Syntaris), both sold over the counter - can prevent symptoms.

Acupuncture has been extremely effective in treating hay fever - it is well worth a try if all other approaches fail.

Prevention

√ Stay indoors if at all possible when the pollen count is high.
√ Stay indoors in the early evening, when the pollen count peaks.

The preceding advise is not very practical for operational officers - particularly rural beat officers - and those who suffer severely should consider whether to ask for indoor duties or even stay away from work.

√ Sleep with bedroom windows closed.
√ Wear sunglasses to stop pollen getting into the eyes - contact lens wearers will say that these help protect the eye from contact with pollen.

Rhinitis
(perennial allergic rhinitis)

If you suffer from a constantly stuffy nose which is not eased by blowing, or year-round cold-like symptoms without fever, these symptoms are likely to be allergic in origin.

Managing rhinitis

Concerted action against dust mites is called for.

√ Use a vacuum cleaner whose suction power and filtration are sufficient to warrant the British Allergy Foundation seal of approval.

√ Replace soft furnishings where possible, eg floorboards instead of carpets, shutters instead of curtains, and cover hanging clothes and open shelving.

√ Air bedding out of doors regularly, as continentals do - ultraviolet light and cold kill mites.

√ Use Astex pillow and mattress covers, which are impregnated with a non-toxic insecticide

√ Buy new pillows regularly; otherwise put them in a plastic bag in the freezer overnight, then defrost and wash at 60 C+ to kill mites.

√ Use blankets which are cotton or synthetic rather than wool.

√ Consider investing in a steam-cleaner to kill mites and clean soft furnishings without chemicals.

√ Reduce exposure to household pets.

√ Keep down humidity, eg avoid drying washing over radiators. To live and breed, mites need water vapour.

Treatment

▶ Steroid nasal sprays or drops, for example beclomethasone (Beconase) - are said to be safe to use regularly for up to five years.
▶ Antihistamine tablets are less effective but may be useful in addition to steroid sprays.
▶ New Era Combination Q tissue salts (available from large chemists and health food stores) are considered to be an effective option.

Asthma

Asthma is the most common chronic disease in the developed world. It affects 150 million people across the globe. It costs the British economy £1,000 million a year in lost working time and health expenditure alone.

Any officer or member of the support staff who develop asthmatic type symptoms - which can be triggered by a 'cold' virus or an allergy - should discuss their problem with the force medical officer. Workplace problems may be identified and may be preventable. (Also visit a GP if necessary.)

Two thousand people die of the condition every year and yet it is calculated that 80 per cent of these deaths could be avoided by following a few simple precautions.

Medical treatment

Respiratory function should be measured by a peak flow meter to monitor the problem and decide when drugs are required. Serious asthmatics may want their own meter at home.

Drugs are of three kinds.

Preventers - which make the airways less sensitive; for example, sodium cromoglycate (Intal, Cromogen) or low dose inhaled steroids such as beclomethasone (Becotide), which reduce inflammation and mucus. If preventers are needed to make physical exercise possible, they should be taken 15 minutes beforehand.

Relievers - are bronchodilators (or betagonists) from hand-held inhalers; for example, salbutamol (Ventolin), terbutaline (Bricanyl).

Controllers - for acute attacks, in the form of steroid tablets (for example Prednisone).

On days when ozone or air pollution is high medication may need to be stepped up. Air quality checks may be made with the Department of Environment, Transport and The Regions (DETR) which monitors the levels of nitrogen and sulphur dioxide, ozone and benzene in the air in different areas of the country.

Alternative treatments

Alternative approaches to the prevention of asthma include homeopathy, biopathy, reflexology and osteopathy.

Homeopathy - has shown in trials that it can significantly relieve asthma symptoms. Learning to breathe more shallowly to prevent hyperventilation - using for example, the Buteyko method - has been recognised as of assistance.

Biopathy - involves a 'biotron' machine to measure energy levels on acupressure points on the hands and feet. The method has been used successfully, particularly in Germany. Plugged into the mains, the biotron is a black box with a metal rod, which the patient holds in one hand while the therapist directs a stylus-like instrument to certain pressure points. The biotron readings indicate in which areas the person is weak.

Reflexologists - manipulate the soles of the feet. Pressure points beneath the foot are said to correspond to various parts of the body, therefore reflexologists massage these points to stimulates the corresponding organs.

Osteopathy - improves breathing, and prevents the pigeon-chested hunched-shoulders posture young sufferers may develop.

Eczema (atopic dermatitis)

Eczema affects one in eight children and one in 12 adults. It is one of the most common skin diseases and in 90 per cent of cases it appears before the age of five years. Nine out of 10 children achieve full recovery.

Managing eczema

√ Get rid of dust mites.

√ Avoid known trigger foods such as dairy products, fish, wheat, nuts and citrus fruit.

√ Wear white cotton clothes next to the skin washed in non-irritant soap.

√ Wash skin regularly with soap-free cleansing oils.

√ Avoid extremes of temperature.

√ Provide young children with all-in-one romper suits in bed to prevent scratching.

√ Keep fingernails short.

Whether red and weeping or scaly and dry, eczema is intensely itchy. Reddish patches with small blisters may eventually merge, sometimes leaking liquid mixed with blood, which forms yellow or brownish scabs. Likely to start in the elbow creases, behind the knees, in front of the ankles, and on the neck and face, it is unsightly and intolerable in its severe stages.

Treatment

- Keep skin moist with emollients; in severe cases, wrap the skin in moist bandages.
- Use Cortisone ointments for inflammation and cover the affected area with a cotton gauze bandage.
- Take antihistamine tables to relieve itching.
- Apply antibiotic ointment or take tablets if sores become infected.
- Chinese herbs have proved to be of benefit, but they may damage the liver and are not recommended for young babies.
- High doses of evening primrose oil capsules can be beneficial.

See also Chapter 14, Checking Your Change, on how best to deal with dermatitis which can occur at any time due to contact with irritants and allergens at work and in the home.

Food allergies

A true food allergy occurs when the immune system responds to a particular food by producing large quantities of antibodies in the blood. The whole body is affected. It is a cruel irony that food, the very stuff of life, can cause illness and, in extreme cases, cause deaths.

Allergies to food provide a vast array of symptoms from a constantly running nose to irritable bowel syndrome. Symptoms may include swollen lips and tongue, itchy throat, urticaria (hives), increased salivation, nausea, explosive vomiting, colic, swollen abdomen and diarrhoea. Sometimes attacks of asthma or allergic rhinitis may be precipitated.

Symptoms of a food allergy may also include food cravings, fluid retention, lethargy, difficulty in losing weight, mood swings, difficulty in sleeping, skin irritations, cold hands and feet, headaches and chest pains.

Some sufferers find they have bad migraine headaches, other aches and pains, fatigue, irritability or skin problems which can, in some cases, be helped by a change of diet.

A food allergy might not be the culprit of these conditions - but if a problem is persistent and troublesome, it might be worth seeking advice on the possibility that an allergy may be a cause.

Some allergies to food can increase weight. They slow down the metabolism which, in turn, causes weight gain. They can also cause water retention so that when the excess water is eliminated, people find that they lose weight.

Foods which are most often found to be causing problems are listed overleaf.

Cow's milk - The allergy usually starts in early infancy and is outgrown by the age of four. Breast-feeding is the best protection. Alternatives to cow's milk are Nutramigen (specially treated cow's milk formula), or soya milk, though some children may become allergic to soya.

Eggs - The allergy often coexists with cow's-milk allergy and is usually outgrown by the age of two. The white of the egg is more often a problem than the yolk.

Cereals - Wheat, oats, barley and other grains can cause allergies at any age. Coeliac disease is a sensitivity to gluten (found in wheat, oats and rye but not in corn or rice), which must be avoided for life.

Fish - White fish (for example, cod, sole or trout) causes more problems than blue fish (for example, sardines, salmon or tuna). A severely allergic person reacts merely to touching a surface that has come into contact with fish. Crustaceans (prawns, crabs) and molluscs (mussels, oysters) are most often implicated.

Fruit and vegetables - Apples, peaches, cherries and kiwi fruit are the most frequent offenders.

Nuts - Walnuts, brazil nuts and almonds are common allergens. Nut allergies may be serious enough to prove fatal and usually persist well into adult life.

Other regular culprits are instant coffee, yeast and chocolate.

There is a definite upward trend in food allergies, but experts still cannot agree on reasons for it, let alone the best treatment. The trouble is there are no official figures showing how many more people suffer today compared with, say, 10 years ago. All the evidence is anecdotal, and nobody has yet been able to pinpoint exactly why we appear to be experiencing increased sensitivity to food.

Early childhood exposure to allergens, the widespread consumption of processed foods and the increased use of antibiotics are all blamed, but there is no real evidence for one or the other. To complicate matters further, there is the prevalence of a condition known as food intolerance (see later) and medical disagreements over traditional and progressive treatments.

A sufferer from a classic food allergy, will probably have known about if for years. Most true allergies begin in childhood and often run in families. A patient with multiple symptoms may on separate occasions see an ear, nose, and throat specialist for rhinitis, a chest specialist for asthma, a dermatologist for eczema and a gastroenterologist for bowel disorders.

Therein lies the problem of treatment. The result of this separate specialist approach to diagnosis is that there is no one doctor considering the whole allergic picture. At least when a person is referred to an allergist, the mechanism of true allergy is understood. The body's immune system over-reacts to a substance (allergen) it believes to be a threat by producing antibodies. These then trigger the release of chemicals (histamines) which then cause the familiar allergic reaction.

Prevention

Food allergy patients are often treated with drugs such as steroids and antihistamines, but the key and the cure to what is often referred to as 'immune response allergy' is the simplest and most obvious thing - eliminating the allergen from the diet. Because a large number of common foods are often implicated, however, discovering the true culprits can be time consuming and difficult. Overcoming the problem is often a lengthy process.

The tried and tested method is to exclude foods from the diet and then reintroduce them one at a time. Often conducted under medical supervision where reactions are extreme, detecting an instant reaction to specific products is fairly easy. Using this approach, sufferers often discover that a food or drink they have had all their lives is causing their problem - in some cases since childhood. Discovering which substance is at fault is of course only the route to 'curing' the problem. The removal of the offending product from the diet is the solution to avoiding the allergen.

Treatments

A pioneering treatment known a 'Miller-technique neutralisation' claims to allow food allergy sufferers to eat the very foods which make them ill, by first desensitising them to their allergens. Named after the American doctor who developed it, the neutralisation technique involves injecting precise dilutions of allergens.

A suspected allergen is diluted with saline to a one-in-five strength. The diluted allergen is then diluted again on a one-to-five basis. This is then repeated over and over again.

It is contended that patients show a positive allergic reaction to most of the dilutions, but that their symptoms are turned off by one specific dilution. This is known as the neutralising dose and, once identified, can be self-administered at home as a drop under the tongue. Allergists who use neutralisation admit that they do not really know how the technique works, which is enough for the sceptics to decry its value.

Peanut allergy

Peanuts actually belong to the pea family and are not strictly classified as nuts.

The incidence of peanut allergies is rising. One child in 75 born in the UK may now be sensitised to peanut by the age of four, and 92 per cent of those allergic will have their first attack by the age of seven.

For allergics, the minutest trace of peanut may trigger anaphylaxis (see later). Even mild symptoms, such as tingling of the lips or tongue, should not be ignored - they could become more severe in the future.

Prevention

- Scrupulously read all food labels, avoiding 'peanut', 'groundnut' or 'arachis'.
- Do not be embarrassed to ask staff in restaurants or canteens if foods contain peanut.
- Keep any child in an allergy-prone family away from peanut products until the age of three years, after which the immune system is better able to cope with such a complex protein.
- Pregnant or breast-feeding women should try to avoid peanuts and their products; nipple creams containing peanut oil should not be used.

Treatment

As for anaphylaxis (see later).

Every person with even a mild allergy to peanuts or other nuts should be referred to an allergy clinic. (This is official UK Government policy.)

Food intolerance

Food intolerance in some form is thought to affect 10 to 25 per cent of the population.

The easy way to differentiate food intolerance from classical food allergy is by the reaction time. Food intolerance reactions take up to 48 hours to manifest themselves, whereas food allergies are instantaneous reactions.

For a long time doctors refused to believe that the food intolerance condition existed. Even today it is often diagnosed as a psychosomatic illness.

The reluctance of many mainstream allergists to recognise the condition is because it is not caused by any clear-cut immune system mechanism. As a result it is sometimes known as 'false allergy'. But the symptoms are real enough. Though not life-threatening, food intolerance can be very distressing and is the cause of chronic disease.

Irritable bowel syndrome is a common form of food intolerance. It can also be the trigger or exacerbater of allergies (for example allergic rhinitis and eczema), as well as complaints that are not primarily allergic in origin, such as rheumatoid arthritis and migraine.

The mechanism is still poorly understood, although some clinicians believe it may be due in part to 'leaky gut syndrome'. In this condition an abnormal gut allows larger than usual molecules of food to leak into the bloodstream, from where they can cause symptoms in any part of the body, including the brain.

Prevention

Food additives are also strongly suspected to be responsible for causing food intolerance. The worst culprits to be avoided at all costs if food intolerance is suspected are 'E' numbers. These include the colouring, tartrazine (E102); emulsifiers; glutamate flavour enhancers (E621-E622); sulphites (E220-E227), nitrates and nitrites (E250 to E255), used as preservatives; and the whitener potassium bromide (E924).

Treatment

Various blood tests have been devised that purport to diagnose food intolerances, but because of the delayed reaction to food, identifying the cause is far from easy. The foolproof way - although it is recognised as a lengthy process - is the exclusion diet, preferably carried out under medical supervision.

Used to establish which foods are causing allergy or intolerance, the method involves having nothing except lamb, pears, rice and bottled water for at least five days, to clear the system of likely allergens.

These foods are specifically chosen because few people in the Western World are allergic to them.

After five days, one new food is introduced every 48 hours, in strict order, starting with the least likely to cause a reaction. Three clear days are required after each potential reaction-causing food has been eaten before introducing any new ones

The surest treatment for food intolerance is the avoidance of offending foods. Remarkably, after three to six months' avoidance, many sufferers find they can tolerate a food again, so long as they do not consume it routinely and/or in large quantities. A rotation diet, in which problem foods and foods from the same family are eaten only once every four days, is sometimes recommended.

Latex allergy

Latex (rubber) came into routine use 50 years ago. Allergic reactions followed some 30 years later. Severe reactions to latex, including anaphylaxis (see later), are becoming more common among patients and health-care workers.

Latex is widespread in medical products, from adhesive tape to masks, blood pressure cuffs and anaesthetic equipment, and especially latex gloves which are so widely used since the advent of AIDS. In the US it has been calculated that 7.5 per cent of operating room doctors have latex allergy while 5.6 per cent of operating-room nurses, and 1.3 per cent of dentists throughout the country are affected by it.

As force-issue protective gloves are likely to be made of latex, the possibility of allergic reactions is something officers should be aware of.

Prevention

Carrying a pair of non-latex surgical gloves (on sale at chemists) is a wise precaution - both for your own use and for use by health professionals when treating you!

Treatment

As for anaphylaxis (see later)

Insect stings

Between two and four per cent of the population are hypersensitive to bee, wasp and hornet stings. A normal reaction involves pain, swelling and redness confined to the sting site. In more severe reactions, the inflammation spreads and a sting on the arm may make it swell to double its normal size.

Hypersensitivity can lead to *anaphylactic shock (see later)* and requires immediate action. Elderly people are often more sensitive to insect stings.

Prevention

Do not wear bright/shiny clothing or accessories outdoors which will attract insects. Use an insect repellent containing diethyl-m-toluamide.

Treatment

Care should be taken when removing bee stings not to squeeze the end of the sting and so empty the poison sac into the skin. Try to 'flick' out the sting with the edge of a credit card for example rather that gripping with tweezers. After removing the insect and the sting, place a bag of ice on the area.

Also see treatment for anaphylaxis (see below).

If you have suffered anaphylactic shock as a result of a sting, ask your doctor about a course of desensitisation injections at a NHS allergy clinic.

Inflammatory reaction (Anaphylaxis)

Anaphylaxis is a potentially fatal medical emergency in which the immune system triggers the release of histamine and other agents that cause a massive inflammatory reaction. It is caused when the body's immune system over-reacts to the presence of a foreign body which it wrongly perceives as a threat.

For some people a bee or wasp sting can induce this instant life-threatening danger, while in others latex allergy can bring on the symptoms. In others immunisations or injections of antibiotics and even strenuous exercise can precipitate the condition. For some, shellfish, nuts, eggs, and even penicillin, can cause anaphylaxis.

An allergy specialist can carry out tests which may provide clues to an individual's potential for allergic response, but there is no foolproof way of determining susceptibility.

Many hypersensitive people may not realise their problem until it is too late, so it is worth knowing the symptoms of anaphylaxis, which start within minutes and, if untreated, can lead to loss of consciousness and cardiac arrests. So serious is the condition that two to three per cent of the 30,000-plus people in the UK susceptible to the condition who suffer an anaphylaxis attack will die from it.

Inflammatory allergic attacks

can take between a minute and two hours to take effect and cause a range of reactions. The symptoms to look for are a combination of the following (though not all need be present at the same time).

Symptoms

- itching or a strange metallic taste in the mouth;
- swelling of throat, mouth and tongue, and/or puffiness around the eyes;
- difficulty in swallowing, breathing or speaking;
- hives (red blotches) anywhere on the body, especially large or multiple hives;
- generalised flushing, swelling and itching of the skin;
- abdominal cramps, nausea, or vomiting;
- increased heart rate;
- dizziness and weakness caused by a drop in blood pressure;
- experiencing a 'sense of doom';
- collapse and loss of consciousness.

If you suspect an anaphylaxis reaction...

This is covered in police officer's first aid training. Officers should ensure they are aware of anaphylaxis in case they are involved in or called to a situation in which someone is suffering an attack.

- Establish whether the sufferer is carrying adrenaline, and if not, obtain some as a priority.
- Administer adrenaline if the attack is severe enough to cause collapse/fainting and/or if breathing becomes difficult.* (Administering antihistamine tablets may also help.)
- Telephone for an ambulance or ensure that this is done - ensure the controller is told the problem may be anaphylaxis.
- Lie the affected person down in the recovery position and stay with them.
- If the effects are limited to itching, blotchy skin, vomiting or diarrhoea, adrenaline need not be used.

Adrenaline

People who know they are likely to suffer severe reactions take the precaution of carrying adrenaline with them at all times. This is usually carried in auto-injectors (such as EpiPen) or inhalers. Sufferers should wear bracelets or necklaces (such as MedicAlert pendants) indicating they are prone to anaphylaxis. Adrenaline acts swiftly to constrict blood vessels, improves breathing, stimulates heartbeat and helps reduce swelling.

* **Note.** Adrenaline is produced naturally by the body which can dispose of it easily without harmful effects. If in any doubt, give adrenaline.

File 6.1 Allergy testing

Three basic methods are used in testing for allergies, *viz* skin tests, blood tests and 'provocation'.

Skin tests

The standard test for allergy is the skin prick test, which determines how the skin reacts to a range of common allergens. Small amounts of a suspected allergen are pricked into the skin of the arm or back to test for any reaction to them. Any weal - its size, colours, hardness - is an indication of how severe the allergy is. The test is, however, less reliable for foods than other allergens. The skin test can give false negatives; a more accurate measurement of the level of antibodies being revealed in the blood test.

Blood tests

The most accepted blood test is the RAST (radioallergosorbent test), which measures the level of immunoglobulin E antibodies (IgE) in the blood to specific allergens. The results are graded from one to six, but there may be false positives as well as false negatives in the test results. The total level of IgE antibodies in the blood (total IgE) may also be measured as an indication of the patient's overall allergic status.

Provocation

This method should only be undertaken under medical supervision because of its inherent risks. The patient is given a small amount of the suspect substance in a controlled environment. A provocation test or 'challenge', is useful when the results of skin and blood tests are unclear or contradictory. If a patient is being challenged with peanut, resuscitation equipment must be at hand in case of a reaction. Some doctors put patients on an exclusion diet for a few days before challenging them with foods and chemicals to aid diagnosis.

Desensitisation

Desensitisation is a process in which known allergic substances are used to precipitate immunity. Desensitisation takes two forms; 'incremental' and 'enzyme-potentiated' (EPD).

File 6.1 Allergy testing (cont...)

Incremental desensitisation is the standard type used in clinics. It works by gradually building up the level of a known allergen. In the UK it is used for a very few allergies (not foods) and its drawback is that only one allergy can be treated at a time. Resuscitation equipment must be readily available in case the system induces anaphylactic shock (described earlier).

Enzyme-potentiated desensitisation (EPD) is the alternative system, in which minute doses of allergens are administered. Injections consisting of allergens, primed with the enzyme beta-glucuronidase, are given about four times in the first year, then less frequently over a course of treatment lasting from three to five years. The precise mechanism by which these tiny quantities of allergens function is not know, but EPD is known to be effective in the whole spectrum of food precipitated and inhaled allergies. Trials have proved EPD's efficacy in allergic asthma, hay fever, and even hyperactivity in children. A great advantage of this system is that patients do not need to have separate injections for each different allergen.

PART THREE

OCCUPATIONAL AND OPERATIONAL HAZARDS

7. Staying immune

Managing the risks of HIV, AIDS and Hepatitis

Police officers and support staff are at the cutting edge of contact with high risk groups for carrying the infectious viruses, Human Immunodeficiency Virus (HIV) and Hepatitis viruses.

A virus differs from bacteria by being smaller having a simpler structure and being able to multiply more simply. Bacteria can live on surfaces where as viruses can only live in cells. There are many types of virus. In general, they can enter the body in the following ways.

Viruses enter the body via:

▶ the nose, mouth and lungs - inhaling infected water droplets, ingesting infected food or drink, kissing or other oral contact with infection;

▶ the skin or bloodstream - through a cut, graze or scratch, from biting insects or animals, or from infected needles;

▶ the eyes or ears - oral contact with body fluids or infection;

▶ the genitalia or anus - through intercourse or other invasive infection.

HIV belongs to the retrovirus type which, in order to replicate itself, invades a cell and makes an enzyme. It is hoped that by studying this enzyme that the key to unlocking the HIV mystery will be found.

HIV and AIDS

HIV is the virus that infects people via body fluids. It is called the primary disease which lowers the body's immunity. Then one or several unrelated diseases attack the body and often prove fatal. This second stage is known as the Acquired Immune Deficiency Syndrome (AIDS).

AIDS was first experienced in central Africa around the 1970s. Western doctors became aware of the disease in 1983. By that time AIDS had spread from Africa to the Caribbean and on to the US. AIDS was found among young male homosexuals in Los Angeles as early as 1979, was first diagnosed in the UK in 1982 and had spread worldwide by 1987.

Various suggestions as to the source of the HIV have been put forward, but the one concerning monkeys and viruses similar to HIV seems feasible. A monkey virus could have been transmitted to people via a monkey bite, bestiality or by eating monkeys, and then could have developed into HIV.

The early eighties saw HIV and AIDS spreading in Europe. As in the US it first spread among homosexual men. Sharing and re-using needles was also helping to spread HIV among the drug-using fraternity of Europe. In the US, UK and the rest of Europe, haemophiliacs and others requiring transfusions were unfortunate victims of HIV infection via contaminated blood.

From a toe-hold among homosexual and bisexual men, prostitutes of both sexes, drug users and haemophiliacs, HIV began to spread to the heterosexual community. Western countries adopted a tough stand against HIV and AIDS during the eighties. Sex education was intensified and included HIV and AIDS information. Schools, colleges, and prisons, were all included. Expensive advertising was undertaken throughout the media.

'USE A CONDOM FOR SAFE SEX'

'DO NOT REUSE NEEDLES
GET FREE NEEDLES FROM CLINICS'

'WORKERS IN HOSPITALS, DOCTORS
DENTISTS TAKE PRECAUTIONS WHEN
HANDLING BLOOD'

'POLICE AND PRISON OFFICERS TAKE
EXTRA CARE WHEN HANDLING BODILY
FLUIDS FROM PRISONERS'

Given the close contact sometimes necessary with infected prisoners, the police were at the forefront of awareness training,

A recent study in the US has show that AIDS caught from sexual contact is on the increase among the over fifties - the combination of high divorce rate and viagra is thought to be responsible. The retirement community of Florida is targeted with health posters proclaiming: 'Sex is not only for the young... Neither is HIV.'

How HIV enters the body

HIV is normally contracted via:

▶ sexual contact;

▶ blood and blood products;

▶ mother to child.

Sexual contact - Unprotected sex - be it vaginal, anal, or oral - can transmit the virus from an infected partner. Logically the receiver of the most volume of fluid, ie semen, would appear to be most at risk. Anal intercourse can also cause tearing and bleeding around the anus (or of the penis) and a mixture of blood may take place. Again any ejaculation into the rectum will leave sufficient fluid to enter any bleeding area of the rectum or anus.

There is a theoretical risk of transmission via kissing, particularly 'French' kissing where the tongue enters the partner's mouth, as the HIV virus has been found in saliva, but there is no conclusive evidence of this. 'Normal' kissing on the lips or cheek should be harmless provided there are no open cuts or sores.

Blood and blood products - Blood from shared needles, ie using someone else's 'works' (prison slang for syringes, needles, cutting equipment etc); coming into contact with blood at a road accident, when dealing with a fight possibly between prisoners, at a hospital or when delivering a baby - are all possible sources of HIV. Police officers also have to be aware of the risk sources outside work - eg needles used for acupuncture, body piercing, tattooing etc, sharing toothbrushes, sharing razors. Childhood games of becoming blood brothers or sisters could now prove fatal.

Blood donors in the UK are now screened for HIV and blood products are pasteurised, that is heat treated. (If a blood transfusion is needed in a third world country - possibly while on holiday - the risk of receiving contaminated blood is greater.)

Mother to child - Ninety five per cent of mothers infected with HIV are thought to pass the virus on to their babies - either before or during birth. The babies not infected at birth could be given the virus later via their mother's breast milk.

HIV can easily be destroyed outside the body - by treating any suspect bodily fluid with household bleach, or washing utensils or clothes at 56° C or over. Normal chlorinating of swimming pools will destroy HIV.

The two main factors in preventing infection at the prisoner stage are:

1. intelligence on the prisoner;

2. covering any break in your skin, such as a cut, graze or spot etc.

Preventing infection

Police duties involve contact with many high risk groups - prostitutes of both sexes, drug users, homosexual men etc. The danger areas include dealing with prisoners, searching people's clothing, cars, houses and bodies etc, giving first aid, clearing spillages of bodily fluids especially blood, and dealing with sudden deaths involving HIV positive or AIDS sufferers.

Dealing with prisoners

Most duties involving the movement of prisoners have been privatised - collections from prisons and police stations for delivery to court are now undertaken by contractors.

These privatised prisoner custody officers (PCOs) are trained in searching and hygiene techniques and should notify police personnel as soon as they know a prisoner is HIV positive or suffering from AIDS. They will normally wear rubber surgical gloves when handling infected or suspect prisoners. Police personnel would also be expected to inform the PCOs when handing over a suspected HIV positive prisoner.

The duties involving prisoner contact remaining in the police domain are the initial arrest, the search, gaoler duties and possible escort duties in the absence of the privatised PCOs, or for example, for high risk prisoners. Also answering bail and taking such persons back into custody could present risks as another search would be necessary.

Intelligence should be sought from any friends or relatives of the prisoner whenever possible - from the national computer (PNC), or from local records.

If nothing is known of the prisoner you should err on the side of caution and treat her or him as HIV positive - especially if the prisoner belongs to one of the high risk groups or associates with such groups.

When going on duty

If you have any cuts or grazes, these can be covered with a simple waterproof adhesive dressing before going on duty. Do not overlook what you might consider trivial such as scratches from pruning rose bushes, from your cat, or small burns or scalds which may leave blisters. Burns take a long time to heal and are open sores for most of that time.

It is essential that these 'trivial' injuries are covered when on duty and potentially in contact with sources of infection.

You need to know where you can obtain medical plasters when on duty - for example the location of the car or station first aid box - or better still always carry a few plasters in your pocket. You may well be involved in a struggle with a prisoner and knock some skin off your knuckles etc. These types of minor injuries should be covered at the first opportunity.

Searching

Searching the prisoner as soon as possible is a top priority to check for weapons, drugs or any evidence of the suspected crime.

One rule of searching is:

'Do not put your fingers where you cannot see...'

in pockets, under belts, inside socks etc.

Always ask the prisoner to turn out pockets or remove belts or socks. Then double check once the suspect areas have been exposed. Drug needles are the obvious danger although razor or small knife blades can be concealed.

Other occasions to search prisoners are when the privatised PCOs hand the prisoners over at the police office; being brought into custody or when answering bail, and after the prisoner has received a visitor.

Any vehicles the prisoners have been in should be searched and care taken as contaminated needles could have been hidden.

Booby traps - Be aware of the occasional 'booby trapped' property in which contaminated hypodermic needles and other sharp objects may have been placed specifically to injure officers. Examples include leaving razor blades in pockets or embedding hypodermic needles into the seats of vehicles about to be recovered or seized by the police.

When searching prisoners, the normal 'rub down' search is used in most cases, but the intimate search and strip search may be necessary.

Strip searches

Strip searches are dealt with in the Police and Criminal Evidence Act Codes of Practice Code C 4.1 and Annex A.

(See File 7.1.i at the end of the chapter)

Condoms full of heroin or cocaine have been found concealed in the rectum or vagina and if these are on the person of an HIV positive prisoner the risk of infection is high. Other prisoners have swallowed the condom containing drugs and x-rays have shown the package in the stomach or intestines.

In such cases the searching staff have to wait for the normal bodily functions to work before the evidence can be seized. These cases are difficult in as much as the prisoner's excreta has to be searched and disposed of with the added danger of HIV infection.

Prostitutes have been known to hide rolls of bank notes in their vagina and anus and it is suggested that arrangements should be made to take such money out of circulation after evidential purposes have been served.

Searching dead bodies

When searching apparently dead bodies for signs of life, signs of foul play and for property or evidence, you should try to establish whether HIV or AIDS is involved. When there is any doubt, exercise extreme caution.

Checking breathing and pulse for signs of life brings the officer into close contact with the body. Fluids in the mouth or nose can be expelled as the body is moved and air or gasses are disturbed in the lungs or stomach. The contents of the bowels and bladder sometimes involuntarily discharge when a person is dying.

You should protect your eyes, mouth and other areas where infection could enter your body. If nothing else is available, tie a handkerchief around your nose and mouth.

Examining the body for any marks or signs of violence is another 'at risk' activity. Surgical masks and gloves should be considered and most forces make these items available. The same considerations apply when searching, undressing or moving the body.

Consider, for example, the possibilities of people hanging themselves - these bodies have to be cut down and normally one officer will have to support the weight first, possibly coming into close contact with bodily fluids.

Cleaning cells and vehicles

Gaoler and escort duties include cleaning after a 'dirty' prisoner has been in the cells or cellular vehicles. If the cleaner is absent then a mixture of bleach and water (about one part bleach to 10 parts water) can be used to kill any lingering HIV in the cells or in police vehicles.

Blankets can be destroyed if badly soiled - or sent for cleaning with a warning note to put the cleaning firm on guard.

When the prisoners shave after a night in the cells, make sure the razor used by a HIV positive prisoner is not used by anyone else - sometimes prisoners will pass the razors on to each other.

Giving first aid

All police officers are expected to perform first aid when necessary. One of the primary duties is the preservation of life. However, officers are not expected to place themselves at risk, as giving first aid can be dangerous in itself. Quite apart from the possibility of HIV infection as we are discussing here, the immediate situation may pose dangers - from motorway or other road traffic, collapsing buildings, a build-up of toxic fumes, risk of fire or explosion or noxious chemicals etc.

However, while all first aid brings the officer close to the casualty the more problematic treatment with regard to HIV concerns unconsciousness and resuscitation, wounds, miscarriage and childbirth.

The unconscious casualty

When listening for sounds of breathing, or trying to detect the feel of the casualty's breath on their cheek, there is the risk of saliva, vomit or blood being coughed onto the aider's face. Again a handkerchief could be tied round the nose and mouth.

In cases when then in no detectable pulse or breathing, the first aid officer should give mouth-to-mouth ventilation and chest compression (cardio-pulmonary resuscitation - CPR). (See File 7.2 at the end of the chapter for an update on resuscitation techniques.) Some forces issue a type of non-return valve appliance which is specially designed for mouth-to-mouth resuscitation - and provide the necessary training to use it.

Force instructions should be followed in this situation, but where there are no force instructions and the casualty is known to be HIV positive, the decision is a personal one.

Mouth-to-mouth resuscitation

To help make the decision it is said that no HIV infection from giving mouth-to-mouth has ever been recorded, despite the theoretical risk. (Hepatitis B is much more infectious - make sure you are immunised - see following section.)

The wounded casualty

One of the greatest risks of HIV infection is via blood. Any bleeding from the casualty must be treated with the utmost caution.

Whether the bleeding is a nose bleed at a road traffic accident, or menstrual blood, the same precautions should be taken. Try to avoid touching the casualty with bare hands - especially if you have a cut or open sore on your hand. Ideally, wear rubber disposable surgical gloves, although force-issue leather gloves will probably suffice if nothing else is available, or put plastic bags over your hands. Alternatively, consider asking a casualty who is not seriously wounded to dress their own wound under your supervision. If, as a last resort, you have to use your bare hands, ensure they are thoroughly washed afterwards.

First aiders are taught to control the bleeding by putting pressure over the wound and, where possible, to elevate the injured part to enlist the help of gravity to stem the bleeding. A dressing should be applied as soon as possible to keep infection out of the wound. As pressure is being maintained and dressings

applied, blood could come into contact with the first aider. It may contaminate clothes, towels, sheets and furniture etc.

In such situations, hygiene considerations must be paramount. Anything that can be thrown away, - soiled disposable gloves, used dressings, blood soaked clothing etc - should be sealed in a polythene bag and burnt. Other articles should be cleaned and the cleaning staff or company warned of contamination with possibly infected blood. Any pools of blood or blood on car seats or any police property or equipment should be cleaned with diluted bleach - one part bleach to 10 parts water.

If any injections were necessary for the prisoner, take extra care in disposing of the needles and syringes.

Miscarriages and childbirth

Police officers are quite often the only source of help or knowledge of first aid at an emergency childbirth or miscarriage and in such situations could be at risk of infection. As around 20% of pregnant women miscarry, an officer should know what to do (see File 7.3 at the end of the chapter.)

The officer should whenever possible wear rubber gloves, or improvise as mentioned above. A mask should be worn (or one improvised out of a handkerchief, or a triangular bandage from a first aid kit). The same applies for emergency childbirth as blood, vaginal secretions and excreta may be present (again see File 7.3 at the end of the chapter).

In summary... prevention, no cure!

As the research into HIV and AIDs treatment stands, every effort of the police officer must be directed towards prevention of infection.

Hepatitis

Hepatitis is the inflammation of the liver which causes the destruction of small patches of liver tissue. It is mainly caused through viral infection, but also can be caused by alcohol, drugs, bacteria, chemicals, poisons, fungus and parasitic infection.

We are concerned with the viral infections in this chapter, but it is worth bearing in mind that Hepatitis can result from overdosing with certain drugs, eg Paracetamol, and by heavy drinking (see Chapt 5: Drugs of First Choice).

There are several Hepatitis viruses, known by the letters A to G - although A, B and C are the most common. The viruses differ both in how they are spread and the effects they have on your health.

Hepatitis can occur in either acute or chronic form. An acute illness is a short sharp illness and a chronic illness is one that lasts a long time, sometimes coming and going.

As all types of Hepatitis affect the liver, here are a few facts about one of the body' most vital organs.

The liver

The liver is the body's chemical factory and performs hundreds of complex functions vital for life:

√ Converts food into chemicals necessary for life and growth;

√ produces quick energy when needed;

√ manufactures new body proteins;

√ prevents shortages in body fuel by storing sugars, vitamins and minerals;

√ aids the digestive process by producing bile;

√ digest fat;

√ neutralises and destroys poisons;

√ controls the production of cholesterol;

√ maintains hormone balance;

√ stores iron throughout life;

√ helps the body resist infection by producing immune factors;

√ regenerates its own tissue.

The liver has the capacity to carry on its functions with only a small part in working order. Most people do not know that it is not working properly until more advanced liver disease has developed.

What is cirrhosis?

Cirrhosis is the result of long term continuous liver damage. Normally, when the liver is damaged, the cells die and the liver re-grows without scarring. When the damage is severe and continuous, the re-growth results in scar tissue which impair the liver's efficiency. Cirrhosis is irreversible and, if advanced, people may develop complications.

Ascites is a build up of fluid in the abdomen; oesophegal varices are varicose veins in the gullet caused by increased blood pressure in these veins; encephalopathy is impaired mental function and is thought to be caused by waste products which are normally broken down by the liver, entering the circulation and affecting the brain. A further complication can be liver cancer.

Hepatitis B (HBV)

Preventing infection

The same precautions as outlined for HIV and AIDS also applies to the Hepatitis viruses, particularly B and C.

It is worthy of note that Hepatitis B (the most notorious and virulent of the Hepatitis viruses) is over 100 times more infectious than HIV.

It was mentioned above that HIV did not survive for very long when out of the body. HBV is by contrast a very stable virus which means it can survive outside the body for a much longer period than HIV (though it is not known for how long).

People most at risk of catching Hepatitis B are

▶ injecting drug users;

▶ babies born to infected mothers;

▶ close family members and partners of an infected person;

▶ those whose professions bring them into direct contact with blood - including police officers;

▶ prisoners, because they frequently come from other groups defined as high risk, and because of sharing cells;

▶ people who have unprotected sex with many partners.

▶ people travelling and working in countries where the virus is endemic, (particularly if having unprotected sex).

The spread of HBV

Evidence from research suggests that the amount of virus and body fluid needed for an infection to occur is a great deal less for Hepatitis B than for HIV, and Hepatitis C lies somewhere between the two. How infectious a person is depends on how much virus there is in their blood.

The virus is mainly transmitted through blood-to-blood contact but it can also be passed on sexually. The virus may also be detected in other body fluids such as saliva.

All blood donated in the UK is now screened for Hepatitis B. However, dental or medical treatment in countries where blood is not screened or where medical equipment is not adequately sterilised may still be a route of transmission. Vaccination is therefore advisable before travelling to such destinations.

Infected mothers can also pass the virus on to their babies around the time of the birth.

Managing the risk

Again we must emphasise that the same precautions as outlined for HIV and AIDS apply to the Hepatitis viruses.

Take the utmost care in any situation in which there is a risk of encountering dirty needles. Remember to always carefully clean and cover cuts, scratches and open wounds with a sticking plaster and clean any spilt blood with undiluted household bleach.

The virus is thought to be killed by a normal hot wash in a washing machine and by hot water and washing up liquid on cutlery and plates.

There is no risk of infection from normal social contact. For example you cannot catch Hepatitis B from a toilet seat or just by touching an infected person.

It is a good idea to advise anyone known to have Hepatitis B to go to a doctor for a blood test to check how infectious they may be.

Vaccination

There is a three-stage vaccine to protect against Hepatitis B. Three doses of the vaccine are needed to give full protection. It is important to receive all three doses as protection is not complete until after the third injection. A blood test to check antibody levels is sometimes recommended two to four months after completion of the course to ensure immunisation is complete.

Medical staff and anyone whose occupation may involve contact with blood or other body fluids should be vaccinated.

> Most forces have a policy on vaccination and usually advocate such precautions for gaolers, custody office staff, drugs squad officers and vice squad officers etc.
>
> Officers should check their force policy and ensure they are vaccinated themselves where necessary.
>
> Officers vaccinated against HBV (and/or HAV) must, of course, not relax their vigilance in guarding against infection. They have no reduced risk of contracting HIV or Hepatitis C (see relevant sections).

There are a few people who do not respond to the HBV vaccine and they may need a repeat course. Also those who continue to in an high risk role or environment are given a single booster dose five years after the first course of injections.

It is a good idea for partners, children and other household members of Hepatitis carriers to be vaccinated. Friends and occasional visitors do not need vaccination - remember there is no risk of infection through normal social contact.

It is important for babies to be protected by vaccination at birth if it is known that the mother is a carrier. For further information about infants infected at birth you could contact the Children's Liver Disease Foundation, 138, Digbeth, Birmingham B5 6DR.

If officers believe they may have been exposed to the HBV virus...

If officers who have not been vaccinated against HBV believe they may have been exposed to the virus - for example, through injury with a contaminated needle - there is a measure which can be taken immediately.

An injection of immunoglobulin must be given as soon as possible after the exposure. At the same time a Hepatitis B vaccine is also given, followed by two more injections at monthly intervals, with a booster at 12 months.

This is an accelerated schedule to speed up the immunisation process.

Immunoglobulin is given to people who have been recently exposed to the virus when there is not enough time to wait for the vaccine to take effect... and also given to children born to infected mothers.

How common is HBV?

The World Health Organisation estimates one third of the world's population has been infected with Hepatitis B and there are around 350 million chronic carriers worldwide. In Europe there are estimated to be one million infected people every year.

In the UK approximately one in 1,000 people carry the virus. In some inner city areas where there is a high percentage of ethnic mothers the prevalence in pregnant women varies from one in 50 to one in 2,000. There is also a higher than average prevalence in homosexual men.

Hepatitis B is common in parts of the world such as South East Asia, the Middle and Far East, Southern Europe and Africa.

Hepatitis C

Hepatitis C is highly infectious, more so, current research suggests, than HIV. Again the same precautions as those taken to preventing HIV and HBV infection generally apply.

Although vaccines are available to prevent infection from Hepatitis A and B, there is no vaccination currently available for Hepatitis C.

Hepatitis C, also known as Hep C or HCV, is one of the more recently discovered hepatitis viruses. Doctors are learning more about the viruses all the time and some of the information about Hepatitis C, particularly about how infection occurs and treatment may change in the light of further research.

The spread of HCV

The HCV virus is similar to the HBV virus in the way it is carried and transmitted, but the levels of risk varies for some methods of transmission. The virus is mainly transmitted through blood to blood contact.

People most at risk of catching Hepatitis C are:

▶ injecting drug users;
▶ those who received blood or blood products prior to September 1991.

Blood donors in the UK have been screened for HCV since September 1991 but blood or blood products in countries where screening does not take place carries a risk of infection.

HCV has spread rapidly through the injecting drug using community and users are thought to be the main source of new infections. There are varying estimates that between 10 and 45% of those with chronic Hepatitis C infection do not know how they caught it. However many doctors believe that in most cases, careful questioning will reveal a past experience with injecting drugs.

HCV can be transmitted sexually but this is thought to be unusual. There are a few cases of the virus being spread through other body fluids such as saliva but the risk is also thought to be low. Experts are unsure whether infection occurs between partners because of sexual exposure or because of sharing a personal item such as a razor, toothbrush or scissors.

Mothers with HCV may possibly pass the virus to their babies but again the risk is thought to be low - and it is presently believed that the disease if passed to the baby will not go on to become serious. It is not known whether the infection happens during pregnancy or during or immediately after the birth.

Managing the risk

As for HBV… take the utmost care in any situation in which there is a risk of encountering dirty needles. Remember to always carefully clean and cover cuts, scratches and open wounds with a sticking plaster and clean any spilt blood with undiluted household bleach.

As with HBV, there is no risk of infection from normal social contact and again, the virus is thought to be killed by a normal hot wash in a washing machine and by hot water and washing up liquid on cutlery and plates.

How common is HCV?

The prevalence of Hepatitis C worldwide is largely unknown as most people have no symptoms. The World Health Organisation estimates that three per cent of the world's population has HCV and that 200 million people worldwide are chronically infected.

> Levels of HCV infection in injecting drug users in the UK are estimated to be from approximately 60 to 90%.

Hepatitis A and its spread

The spread of HAV

Hepatitis A, also known as HAV, is caught by eating or drinking food or water which is contaminated with the virus. Infection also occurs as a result of close contact with an infected person. The virus is spread because of poor personal or public hygiene. It can be caught where standards of hygiene are low, both in this country and abroad. Infected water, hands and cooking utensils are also sources of infection.

HAV is more common in countries with poor sanitation and low standards for drinking water, such as southern and eastern Europe, Africa and the Middle and Far East. The prevalence in the UK is low - approximately 7,500 cases were reported in 1991 - but the disease is likely to be under reported as many people with mild symptoms never consult their doctor.

Hepatitis A is spread quickly in communities. Outbreaks may occur in nurseries and schools where children are not yet toilet trained. Infected children may introduce the disease to adult carers, In is also more common in homosexual men and injecting drug users.

There is a very rare risk of transmission via blood transfusion or blood products. Those known to be at risk of infection by this route, such as haemophiliacs, can be protected by vaccination.

General guidelines to avoid HAV infection are:

√   Maintain a high standard of personal hygiene.

√   Ensure you are vaccinated if visiting high risk countries.

√   When in high risk countries - avoid raw or inadequately cooked shellfish, raw salads an vegetables, untreated drinking water, ice cubes and unpasturised milk.

Vaccination

For officers who have been in close contact with Hepatitis A, or who may be imminently working in or travelling to areas where infection is more widespread, immediate short term protection is recommended. This can be provided by a single injection of immunoglobulin which lasts for about three to six months.

Officers and their families who are planning to travel to high risk countries such as parts of southern and eastern Europe, Africa, India and the Middle and Far East should consider long term protection. One injection is given two to four weeks before travel. Most people will be protected after one injection. A final booster injection given six to 12 months later provides protection for up to 10 years.

Recently a combined Hepatitis A and B vaccine has been introduced.

The British Liver Trust

The authors wish to convey their thanks to the British Liver Trust who donated information for this chapter.

The Trust runs support groups for people with liver disease and a telephone information service. It also produces a range of leaflets which cover specific aspects of liver disease. For a list of support groups and information leaflets write enclosing an sae to:

British Liver Trust
Ransomes Europark
Ipswich IP3 9QG

Tel 01473 276 326
Fax 01473 276 327
Information Line 01473 276 328

The British Liver Trust is the only national charity in this country dedicated to fighting all adult* liver diseases through research, education and patient support. It raises funds by voluntary contributions and should you wish to support the Trust please ring or fax the above numbers for information.

* The Children's Liver Disease Foundation deals with all aspects of paediatric liver disease.

Children's Liver Disease Foundation,
138, Digbeth
Birmingham B5 6DR

The CLDF can be contacted on:
0121 643 7282

Experts estimate that more than half of all liver diseases could be prevented if people acted upon the knowledge we already have.

File 7.1.i: Strip searches

PACE Code C 4.1 and Annex A
(England and Wales)

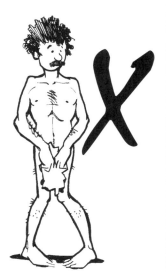

A strip search is a search involving the removal of any-thing more than outer clothing. This search operates on the 'necessity principle' ie not carried out as a mat-ter of routine and only as necessity demands.

A strip search must be authorised by the custody officer only when he reasonably considers that an article might have been concealed which the person would not be allowed to keep, eg drugs. PACE Code of Practice Annex A(B) sets out a programme for strip searches.

- **Same sex** - the officer searching must be of the same sex.
- **Privacy** - the person searched must not be seen by anyone except the person(s) necessary for the search and an appropriate adult where necessary.
- **Two present** - except in urgent cases - there must be at least two persons present in the following circumstances:
  - risk of serious harm;
  - exposure of intimate parts;
  - juvenile, mentally disordered, mentally handicapped (extra person must be an appropriate adult, though the appropriate adult need not be present if both the juvenile and appropriate adult agree).
- **Sensitivity** - whenever possible, allow the person to remain partly clothed at all times, eg replace upper garment before removing lower ones;
- **Visual** - require the person being searched to spread arms and legs and bend to facilitate the examination of genital and anal areas. There must be no physical contact with any orifice which could constitute an intimate or non-intimate search.
- **Removal of articles** - article found must be handed over by the prisoner as removal could constitute an intimate search under Annex A(A), the exception being the mouth (search upon arrest).
- **Speed** - the search should be done quickly to allow the person to dress as soon as possible.

When the subject is a HIV suspect this must be borne in mind throughout the whole search.

File 7.1.ii: Intimate searches

PACE Code C 4.1 and Annex A(A)
(England and Wales)

Once again this type of search operates on the principles of necessity and account-ability. In practice, common sense and decency are the watchwords of the custody officer.

Body orifices other than the mouth may be searched by a medical practitioner or nurse only when a superintendent or above has reasonable grounds for believing that:

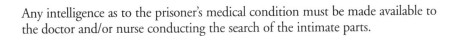

▶ an article which could cause physical injury is concealed; or

▶ a Class A drug, intended for supply or export is concealed; and

▶ an intimate search is the only practicable means of removing it.

Any intelligence as to the prisoner's medical condition must be made available to the doctor and/or nurse conducting the search of the intimate parts.

File 7.2: Update on resuscitation techniques

Mouth-to-mouth ventilation

1. Lay the casualty down and make sure the airways are open and unobstructed. Tilt the head back and lift the chin.

2. Pinch the casualty's nose and, after taking a good breath, blow into the mouth until the chest rises. It should take about two seconds to inflate the casualty's chest.

3. Allow the chest to deflate and repeat the process at the rate of about 10 inflations per minute.

Chest compressions or CPR

1. Lie the casualty down on a firm surface - the floor as opposed to a bed - measure two finger's width up the sternum (breastbone) and place the heel of the other hand over the breast bone against the two fingers.

2. Placing the other hand over the heel of the first hand, press down with straight arms while kneeling at the casualty's side. Depress the chest one and a half to two inches (four to five centimetres) and then release.

3. Repeat this process at the rate of about 80 depressions per minute, ie less than one second per depression.

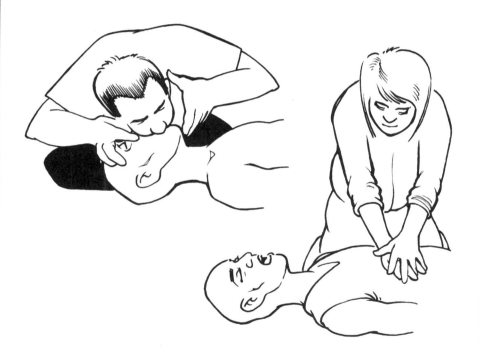

In combination...

To combine mouth-to-mouth with CPR, inflate the chest twice using mouth-to-mouth and then compress the chest 15 times with CPR. The two inflations to the 15 compressions should be continued until the ambulance etc arrives or until the casualty recovers.

File 7.3: What to do on attending an emergency childbirth or miscarriage

Any sudden and heavy vaginal bleeding could herald a miscarriage, especially if accompanied by painful cramps in the area of the womb. If an officer comes across, or is called to a woman who is believed to be miscarrying, the officer should help the woman into a semi reclining position, give her something with which to clean up any blood; save anything that is passed out of the vagina for later examination and arrange for medical assistance as soon as possible.

Emergency childbirth and miscarriage are similar situations as they apply to potential infection - blood, vaginal fluid secretions and excreta may be present. Officers should take precautions to protect themselves from infection as outlined in the main body of the chapter.

The mucus plug at the entrance of the womb may be discharged as a 'show' starting the birth process. The waters breaking is a sign of labour and may occur quickly or as a trickle. As contractions increase, the bowels may involuntarily discharge. To prevent this contaminating the baby, as soon as contractions start, place a pad over the anus area. Sufficient towels or sheets or even newspaper should be placed under the woman's body to catch these discharges. The baby will be extremely slippery when born and should be handled with care.

The do's and don'ts of childbirth

Do

√ Wash your hands thoroughly before and after delivery.

√ Ask the woman to remove all clothing that could hinder the birth.

√ Male officers should try to find a chaperone if possible.

√ Check that the baby's breathing is not restricted by a membrane or the umbilical cord around its neck etc.

Don't

x Do not try to delay the birth.

x Do not let her bath if her water have broken as this may bring risk of infection.

x Do not give her any food or drink, but moisten lips if necessary.

x Do not pull the baby's head or shoulders.

x Do not cut the umbilical cord or smack the baby.

File 7.4: Symptoms and treatment for the viral infections discussed in this chapter

File 7.4.i: HIV and AIDS

How HIV affects the body

Once the HIV is in the body it infects a type of white blood cell called T4. This cell is important to the workings of the immune system. Once the cell is infected the virus can become a 'sleeper' - to activate at some time in the future - or could kill the cell. The body seems to recover after the initial invasion and slight decline in T4 cells. It makes antibodies against HIV and builds its T4 cells nearly back to square one. People at this stage would test positive in relation to HIV antibodies, although they would not be defined as having AIDS.

Apart from a short lived flu-like complaint, sweating or fever, the infected individual will show few signs of being infected. HIV can then take between two and 10 years to weaken the immune system, by destroying the T4 cells, to such a degree that the individual has Acquired the Immune Deficiency Syndrome.

The initial disease caused by the invading HIV is called the 'primary' illness and the symptoms are caused by the body's reaction to the HIV virus. Full blown AIDS is diagnosed when the HIV has made the immune system so low that 'opportunist' illnesses attack the undefended body.

Signs and symptoms of HIV

Some people do not seem to be affected at all, while others will suffer symptoms of cold or influenza. Also inflammation of the skin may occur, particularly on the face. Other more serious symptoms may be coughing, glandular fever, thrush, diarrhoea, or a substantial weight loss.

These are the symptoms when first infected by HIV. The next stage before full blown AIDS is AIDS-Related Complex (ARC). This is used to describe a pre-AIDS condition, for example, weight loss, fever and enlarged lymph nodes, but without the full blown AIDS illnesses. Usually those diagnosed as ARC will progress to AIDS.

Signs and symptoms of AIDS

AIDS symptoms are a range of 'opportunist' illnesses which eventually cause the victim's death. The complaints are called 'indicators' and include:

> Diarrhoea (may cause dehydration which can be fatal) - Tuberculosis (TB) - Leukoplakia (white patches develop on the mucous membrane or moist skin areas which are generally harmless) - Kaposi's Sarcoma (skin cancer characterised by blue-red nodules) - Pneumonia - Herpes viruses including shingles.
> Many other fungal and bacterial infections can affect the AIDS victims and the signs and symptoms of all the above-mentioned can vary greatly from individual to individual.

Treatment for HIV and AIDS

Scientists are undertaking one of the most involved research programmes ever launched to find a cure. The first drug used on AIDS patients was AZT (Azidothymidine) which slowed down the progress of the illness. Another was DDL (dideoxyinosine). Neither were cures and both had damaging side effects. Other drugs on trial slow down progression of the illness to varying degrees and with varying side effects. A main area of research is devoted to developing a vaccine against HIV. Like other vaccines an effective one would promote the production of antibodies within the body to block the virus before it could become established.

As emphasised in the main body of this chapter:

> *As the research into HIV and AIDs treatment stands, every effort of the police officer must be directed towards prevention of infection.*

File 7.4.ii: Hepatitis B

Symptoms of HBV

There is an incubation period of between six weeks to six months before any symptoms may appear. However, many people may never have any symptoms and do not feel ill - although they are still infectious. If there are symptoms, most adults notice a short, mild, flu-like illness which may include a cough, sore throat, tiredness, joint pains and loss of appetite. Some may have nausea and vomiting. Occasionally the acute infection can be severe with abdominal pain and jaundice.

How serious is HBV?

The majority of adults infected with Hepatitis B recover fully after a few weeks.

People who have the virus for longer than six months are described as chronic carriers. Less than 10 per cent of adults become chronically infected (though approximately 90 per cent of infected babies go on to become chronic carriers).

A few infected people who have no symptoms continue to carry the virus in their body for many years and remain infectious. They may not necessarily have Hepatitis and are known as healthy carriers.

However for those who do suffer from chronic HBV, the continuing liver inflammation and damage may lead to cirrhosis and, over time, liver cancer. People with cirrhosis need careful monitoring by a specialist in liver diseases - a hepatologist or gastroenterologist - to detect whether liver damage is occurring.

Treatment for Hepatitis B

Most acute sufferers of HBV do not need treatment as they do not develop any significant liver inflammation. They may feel more tired than usual and need rest, but eventually recover and acquire life long protection against the virus.

Chronic sufferers who are infected for longer than six months may benefit from treatment. The current treatment is with an antiviral drug called Alpha Interferon. It mimics naturally occurring interferon in the body which is produced as part of the body's immune response to infection and may be used in combination with other antiviral drugs. However it usually produces unpleasant flu-like side effects. The aim of the treatment is to prevent the virus replicating and causing further liver damage. Some people respond better than others - those born with the virus tend to respond less well, but it is still sometimes recommended to help prevent cirrhosis developing and to reduce the chance of the infection being passed on.

File 7.4.iii: Hepatitis C

Signs and symptoms of HCV

> Mild to severe fatigue - anxiety - weight loss - anorexia - alcohol intolerance - joint pains - pain in the area of the liver - concentration problems - nausea - flu-like symptoms such as fever, chills, nightsweats and headaches.

Some of the symptoms come and go and it is not unusual for people to be wrongly diagnosed as having ME (myalgic encephalomyelitis). In HCV infection there is usually a long latent phase in which people feel quite well before more serious liver disease may become apparent.

How serious is HCV?

Only a few infected people develop an acute illness - such as jaundice - shortly after being infected.

However it is thought that around three quarters of infected people - whether they develop acute symptoms or not - go on to develop chronic HCV (that which lasts longer than six months).

For chronic HCV sufferers the liver remains inflamed and causes damage to the liver cells. Unfortunately doctors cannot predict who will go on to develop serious liver disease. Most will have a mild disease, either stable or only very slowly progressive. Others will eventually develop cirrhosis - some 20, 30 or even 40 years after contracting the virus.

Tests for HCV

The virus is detected by a specific blood test, usually an ELISA-3. Sometimes called an anti-HCV test, it looks for Hep C antibodies in the blood. A positive result (anti-HCV positive) reveals exposure to the virus at some time during life. It does not tell whether the virus is still present or whether you are infectious.

A further test is needed to detect on-going infection. However it does take time for antibodies to appear in the blood after infection. This 'window period' is called seroconversion and is usually eight to twelve weeks after exposure to the virus, but can take up to six months. Blood tests taken too early may not detect HCV.

Treatment for HCV

Treatment for HCV is the same as that outlined for HBV. Doctors are learning more about who is likely to respond and several factors may be taken into consideration before treatment is advised, These will include, age, which of six strains of Hepatitis C is present, low long a person has been infected and whether cirrhosis has developed.

However it is important for those with Hepatitis C to be seen regularly by a specialist whether treatment is considered appropriate or not. Regular assessment is needed to detect whether damage is occurring and if therapy is appropriate.

File 7.4.iv: Hepatitis A

Signs and symptoms of HAV

Some people may have no symptoms at all whereas others develop serious illness. There is an incubation period of between 2 and 6 weeks. after which symptoms may develop, such as headache, fever, nausea, vomiting , diarrhoea, and abdominal pain. These symptoms may last for a week or more before jaundice develops. Jaundice is easily noticeable as the skin and whites of eyes turn yellow, urine turns dark and stools become pale.

How serious is HAV?

Most people recover in a few weeks and it is unusual for people to be admitted to hospital. However, fatigue and debility may last in some people for many months, In a few, the illness may be more prolonged and severe but eventually recovery does occur. Some people may have abnormal liver function test for several months after the illness, although it is not thought to cause long term liver damage. The severity of the disease increases with age and there is a small risk of death in the acute phase, particularly in people over the age of 60. In infants and young children, the infection can be mild or even pass unnoticed, Once a person has recovered from Hepatitis A they are immune for life.

Treatment for HAV

Once infected, as with most viral illnesses, there is no specific treatment. For those who develop jaundice and itching this can be treated with a short course of cortisone tablets. It is important for people to eat and drink as well as possible. Light food may be easier to digest but there is no reason to omit fat from the diet. Alcohol and heavy exertion should be avoided.

File 7.5: Terms of the drug-using fraternity

Back loading - a method of preparing and sharing drugs for injection to reduce waste, using two syringes. The drug solution is drawn up in one syringe, the plunger taken out of the other and some of the solution squirted in.

Flushing out - used to ensure all the drug is injected into the vein. While the needle is still in the vein, the plunger is withdrawn to draw up blood into the syringe. This is then injected back to flush out any drug particles.

Front loading - Similar to back-loading but in this case the needle is taken out of the second syringe so the solution may be squirted in from the top.

Sharps - term used to describe needles and syringes.

Skin popping - injecting drugs in between skin and fat layers.

Works - term to describe injecting equipment used particularly in prisons.

8. Mind out

Coping with stress and psychological problems

For operational police officers, who are trained to be self-reliant and solve problems under pressure, it can be a bitter experience to discover that personal resources are sometimes no match for the complex alterations in emotion, mental competence and health that can be triggered by change, uncertainty and trauma.

At such times it takes a special blend of courage and humility to seek professional advice.

On the professional side a wealth of experience has been accumulating in connection with helping both police officers and support staff to restore and maintain their health. The latest developments in health psychology and treatments can now offer increasingly efficient and effective solutions for a wide range of problems that adversely affect work performance and attendance.

For psychologists, police employees comprise an interesting occupational group. Not only does their organisation and culture have some distinctive features, but it is difficult to find another set of employees who through their careers can be engaged in such diverse tasks and who can end up experiencing such a wide variety of psychological problems.

The following case history (reported with the officers' permission) illustrates one of the more important new treatments now available for dealing with a potentially devastating consequence of operational police work.

Case history: a police officer forced to abandon his colleague

At the height of the miners' strike in 1984, two police officers on duty at an isolated station saw a crowd of about 70 hostile miners streaming toward their building. Fearing the worst, the two officers ran out of the rear entrance and climbed over a fence with the intention of making their escape across a field.

However, the leaders of the mob soon caught up with the female officer who had been hampered by her skirt. One brought her to the ground with a rugby-tackle, and another kicked her so forcibly in the chest that she was lifted through the air.

The male officer stopped in his tracks and the developing scene became etched on his memory - the imploring look on the woman's face as the kicking continued, and then further shouting and chanting as the miners re-grouped and set off in his direction.

He figured that if he were to go to the aid of his colleague he would be as good as dead, so he turned and ran for his life.

Case history continued...

Months of intense psychological and physiological disturbance followed the incident, and for a period the officer became housebound. Eventually, enforced medical retirement became the only option as far as his career was concerned but even that did not resolve his problems.

Over the next 10 years, despite excellent support and many hours of counselling, he remained deeply troubled by intrusive images of the final moments before he deserted his colleague and the guilt feelings that accompanied them. Recurring nightmares of being chased by a faceless lion would awake him in terror once or twice each week in physical distress from chronically hyperventilating.

Following further assessment and as a last resort and he had agreed to subject himself to a quite different kind of treatment - Eye Movement Desensitisation and Reprocessing (EMDR) - developed by the American psychologist Francine Shapiro. With an air of politely sceptical resignation the former officer sat down and the process was initiated.

Eye Movement Desensitisation and Reprocessing

During this treatment, memories of past experiences and anticipations of future events are 'reprocessed' in a person' s mind into different and more acceptable forms. EMDR is non-hypnotic, and it is particularly useful for situation in which a person does not wish - or is simply unable - to disclose many details of the traumatic experience.

The 'reprocessing' is most obviously triggered when attention is split for short periods of time between physical stimulation and previously selected psychological 'target material'. The target material will include the past experiences at the root of the pathology, along with present situations that currently trigger the disturbance. The visual, cognitive, affective and body-sensation components of each target are also specified and to do this the officer must relive the physical and mental sensations associated with the remembered experience.

For some people the 'reprocessing' may happen quite peacefully, but for others it may bring high levels of disturbance as they re-live or re-enact distressing experiences. Sets of bi-directional eye movements are commonly used as the stimulation, but alternating hand-taps or auditory cues will also work. Talking, at least in the form of active listening or modest interpretation, actually seems to inhibit the reprocessing and so is discouraged.

Case history continued...

Forty minutes later the former officer was a puzzled man. Try as he might, he could not recall the troublesome images. Instead, all that he could see was the fence and the field as they had looked on peaceful summer days.

He knew precisely what the original images had contained, but he was now retaining that information in a different form. The pattern of physiological responses that normally accompanied any focus on the experience was not present, and for the first time since the incident he felt deep down that there had been nothing wrong with the decision to leave his colleague.

Over the next few days he felt very sleepy and sometimes nauseous, and noted that a lot of changes seemed to be going on in his mind. Even though the nightmare had not been specifically targeted during the treatment he never experienced it again. A six-month follow-up assessment showed the initial treatment effects had been maintained.

The chronic hyperventilation and associated physical and psychological symptoms required separate treatment, but they were rectified. With less entrenched cases such breathing disorders can spontaneously begin to correct themselves after EMDR, but it seems that chronically traumatised people, such as this officer, need to work harder to re-set the relevant physiological parameters.

Focus on EMDR

Apparently intractable problems that can be resolved as quickly and easily as this are very common for those who practice EMDR regularly. More complex problems will of course take far longer. There will also be situations in which EMDR may be used as just one component of a wider treatment plan, and others in which it will be altogether irrelevant.

Fortunately, EMDR has developed within mainstream psychology in the US and among the 20,000 or so trained users world-wide are some very eminent scientists and practitioners.

'Those involved in its dissemination have actively encouraged research, and have sought to comply with best practice in matters of training, informed consent, client safety, and related professional issues. Now, eight years after its inception, the growing scientific evidence is confirming the hopes raised by numerous published case studies that EMDR is indeed a treatment of great promise for event-related disturbance.'

(Wilson S, Becker L and Tinker R (1995) 'Eye movement desensitisation and reprocessing (EMDR) treatment for psychologically traumatised individuals' *Journal of Consulting and Clinical Psychology*, pp 928-937).

Further reading

For those interested in pursuing the subject beyond the anecdotal level, a detailed description of all aspects of EMDR is now in print, along with a review and critique of recent controlled evaluation studies:

Eye Movement Desensitisation and Reprocessing: Basic Principles, Protocols, and Procedures. New York: Guilford.

An introductory book is available for lay people:

EMDR: The Breakthrough Therapy for Overcoming Anxiety, Stress and Trauma. New York: Basic Books (Harper Collins).

An advanced text is also in preparation.

The remainder of this chapter will focus, as a case study, on one particular English police force - West Yorkshire Police (WYP).

This case study examines the history and operation of an external psychological support service developed over the past 10 years, and then considers the types of problems that can be addressed by a service of this kind.

These problems - and what can be done to address them - are illustrated by range of diverse case histories.

Case study

Psychological support for West Yorkshire Police

The beginnings

Shortly before the Bradford football stadium fire in 1985, WYP decided to form a group to establish methods of implementing Home Office recommendations on managing stress in the police service.

The pressing need to implement some of these recommendations came sooner than expected and in the weeks following the Bradford fire the author of this chapter was invited by Chief Constable Sampson to set up a confidential screening and counselling programme for officers adversely affected by their experiences, (Duckworth D H 1986 'Psychological problems arising from disaster work' *Stress Medicine 2*, 315-323).

The WYP Committee on Stress had its inaugural meeting on 14 November 1985, in the wake of the fire. It reviewed the operation and outcomes of the experimental programme, and decided to recommend to the Joint Advisory Committee in 1986 that a more permanent confidential, occupational stress-counselling service be established for police officers.

In due course, this service became known as the Force Confidential Counselling Scheme. It was intended to cater for both traumatic and more routine problems, and was to be supported by awareness training or briefings for all officers of the rank of Inspector and above.

The Committee sought expert advice from outside the force on the proposed plans, costs and so forth, including that of Dr Ann Fingret, Chief Medical Officer at the BBC and President of the Society of Occupational Medicine.

At that point the author was formally invited to take on the role of consulting psychologist to WYP, in order to help provide this service in conjunction with the Force Welfare Officer. At first the scheme was restricted to police officers, but after a few months it was extended to civilian employees.

Detailed operating protocols included procedures for referral to the external psychologist. The initial attempts to satisfy the conflicting requirements of accountability and confidentiality produced a rather cumbersome procedure involving designated referral officers. However, this procedure was subsequently to allow officers and members of support staff to refer themselves directly.

The Force Confidential Counselling Scheme underwent an initial 12-month evaluation and then for the next few years each user completed an anonymous evaluation form to be returned in a pre-paid envelope to the Welfare Officer. The response rate was very high, and several hundred forms were returned. In due course this procedure was discontinued as the response to the Scheme was consistently satisfactory and yielded no new information.

As events turned out, the Bradford football stadium fire was just the first in a series of disasters in the latter half of the 1980s which had a large police involvement.

Several other forces were compelled to address the same or even more complex issues sooner than they might have chosen, and most forces began to set up coherently planned systems for dealing with the psychological sequelae of major incidents and other types of psychologically-disturbing situations.

It became more widely accepted that these work-related health problems were both operationally and commercially important due to their potentially serious effects on performance and attendance at work.

It proved necessary to develop in-house solutions because then as now, prompt and suitably specialised assistance was difficult to obtain through traditional National Health Service (NHS) routes.

The Scheme in operation

The WYP Confidential Counselling Scheme began in 1987. Since that time there have been far-reaching organisational changes throughout the force and a well-staffed Occupational Health Unit (OHU) has been established.

The Scheme continues to provide an external, specialised psychological support service for the force, but where appropriate it now liaises closely with welfare and medical staff in the OHU. The OHU may prove influential in persuading an employee to use the Scheme - similarly an employee can be referred to the OHU for welfare or medical attention. There are no formal links with the OHU, however, and client records are not shared.

Can it be confidential?

Police staff can use the Scheme in the knowledge that nothing they say will be disclosed to any third party, that nothing from their transactions will find its way on to any personal records, and that nothing at all about their identities or problems will be divulged to anyone in the Service or the NHS - *in normal circumstances.*

In exceptional circumstances - those in which it is judged that a person could constitute a danger to him/herself and/or to others - there is a professional and ethical responsibility to manage this appropriately.

A potential conflict between public interest and confidentiality is particularly obvious when an officer in a high-profile role such as firearms, underwater search, motorway pursuit or undercover work has a problem that is serious enough to constitute a danger to life.

In such circumstances, and when it has not already come to the attention of supervisors, the officer concerned is given the opportunity to handle the matter in a professionally dignified manner by going and disclosing his or her predicament to a supervisory or medical officer. The only proviso is that the supervisory or medical officer within an agreed time limit must communicate confirmation of the disclosure back to the psychologist. Failing this, the psychologist has a duty to report the problem.

In the few instances when this situation has arisen, there has never been any difficulty in persuading an officer to take the appropriate steps.

It has also been reassuring to see that the organisation has not treated such problems as signs of irremediable flaws in the makeup of the officers in question, and that once fully recovered the officers in question have - when appropriate - been given a chance to resume their normal duties.

'TREATMENT-ONLY'

When first designed, the Scheme was intended to have a strictly 'treatment-only' focus, and fortunately that has been maintained.

No assessments of individuals are carried out in connection with injuries on duty or fitness for duty, and no reports are prepared for use in litigation or disciplinary hearings.

The purpose of this single-function design was to ensure that staff would only use the Scheme if they really wanted to get over their problems. As things stand, for example, a person has nothing to gain by trying to use the Scheme to show how 'permanently unfit' she or he is!

How can employees be persuaded the Scheme is worth trying?

It is important to remember that only a very few individuals actually *want* to make use of the Scheme.

At first, potential users are typically reluctant to avail themselves of the facility because of what they imagine it signifies about themselves, and also because of what they think it might involve. They only relent because of their pressing needs. When self referral was first introduced and publicised in 1990, there was no sudden flood of additional cases.

Simple psychophysiological indicators commonly evident at the first visit, such as heavy use of the toilet, pronounced body odour, and clammy handshakes confirm the anxiety that most people feel when going to see a psychologist about personal matters for the first time. For some, this anxiety has been so acute that they have later confessed to vomiting or lack of bladder control before the first session.

The problem has never been how to bring the Scheme to the attention of staff so that they can simply use it when they want to. Rather, it has been how to identify and reach those who need it, and persuade them that it is relevant and worth trying.

In management terms, the successful operation of the Scheme constitutes a delivery rather than a marketing system.

The web of referral influences that has developed over the years, therefore, is critically important to the successful operation of the Scheme. Past users of the Scheme, supervisors, OHU staff, General Practitioners (GPs), and staff association representatives are some of the important players in this system.

As all those involved become more familiar with the kinds of problems the Scheme specialises in, they have all made increasingly appropriate referrals. Ultimately, this situation is far superior to one in which employees only come as a last resort, because all other sources of help have failed them.

Another significant component of the delivery system is the proactive professional support that is now provided for officers in 'high risk' roles - undercover officers, Witness Support Scheme officers, staff in the Domestic Violence and Child Protection Units, and a number of other individuals in demanding posts. For these officers, health-maintenance is achieved through periodic, scheduled consultations for each individual, and the development of a suitably trusting, professional relationship that makes it easy to home in on incipient problems and deal with them so that they never develop into management issues.

Recent findings from the Scheme

Use of the Scheme in 1997

Attendance

Total WYP staff using the scheme during the year
260 employees.

Of these 260:
78% - police officers;
22% - support staff.

Referrals

40% - OHU staff;
15% - directly by supervisors;
45% - self referral.

Use of the Scheme in 1997 (cont...)

Although 45% ultimately referred themselves, in most cases they had been influenced by multiple sources over a period of weeks or months: colleagues, supervisors, staff association representatives, OHU staff, GPs, and the like.

Outcomes

90% dealt with within four sessions;
90% stayed at or returned to work - rather than going or staying off sick or leaving the Force.

This latter figure has slowly increased over the preceding years.

Source of problem

39% - work;
61% - domestic/personal.

Work-related problems

Employee's problems which (broadly) could be classified as work-related yielded three broad categories.

An 'incidents' category included problems arising from road traffic accidents, crowd-control problems at football matches, assaults, head-injuries, shootings, and public order situations.

Occasionally, it was necessary to treat the intensely distressed partner of a police officer who had been injured on duty. Consider that this can make all the difference between an officer returning to duty rather than coming under pressure to leave the job.

A 'treatment' category included problems arising from harassment or bullying by peers and superiors, disciplinary investigations, enforced transfers and instances of what was perceived to be poor management.

A 'job' category included exhaustion problems arising from work overload, aggression toward prisoners and members of the public, 'loss of bottle' in the face of confrontational situations, over-obsession with particular criminals, and loss of confidence at work.

Domestic/personal-related problems

It is difficult to truly separate many job-related and personal problems and this classification includes a wide variety of problems whose sources could be in either or both.

The category includes a wide variety of phobias - for needles, flying, driving on motorways, passing through wide-open spaces, and several so-called 'social phobias' (eg acute fears of vomiting in briefings, courtroom settings, and meetings).

There were many problems (for example, depression; anxiety; panic attacks; emotionality; hyperventilation) related to personal ill health (for example, chronic fatigue syndrome; chest injuries; chronic pain; cancer; caffeine intoxication; heart disease; asthma).

Domestic crises relating to childbirth, abortion, or after surgical errors caused a number of serious psychological problems, as did traumatic bereavements (for example, the sudden death of a person's young child or baby). There were also the usual serious problems arising from domestic violence/abuse, child abuse, rape and other assaults away from the work situation.

Problems addressed by a psychological support service

The general focus

Many factors contribute to the onset of health problems, from genetic vulnerabilities through to factors within a person's work and domestic situations.

Personal psychological vulnerabilities constitute another vital ingredient.

These can take many forms including incompletely processed memories of disturbing past experiences, limited or over-rigid personal philosophies, incorrect beliefs about the maintenance or restoration of personal health, and deficiencies in social skills.

Some 'psychological vulnerabilities' are fairly universal and judged to be 'normal' within society. It is a person's intense desire to stay alive that makes a near-death experience so terrifying; it is a mother's love and feelings of responsibility toward her new born child that makes a cot death so intensely distressing.

Other vulnerabilities can be idiosyncratic and potentially dysfunctional.

The operation of personal vulnerabilities (most of which can be corrected) can be illustrated by the questions overleaf:

Personal vulnerabilities

? Why does one person faced with a perceived gross inequity at work become enraged and progressively ill, while another remains philosophical and healthy?

? Why does one officer with an excellent operational track record gradually become over-anxious and paranoid when he hears that a contract has been taken out on his life, while another remains calm and collected?

? Why can one conscientious person 'switch off' each night and sleep well, while another lies awake reprocessing the tasks of the day to a point of near-exhaustion?

? Why is one hard-working officer capable of remaining healthy throughout a protracted murder inquiry, while another behaves in a manner that precipitates illness?

? Why does one person fall prey to the arts of the manipulative bully, while another simply shrugs them off?

? Why does one officer recruited from the army find that his active service experiences leave him aggressive and dangerous after a drink, while another can leave his experiences behind him?

? Why does one sergeant become anxious and dizzy while giving briefings, while his colleagues remain quite calm?

? Why does one officer feel demoralised and useless after a heart attack, while another looks forward to returning to work and recovering his health?

? Why is one officer able to return to normal driving after a serious traffic accident, while his partner from the same accident remains phobic toward all aspects of driving?

The difficulties of predicting psychological vulnerability

It is important to realise that most individuals cannot predict in advance what their vulnerabilities are, and how they could personally capitulate. That only becomes evident once the decline has started.

Perhaps for this reason, questionnaire surveys that ask an individual to describe those aspects of police work he or she finds most 'stressful' tell us little or nothing about the mechanism through which the person ultimately may break down.

Apart from excluding the most unsuitable employees, personality tests are also of little use in predicting personal vulnerabilities. The roots of the problems are much more specific, varied and complex than the concept of 'personality' can ever hope to encompass.

All of this means that prevention before any decline is very difficult to achieve.

'Training needs' cannot readily be established, and because there are so many potential points of vulnerability and so many possible parallel and serial combinations of vulnerabilities, a person can rarely see any personal relevance in educational programmes that are offered.

To cap it all, even where relevance is perceived, few individuals possess the skills required to translate instruction into personal change at the level of latent vulnerabilities.

The role of the psychological support service

One way of describing the work of a psychological support service, therefore, is to say that:

√ it helps individuals to repair the damage stemming from life events that have interacted with 'normal' psychological vulnerabilities (for example a stabbing or traumatic bereavement), and also

√ it helps individuals to identify and correct dysfunctional psychological vulnerabilities along with any damage they have been responsible for.

This is most effectively and efficiently achieved when a 'biopsychosocial' approach is taken. That is, looking at the whole person in his or her social and developmental context, and intervening from all available angles.

The full constellation of relevant psychological and situational problems needs to be examined, both past and present.

Dysfunctional coping behaviours have to be identified, physiological disturbance as well as psychological disturbance must be assessed, and knock-on effects on health, relationships and work need to be taken into account.

Returning to EMDR

The EMDR treatment illustrated at the beginning of this chapter is particularly useful for repairing the psychological damage arising from incidents which have traumatised police officers.

The main problem in such cases is often that officers are left with disturbing and incompletely processed memories of their experiences.

In a recent study of traumatic memories Van der Kolk and Fisler confirmed what has been observed clinically for at least a century: that there are critical differences between the ways people form memories of traumatic events, and memories of other significant but non-traumatic events (Van der Kolk B A and Fisler R 1995 'Dissociation and the fragmentary nature of traumatic memories: Review and experimental confirmation' *Journal of Traumatic Stress*).

Developing a personal story

When people receive ordinary, non-traumatic sensory input, they automatically synthesise this information into a personal story that can be evoked at will, that can be condensed or expanded according to need, and that can be modified over time.

Disrupting the story by a traumatic experience

During the excessive arousal associated with a traumatic experience, normal memory processes are often disrupted and many aspects of the experience are stored in a disorganised way as 'fragments' - images, sensations, feelings, behavioural responses, and so forth.

Most of these cannot be evoked at will, but instead are triggered by certain internal or external circumstances.

They show up as intrusive recollections (for example, flashbacks, nightmares, images) and sudden intense feelings. They have an adverse influence on day-to-day behaviour, and support feelings of insecurity. They cannot be condensed or expanded, and they do not change very much over time.

Even when a person develops a personal story that covers the main events, the fragmented memories still tend to have a life of their own.

This breakdown in information processing during trauma that leads to the fragmentation of memories is considered by most experts in the field to be at the very core of the pathology of Post Traumatic Stress Disorder (PTSD).

It is precisely this breakdown in information processing that seems to be addressed so successfully by EMDR with its 'reprocessing' of fragmented memories.

Working through EMDR

During EMDR (Eye Movement Desensitisation and Reprocessing) the eye movements - among other things - exert a physiologically soothing effect upon a person's mind, so that it becomes possible to work through even the most terrifying or horrific experiences without becoming overwhelmed by emotion.

Any emotions or physical sensations that are re-experienced during EMDR seem to pass quite quickly, and once they have gone it is almost impossible to get them back.

This is the 'desensitisation' element of the treatment, and it is usually accompanied by spontaneous and extensive cognitive restructuring. The main signs of a successful resolution are that a person can think through the experiences in question without being disturbed, and that external and internal 'triggers' lose their potency.

During all of this, the information in a person' s mind is not being erased, but re-configured. A particular traumatic image may completely disappear, for example, but the person still 'knows' exactly what happened. The information is all there, but it is stored in a new, non-disturbing form.

The parameters of psychological support

At best, for the reasons described earlier, psychological assistance will usually amount to prevention in the early stages of decline, rather than the theoretical ideal of prevention before any decline has taken place. In this process of 'prevention at the point of decline', however, not only can current problems be resolved, but whenever possible, the officer is helped to become more resistant to future problems of a similar kind.

There are of course many types of psychological and psychiatric problems for which a dedicated psychological support service will not be the appropriate agency.

Examples would include the more biologically-driven types of mental illness that require medication or other long-term psychiatric support (for example, manic-depressive disorders; severe depression), substance use disorders (such as drug addiction), paraphilic psychosexual disorders (for example, paedophilia) and other disorders of impulse control (such as gambling) which require lengthy treatment.

When help cannot help

A less obvious type of problem which usually cannot be resolved is one with a 'secondary gain component'.

A classic cases in the police service arises when deep in his or her heart an individual turns against being a police officer and wishes to leave the service, but cannot afford to do so without a medical pension.

At a superficial level, the officer may complain (quite genuinely) of everything from anxiety when facing operational situations through to anguish following bereavement. He or she may express (quite sincerely) a desire to co-operate with whatever treatment is offered.

However, deeper parts of the officer's mind will not allow any recovery process to take place that might jeopardise the escape from the police service. Unless the person has an unusually high degree of self-awareness, attempts at treatment will be doomed to fail.

Examples from the case files

In the case examples that follow, care has been taken to preserve the anonymity of individuals while giving enough detail to illustrate some of the problems that can be dealt with by a psychological support service. No case is uniquely linked to a particular employee and in most instances material has been combined from two or more similar cases.

Unduly complex cases that would require a great deal of elaboration have not been included and no attempts have been made to give a full explanation of either the symptom profiles or the treatments that are described.

Case file 8.1: Residues from operational incidents

Almost any operational incident can leave an active and psychologically complex 'residue' in the mind of an officer - particularly if she or he feels dissatisfied with personal performance during the incident.

Depending on the precise dynamics of the original incident, this can show up either as a 'loss of bottle' and fear of future confrontational situations, or as a potentially dangerous increase in aggressiveness when confronting members of the public.

About a year after successfully completing his probation, a young officer was persuaded by other shift members to seek assistance with his 'change in personality'. From being steady and reliable in encounters with members of the public, he was now fiery and aggressive: His baton was drawn at the least provocation and he did not hesitate to use it with considerable force. His domestic partner (also a police officer) complained about his bad temper, his habit of throwing things when angry at home, and his out-of-character and somewhat paradoxical tendency to weep more often.

These changes were first noticed after a violent incident 12 months before when, along with several of his colleagues, he was involved in a protracted struggle with a particularly large and strong 'body builder'. The officer had been flung against a wall as though he were a rag doll (sustaining a back injury), and his attempts to use his baton to stop the man nearly strangling his partner were to no avail. His blows were perhaps more hesitant than they should have been because a little girl was standing in the doorway watching. When finally apprehended, the man never admitted anything and his eventual sentence was relatively light.

Since that incident, the officer had been beaten up on two further occasions, and each time he had felt helpless. Now, whenever he thought about the original incident or was confronted by someone who looked potentially dangerous, his stomach went tight and he felt a strange mixture of consuming anger and vulnerability. Getting the first blow in - with some force - seemed the logical thing to do.

Following an assessment, it became apparent that the officer's memory of the original incident had never 'settled down' and many aspects of it were still active. These aspects readily intruded into his perception of ongoing and anticipated situations, leading to incorrect risk assessment, inappropriate emotional arousal, and consequent over reaction.

Key elements from the memory of the operational sequence (including visual images, sounds, body sensations, and associated thoughts and conclusions) were therefore 'desensitised' so that the incident could become 'history' in the proper sense. Finally, templates for more desirable future behaviour were installed, and the officer ended up able to feel calm and in control in the face of provocation, rather than angry and vulnerable.

Case file 8.2: Traumatic domestic experiences with officer's own children

Each year, a proportion of staff take maternity leave. For many, the experience is enjoyable or at least satisfactory. For others, however, the experience is more exhausting than they ever imagined possible and in some cases quite traumatic. The medical profession now acknowledges that mothers can suffer from PTSD, but beyond rudimentary counselling little help is usually available locally.

At some point, for some employee, there will be a tragedy. A cot death may take place, or a child may suffer an accident or a life threatening illness.

Sometimes a person's circumstances are widely known throughout the organisation. On other occasions, however, only a tight circle of colleagues and friends have any idea of the depth of suffering that is being experienced. In some cases the details are so horrendous that the person can find no one outside the immediate family who can bear to listen to the story. One officer recently tried in vain to explain (in outline) to his Inspector what had been happening, but the latter broke down and asked him to stop.

The mothers (and sometimes fathers) usually struggle back to work for a time after the initial problems, and then capitulate. This is often the point at which they are steered in the direction of professional help.

A member of staff returned to work following the birth of her twins, but after several months felt too ill and desperate to continue.

During her labour the foetal heart beats had been irregular, and each time they faded she had felt her babies were dying and desperately willed them to recover. She was then rushed to the operating theatre for an emergency Caesarean, and had vivid memories of staring at the surgeon feeling utterly helpless. Part of her wanted to scream in panic, and part of her felt she could just stop breathing and die.

Even when she returned to work, unless she was constantly distracted, she found it very easy to continue 'hearing' the ghostly echo of the foetal monitor: it came from behind her and to the right, the position it had been placed in at the hospital. She was also still scared by her GP having told her that the subsequent haemorrhaging came about because her body had just given up. Two or three times each week she had a nightmare in which she felt she would die if she did not immediately take some medication. She would wake from this frantically trying to work out what it was that she had to take.

Her memory had deteriorated, she was eating a great deal despite not feeling very hungry, she had absolutely no interest in sex, she constantly thought about death, and quite often ended up feeling so desperate that she could only cry and scream. She had to keep checking that her children were all right, everything felt to be an enormous effort, and she felt as though she had no control over anything.

Following an assessment and specification of the problems, her memories of the foetal monitor were first targeted for 'desensitisation'. Deliberately focusing on these memories initially made her start to faint, but in due course both the sound and the spatial awareness of the monitor disappeared. She could remember what the intrusive memory had consisted of, but could no longer experience it.

Heartened by this progress, it was possible in the next session for her to focus on the sequence of events and feelings leading up to the Caesarean. Although highly disturbing at first, the memories gradually re-configured and settled down. By the end of the session she could recall the whole experience without any disturbance or peculiar body sensations, and felt completely calm. The nightmares ceased immediately, the other troublesome symptoms subsided over the following few weeks, and in due course she thoroughly enjoyed returning to work.

Case file 8.3: Chronic fatigue syndrome

Problems can arise when career and operational considerations lead to a person attempting to return to work before having fully recovered, possibly from a serious infection.

The physical and psychological sequelae that eventually lead to a return visit to the GP are vague and non-specific, and when standard tests prove negative the person typically will be offered anti-depressant medication. If the person happens to be depressed, then that component of the problem may ease, but usually little else will change until further aspects of the problem are addressed.

A 'fast-track', middle-ranking officer was off sick after struggling unsuccessfully to regain his health and fitness. His problems seemed to have developed once he returned to work after a particularly serious respiratory infection nine months previously. The fact that one of his children was being treated for a serious illness did not help. He felt exhausted all the time, yet found it very difficult to sleep for more than two hours at a time. Each time he awoke, his mind would be racing. He seemed to catch every infection that he came into contact with. The muscles at the back of his neck felt permanently tense, and as each day wore on the discomfort would gradually develop into a headache.

Even gentle exercise soon led to breathlessness and discomfort. He experienced quite severe muscular cramps in his fingers and calf muscles, was very irritable at home, felt unduly guilty in situations where he might be at fault, was becoming obsessional in his habits, and found himself to be far more emotional when encountering something that was 'sad'. His concentration and memory were very poor, the environment around him periodically would feel 'unreal', and he noticed that his breathing was shallow and interspersed with a lot of sighs.

Fatigue can arise from several different quarters, but a key factor in this case turned out to be chronic hyperventilation. This is something that can easily arise when a person struggles to perform normally while still debilitated after a physical illness.

This was systematically corrected through a regimen of breathing exercises that corrected the underlying physiological problem. Recovery to the point where symptoms had virtually disappeared and a full shift pattern could be resumed took several months, and included a period of gradual rehabilitation and exercise after some intensive rest. Some attention was also devoted to modifying the officer's work style (from 'driving' and Type A, to slower and more well-paced).

Case file 8.4: Nightmares

Recurrent nightmares - when essentially the same terrifying dream is experienced again and again - are very common after traumatic experiences. Many officers and support staff have been unfortunate enough to have experiences at home or work that have led to a period of recurrent nightmares. Sometimes the nightmares themselves are so frightening that they in themselves (as well as the original incident) are a source of trauma. During the day, a person can feel dominated by memories of the nightmare, and react physiologically each time the memories intrude.

The nightmares usually cease once the disturbing elements of the incident-related memories have been dealt with. Failing that, it is quite easy to target memories of the nightmares directly. This is especially useful for those few individuals who have what might be termed 'free-standing' recurrent nightmares. Here, usually as an accompaniment to some physical illness or other debility, an almost random but terrifying theme begins to haunt the person.

An officer who lived on her own had been working very long hours due to staff shortages in her CID office. She also had a neck injury that was playing up. Out of the blue she suddenly started waking from a nightmare around 3.00am, screaming and sweating. This happened up to three times each week, and had been going on for 18 months by the time she sought help.

The nightmare always involved the sensation of lying in a coffin squeezed up against the cold, sticky, smelly body of a murdered vagrant she had seen cut-up at a post-mortem many years before. The body had not bothered her at the time, but now when she woke she could 'feel' it at the side of her. Even worse, she had the sensation of being totally paralysed and at first unable to move or escape.

The initial horror left her very distressed, and each time this happened she had to get up, put all the lights on, and search the house to get rid of the feeling that someone/thing was there.

On the first occasion that an attempt was made to 'desensitise' the key elements of the nightmare, the experience of re-living it was so disturbing that further work had to be postponed until the next session. That next attempt was more successful, and was completed over two sessions.

First of all the total image and associated sensations began to disappear quite quickly soon after she started to think about them, rather than gripping her attention. Then she had a sense of being able to climb out of the coffin without being trapped. This gradually gave way to a feeling of not being in a coffin at all, and then finally she was able to think about the coffin and the body without any sense of personal involvement.

During this treatment period, the nightmare first became less frequent and intense, and then died away altogether.

Case file 8.5: Caffeine intoxication

A person's problems are sometimes sustained or made worse by the very efforts that are made to ease them. Alcohol consumption is perhaps the classic case, but caffeine intake is also something that needs to be checked. There is nothing particularly harmful about the substances that contain caffeine, or indeed with caffeine itself in moderate doses. It is surprisingly easy, however, to cross from stimulation into intoxication as caffeine consumption goes up during times of stress or worry, and then the person begins to experience a set of quite worrying symptoms on top of whatever else is going on.

For about six months an officer had been feeling increasingly jaded. He had been successful in his promotion attempts, though his single-minded pursuit of that goal had cost him his relationship. Although he trained hard and regularly jogged, he was losing his appetite, his weight was falling, he was more on edge and emotional, it was taking him two or three hours to get to sleep and even then his sleep was disturbed, he was getting more headaches, and he felt tired all the time. He had taken sickness absence and been given antidepressant medication by his GP, but had noticed little difference.

He was showing signs of exhaustion and over training, but of particular interest was the fact that his caffeine intake had markedly increased around the time his symptoms worsened. He regularly drank up to 14 mugs of strong coffee each day, which, even calculated on the basis of the most conservative assays, put him well into the toxic zone.

He took it very easy for about two weeks, during which time he weaned himself off the caffeine. By the end of that period there was a marked improvement in almost all of his symptoms. He still experienced 'withdrawal' headaches first thing each morning, but even they were gradually getting less intense. A week later he was ready to return to work and was feeling decidedly positive about life once again.

Case file 8.6: Aversion to Communication Centre work

Staff from Communications Centres can present a wide variety of problems. Loss of confidence and an almost irrational fear of the work and/or the equipment are not uncommon, and in some cases these changes are caused and/or sustained by chronic hyperventilation.

If a person is tired or upset and the going gets tough, it is quite easy to become flustered and start indulging in more thoracic breathing (shallow breathing from the chest rather than diaphragmatic breathing which, for good reasons, is taught in acting and public speaking lessons). This thoracic breathing is usually accompanied by an 'out of breath' style of talking, and the person unwittingly begins to over-breathe or hyperventilate.

In a fairly short time the knock-on physiological effects of this important secondary problem will cause anxiety levels to mount, and the person will feel increasingly uneasy at the work station. For some people, it will then become more and more difficult to face work.

A female member of staff came for help after being off work for three weeks. She had started to break down while at work, and her confidence had dropped to zero. Over the past six months she had felt increasingly poorly while doing her work. Her stomach would churn, she would become light-headed, and she would start to panic and feel that she was going to pass out. Her neck would go rigid, and she felt that there was an obstruction in her throat that made it difficult to swallow.

These symptoms were first evident at work, but then began to occur while she was at home. Then, as she walked toward work, she found that her chest was going tight and her legs were turning to jelly and it took enormous will power to go in and sit down.

Assessment revealed that she had been hyperventilating for some time, and it appeared that this was the most likely cause of many of her troublesome symptoms.

It took nearly a month to correct that problem, but she was then left with the conditioned (learned) aversion to her workplace. Fortunately, this had not reached the stage where she no longer wanted to return to work (which would have been almost impossible to rectify); she wanted to return, but had very unpleasant feelings as she actually anticipated doing so. Her stomach knotted up each time she thought of returning, and she kept thinking that she would inevitably make a major mistake once the pressure was on again.

That series of dysfunctional anticipations had to be desensitised, and although it only took about 30 minutes to accomplish she found it intensely distressing. By the end of the session, however, she felt very calm and positive, and could stay peaceful while imagining going into work and dealing with all the usual tasks. Two weeks later she went back to work and reported that she was feeling 'back to normal'.

Case file 8.7: Victimisation

Bullying takes many forms in an organisation. In some cases it is so subtle that it is hard for even the victim to describe what is going on. Individual instances of unpleasant treatment can sound fairly trivial in isolation, and in any case they usually only hurt because of the special significance they have for the victim.

Unless a person has experienced bullying, they are unlikely to have any idea about the way the bully can get 'inside the head' of the victim, generating disabling levels of fear, anger and self-pity. The face of the bully can appear as a full colour image in the sleepless hours of the night, the scathing tone of voice can intrude into otherwise peaceful thought processes, and the accumulated personal criticisms can begin seriously to undermine self-esteem and confidence.

Despite advances in the grievance procedures, there are many occasions when it makes little sense in the long run to pursue that particular route. The bully may be a fairly senior and respected person, for example, with the reputation of being an effective manager. In such cases, there is still quite a lot that can be done to help a person get out of the victim role.

A Sergeant found that he was becoming the focus of increased attention from a particular Inspector. He was 'needled' and criticised regularly for things that he had played little part in, his work was interfered with, and to cap it all he was required to alter his shifts for some trivial reason with the result that he found it very much harder to complete the duties required of him.

His desk was set at an angle to the door in his office, and he had to look to his left when he heard footsteps approaching if he wanted to see who was coming. He then found that even when he was away from work, if he looked to his left he began to feel disturbed and on edge, and in his mind's eye could readily see the face of his supervisor approaching. He also began to have unpleasant dreams about him.

Four weeks before he actually sought help, he felt so angry that he got up, walked out of his office and did not return to work.

It took just one consultation to reduce this fairly straightforward problem to a more manageable size. The threatening image of the Inspector's face was neutralised to such an extent that it began to look amusing. The various tingling sensations down the Sergeant's back and legs associated with encountering the Inspector were also extinguished, and finally the 'looking left' response was successfully removed. Three weeks later he returned to work and found that he was no longer falling into the victim role.

Case file 8.8: Road traffic accidents

Being involved in a road traffic accident can have far more serious effects on the health of staff than is sometimes appreciated, whether or not it occurs during working time. Perhaps because accidents of this kind are so common, their importance is underestimated.

For example, after a pursuit car has missed a bend and rolled down a bank into a canal or river, the emphasis tends to be on how fortunate the officers are only to have minor injuries. Particularly if a person has been the passenger, however, the fragmented memories of the accident can remain active in the mind, and insidiously undermine future behaviour.

About two years before seeking help, an officer had responded to a call late at night relating to a reported burglary. He arrived at the scene, and was about to get out of his car when, in his rear mirror, he saw the headlights of a lorry approaching at high speed. There was a roaring sound as the lorry driver braked, but in that moment the officer knew what was going to happen and braced himself for the impact.

He was trapped in the wreckage for some time, in considerable pain and with suspected broken limbs. Had to be cut free by Fire Service officers who put some soft sheeting over his face to protect it from the sparks and fumes. Now, merely thinking about the experience under the sheeting made him feel extremely nauseous. It was as though he were drowning.

He found it very difficult to drive at night, especially in poorly lit areas, and was very reluctant to park his car near a road. When working alone at night, he quite often had to stop somewhere to recover from intruding memories of the incident.

He would begin to sweat and shake and his heart would race. Above all, he was terrified of any situation that could culminate in another collision. In the meantime, his supervisors were quite unaware of his problems.

Just before he went to Welfare, and then off sick, he had started to feel really ill. His sleep was brief and broken by nightmares, he was sweating profusely, and he felt nauseous all the time.

This was one of those problems in which the disturbance was so intense and volatile that the treatment process had to be implemented with extreme care and delicacy. It takes immense courage for a person like this to seek help with such a problem, and since facing the problems will at first make him feel worse it would be all too easy for him to 'drop out' of the process.

As soon as he returned home from the first session, he had to vomit. His nightmares intensified, he developed a migraine and was sick each day for a whole week, and then again just before he came to the next session. During the session, as his mind began to explore the most scary parts of the experience - he first developed an intense headache and then had to rush out of the room and vomit again.

By the end of that session, however, he could feel some deep changes occurring within himself, and by the next session he was almost impatient to get on, come what may. Each part of the experience was systematically desensitised. He found that further details came back to mind once the fear began to reduce. For example, he remembered for the first time since the accident that a female paramedic had held his hand and talked with him while the sheeting was over his face. His mind brought this comforting memory back with such clarity and intensity that it began to neutralise the usual sensations associated with the sheeting.

Total contact time with this officer was seven hours. After the treatment was completed, he was able to return to work and drive without all the tension and with hardly a thought about the original incident. His sleep returned to normal, and he could think through the whole accident from collision to casualty department while simply feeling warm and relaxed.

Case file 8.9: Sudden deaths

Dealing with sudden deaths is a routine part of police work, and most officers are fairly inured to the process. Occasionally, however, maybe after several years away from the front line or after the sudden death of a loved one, the experience of dealing with a death can cease to be routine and can become disturbing. Under such conditions, it can be useful for an officer to have access to swift procedures for dealing with the disturbance.

An officer had recently been dealing with the death of his younger brother. As the eldest son his family always turned to him when there was something difficult to do. Now, at work, after three unpleasant sudden deaths in as many days, he had gone to another where a young man had died as a result of excessive alcohol intake.

This one felt to be different. He suddenly wondered if he could cope, and began to experience a mixture of anger and apprehension. He went with the body to the mortuary, which was very busy, and for some reason found himself standing for a while around the corner from the main activity. That turned out to be worse than watching.

He could hear the high-pitched whine of the bone saws in the distance, the smells were very intense, and nearby he could hear the staff undressing the youth whose body made a strange gurgling noise at one point as he was moved. Once home again, the officer found that he could not sleep, his interest in sex had vanished, and he felt very angry toward the controller who had sent him.

This problem was sorted out within a single consultation. Each sensory memory (that is the sounds, smells, sights) was desensitised, along with the associated body sensations (for example changes in heart rate, as he recalled certain details). He was able to resume work and felt little concern thereafter at the thought of dealing with further sudden deaths.

Case file 8.10: Social phobias

Intense and unpleasant experiences involving bodily functions can be the starting point for what are known as 'social phobias'. These are characterised by a deep fear of humiliating oneself in a public place, and they can dominate a person's thinking both at work and at home.

Being stuck on a stranded underground train with a very full bladder, developing diarrhoea while being deployed in a police van to an escalating public order situation, vomiting uncontrollably for several hours with food poisoning while trapped in the middle of a crowded pop-concert stadium, experiencing an inexplicable ejaculation in a totally inappropriate setting, or almost passing out in a supermarket queue are all suitable starting points.

It is very easy to remember the actual or potential humiliation that was involved in these crises and, particularly if a person is tired or debilitated for some other reason, it becomes all too easy to imagine the kind of catastrophes that could happen in the future if the situation were to be repeated.

The individual concerned tends to devote a great deal of thought as to how to avoid situations in which such humiliation might occur. When unable to avoid a particular situation (for example having to give evidence in court) the person usually experiences a panic that is out of all proportion to the actual risk of the humiliation. Unfortunately, of course, such panic tends to stimulate bodily functions anyway, and the person can really feel that he or she is about to the experience the worst scenario. And so it goes on.

Each year a few force employees come forward with problems of this kind. Typically, a person will struggle on for several years before seeking help and by that time the problem is of course fairly entrenched - and secondary problems may have developed that help to sustain the primary problem.

An officer came for help because he was finding certain situations too difficult to deal with. If the door was shut during a briefing, he started to have panic feelings. He could take a local bus that stopped at regular intervals, but could not countenance a coach journey or plane flight. He felt all right in his own car, but terrible in a police van. He could go out for a meal to a restaurant with his wife, but not with friends.

It transpired that 10 years before, shortly after starting a three-hour journey on a very crowded coach, the food poisoning that had started during the previous night really struck hard. He vomited and retched uncontrollably for most of the journey, suffering all the intense embarrassment that might be expected in such a situation. Since then, the thoughts and fears associated with that experience had slowly developed into a full-blown social phobia, and he could recount many other situations in which he had felt nauseous and in a blind panic.

Once the developmental history of his problem had been charted, a procedure was employed to neutralise not only his memories of the original humiliating experience, but also some of the worst experiences since - and the experiences he imagined he might have in future situations.

As would be expected with such a problem, he regularly hyperventilated once he started thinking about the situations that frightened him, which only served to accentuate the panic feelings. This secondary problem also had to be addressed.

Within a fairly short time he was able to go out with friends for the first time in years, and he even booked a holiday involving a plane flight.

Three months later, however, he had a partial relapse. Although no longer fearful of vomiting, while in the middle of a large crowd at a football match he began to feel peculiar, and started shaking and sweating. Further examination of the problem revealed that not only had he become very tired and run down after coping with a series of domestic and work problems, but he had also failed to continue with the regimen that was intended to correct his rather entrenched breathing problem.

Once he slowed down, resumed the exercises he had been given, and addressed the question of how to get more space and time for himself, he immediately began to improve again. He was able to enjoy his holiday and then return to work with no significant problems.

9. Shifting the load

*How to live with shift working
and minimise the danger to health*

The trouble with shifts

The main disruption to police health is caused by working shifts. Normal bio-rhythms are abruptly altered by frequent changes in routine and by disturbed sleep patterns.

The stresses and strains of shift working

▶ Indigestion, fatigue, sleeping problems and constipation are commonplace.

▶ Shift workers suffer an increased susceptibility to illness, particularly digestive problems and stomach disorders.

▶ Female reproductive health may be adversely affected.

▶ Infection and other medical problems may take longer to cure.

▶ Work and domestic relationships become brittle.

▶ Sleep duration is poor despite fatigue.

▶ There is an increased reliance upon drink and/or drugs to induce sleep or provide stimulation.

▶ Smoking is heavier than usual.

▶ Mistakes are made (particularly with paperwork) and judgement is often impaired.

This is not negative thinking - these are facts of life. Very few mammals have evolved to sleep during the daylight hours and hunt or work at night. It is not healthy for humans to reverse their natural order.

Recent research supports this, finding that:

▶ sleep duration is poor around night shifts and best around late shifts and rest days;
▶ there is much lower alertness on nights;
▶ officers smoke more heavily on nights.

However, the problems do not stem from night working alone, but also from the constantly changing cycles of a rotating shift pattern - moving abruptly from a night to day or afternoon shift and then forcing the body back into the night shift pattern again.

For example, when working nights, by the fourth or fifth night, hormonal and chemical changes take place as the body gets used to staying awake at night and sleeping during the day. Thus by the seventh night, the body is ready to continue, but then has to re-adjust all over again.

Shift systems

Shifts are necessary to maintain police cover for every 24-hour period and need to be flexible enough to place more cover on the ground for peak times and emergencies.

It is 'normal' for the 24- hour period to be covered by the early turn shift of 0600 to 1400 hours, the late turn shift of 1400 to 2200 hours and the night shift of 2200 to 0600 hours the following day.

Shift systems can be many and varied eg a 15-week pattern, the 10-week 'Ottawa' system, the usual four-week system or variable shifts. Generally shifts are of eight hours duration, but some staff work nine, 10, or even 12-hour shifts.

The Ottawa shift system is popular as it gives 42 more days off per year - but entails nine-hour nights and 10-hour shifts at other times. Officers work seven nights and than have six rest days.

The Area Superintendent will usually select the most appropriate shift system to provide optimum ground cover - in liaison with the Police Federation representative

Some forces are trying to work fewer consecutive nights with a maximum of four followed by rest days. For example Merseyside Police, who have been researching the problems of shift work for several years, have opted for a variable shift arrangement on a five-week cycle, giving a maximum of four nights followed by three rest days.

The 'quick change'

'Quick changes' of duty often lead to sleep deprivation. The quick changes occur between finishing late turn at 2200 hours and going to bed about 2300 hours only to get up at 0430 hours for early turn starting at 0600 hours. Similarly to finish nights at 0600 hours and go to bed at 0700 hours for five hours to get up at 1200 hours to go to work for late turn at 1400 hours.

Court appearances after night duty cause similar problems. For example, an officer who arrests someone for burglary at 0400 hours may have to go court with the offender for 1000 hours the following day.

Paperwork after the arrest will probably take at least one hour and then, if the officer is lucky, there may be time for a nap between the end of paperwork and court attendance at 1000 hours. Sometimes officers will be at court most of the day and will still be expected to report for night duty at 2200 hours.

Officers also find themselves working a shift until the early hours of the morning which is followed by a rest day. Naturally they wish to take advantage of their time off and the likelihood is they will get up early or not go to bed at all. Thus, sleep deprivation is further compounded.

Living with shifts

Most officers will have experienced the awful sensation of waking up with a start thinking:

'What shift am I working today...?'
'Is it today I am at court...?'

It is even worse to be woken by the phone ringing and then hearing the Sergeant explain that your duty or a court attendance was half an hour ago!

Keep an up-to-date diary

There have been cases when officers have reported for an 0600 early turn when in fact they were on late turn and had arrived for duty eight hours early. Similarly, officers have forgotten to arrive for a course, a court attendance or for voluntary extra duty at a football match.

These (amusing when it is not happening to you) anecdotes illustrate the importance of keeping an up-to-date diary.

The administrative staff or office constable or sergeant will devise up to 12 months of advanced duties for the various teams on the section or sub-division. Some forces computerise the advanced duties for interrogation by officers throughout the area concerned.

Duties are frequently changed however, to cater for officers who report sick or injured, have unforeseen court appearances or last-minute courses to attend. Weekly duty sheets are prepared which reflect all these changes and staff need to make a final check of their shifts.

The experienced officers and support staff always checks the following day's shift before going off duty. Someone could have made a last-minute change and forgotten to inform them.

Method in madness

Staff should be as methodical as possible in procedures at home and at work. Where is the diary kept? If a certain drawer at home and a pocket in the uniform or civilian clothes is adhered to, then misplacing the diary is prevented. This advice also applies to other crucial items such as car keys, pocket book, handcuffs, baton, mobile phone, police radio etc.

The methodical system of putting these items in a particular place pays dividends, especially when fatigue has set in after a number of night shifts or early turns. Some find a little chant as they leave the front door to go on duty is helpful - 'Handcuffs, baton, pocket book, keys, wallet, watch and glasses....'

The importance of having a tried and tested method of keeping pocket books, equipment, court files and/or exhibits together is patently obvious when quick changes arise and time is of the essence. It is equally important to ensure car keys are to hand, there is petrol in the car and, in winter, that de-icing spray for locks and windows is readily available.

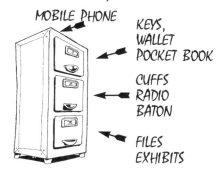

Sleep or the lack of it

Sufficient sleep between shifts is the secret to keeping alert, staying in good health and enjoying the job. It is easy to build up a sleep deficit on any shift system and easy to compound the problem. There is much temptation to stay up longer that is sensible in the evenings when working early turn, or to refrain from going to bed after night duty.

Going without the required amount of sleep has the debilitating effect that most police staff have experienced towards the end of a week of nights or early shifts. Research has shown that, even when officers believe they are not tired, their response times are considerably lower as a result of several consecutive night duties.

Building up a sleep deficit

On early turns, if a member of staff lives a few miles or more away from work, it will not be uncommon to get up around 04.30 hours in order to get ready, travel to work and hope to be at morning briefing by 0545 hours - allowing time to speak to colleagues and obtain a better handover of any incidents that are still 'live'. If you didn't go to bed until midnight-ish, then four and a half hours sleep is all that there is to be had. The missing three or four hours sleep deficit soon accumulates and lethargy and moroseness replace the required vitality.

Working nights bring their own problems. The arrival home is about 0700 hours - assuming you finished duty on time. If you are good at sleeping during daylight hours then six to eight hours' sleep should suffice. But if you are a poor sleeper or if outside traffic noise, children playing inside or outside the house, pneumatic drills etc interrupt your sleep, then you may need longer.

Normally to sleep until 1500 hours after night duty seems adequate, but sleeping until 1700 hours might be necessary occasionally. If you have to get up early for an appointment and interrupt your normal sleep pattern, then an additional three or four hours' nap may be required to 'top up' your rest.

There is nothing worse than working nights after not having had sufficient sleep. Trying to keep awake around 0400 hours is difficult - more so if in a warm patrol car or office. It is in these early hours that you will often find time to write reports which may eventually land on the desk of some eagle-eyed solicitor or barrister. An excuse that the report was prepared at 0400 hours following a week of interrupted sleep will carry no weight with them when the case collapses through lack of attention to detail!

Staff should be aware that, if fatigued, their reaction times and judgement can be impaired. Quick tempers and irritability can also be experienced at home and work - which can land you in hot water!

At the end of a week of nights it is tempting to go without or with very little sleep after the last night duty - as a rest day normally follows the last night you will probably want to socialise with family or friends. This is all very well so long as you remember that driving after little or no sleep can be dangerous, that alcohol can have more effect on a tired person, and that long term sleep deprivation may cause health problems.

To get more sleep...

▶ Some go to bed in the afternoon for a few hours towards the end of a week of early starts. For some a 'napping strategy' is an ideal means of avoiding a sleep deficit - try two to four hours of napping time during the day and just before you go to work.

▶ Though rest days may seem too valuable to waste, to compromise and sleep until 1100 or 1200 hours would seem to be the best course of action.

▶ Family and friends should be made aware of the necessity to keep noise and interruptions to a minimum when you are sleeping during the day (put up 'night worker sleeping' signs and turn off the sound on nearby phones). Disturbance from slamming doors, barking dogs and shouting children should be minimised.

▶ Double glazing, thick curtains, ensuring you are not sleeping at the noisiest side of the house, using earplugs, or playing soft music or 'white noise' (continuous low-level noise) will all help to block out other sounds and created the right atmosphere for sleep.

▶ Stimulating drinks should not be consumed after 0300 hours in order for the body to be ready for sleep after the end of the night shift. Resist the temptation to consume coffee and tea right up to going off duty. Sleeping will be easier if decaffeinated drinks are the norm after 0300 hours. Also bear in mind that drinking chocolate and some soft drinks contain caffeine. Energy-giving pills should not be taken unless under a doctor's supervision.

▶ Milk has been found to have certain components that relax the body ready for sleep. Instead of going home from nights and pouring yourself an alcoholic drink - or a sugar-based drink such as lemonade or coke - milk should be the first choice. Accompanied by a snack of light carbohydrate or low-fat dairy produce, it will aid sleep and guard against being woken by hunger.

Fitness and health

Good health is difficult to maintain when working different shifts. It is impossible for your body to enjoy a healthy routine as the bio-rhythms are constantly upset. The jet-lagged feeling of long distance flyers is experienced weekly.

Under these conditions, minor ailments tend to be magnified out of all proportion. A common cold may seem like influenza at 0330 hours on night duty or a strained muscle or joint like a case for crutches.

There are times with shift work when a visit to the doctors and possible sick leave are necessary in order to 'throw off' a persistent minor ailment. Normal contagious illness can travel through a team or the whole police station quite quickly because of the labour-intensive nature of the organisation.

Police officers and support staff are more likely than the general public to have contact with people who do not look after their health. They may come into contact with persons who are HIV positive, Hepatitis B or AIDS sufferers, and dead bodies - both human and animal - from which disease may by transmitted (see Chapter 7 'Staying Immune').

For anyone working shifts, health, exercise and diet are vitally important.

A healthy diet and regular exercise are a must. Several and regular light meals are better than one heavy one, while light carbohydrate or low-fat dairy products assist sleep.

An exercise routine which includes 'stretching' the cardio-vascular system is a must. Brisk walking, cycling, swimming or 'keep fit' classes are good examples. (For a complete guide to an 'exercise and diet strategy' see Part Two on 'Lifestyle'.)

Fitter and younger workers handle the irregular hours best. As one gets older the shifts become harder. Medical evidence suggests that once past 40, due to physical changes, the body finds it increasing difficult to cope with shifts. Yet the average age of patrol officers has increased over recent years and is now between 35 and 42 years of age.

It is therefore vital to look after your health if the debilitating effects are to be minimised.

The Working Time Directive makes it compulsory for employees to have a free health assessment before being placed on nights. The Police (Health and Safety) Regulations 1999 state that anyone whose health is likely to be affected by working nights should not be put onto night shift. Diabetics who need regular meals are not permitted to work nights.

Ensure you are aware of the relevant legislation and ensure you take advantage of any Occupational Health facilities provided by the service - or visit a doctor for advise.

There is growing evidence that women who work nights are less likely to conceive. Woman officers who do become pregnant should notify their line manager to undertake a risk assessment. It is advisable to stop working nights as soon as possible under the terms of the Police (Health and Safety) Regulations in view of the stresses and strains to be endured.

In terms of safeguarding general health and fitness, shift workers particularly should seek to avoid unhealthy eating and drinking habits.

Avoid...

X the temptation to drink alcohol after night shifts as a means of getting to sleep;

X eating takeaway food in the early hours of the morning when the digestive system is practically on shutdown;

X drinking excessive quantities of tea, coffee and soft drinks which contain caffeine - particularly towards the end of a night shift.

Further reading

Further reading in this area can be found in an article entitled 'The Working Time Directive: Officer Health and Safety and Police Efficiency.' This appeared in *The Police Journal*, January 1999 published by Butterworths UK. It was written by Carl Mason of the Merseyside Police Management Development and Training Unit and Kevin Wardman, senior lecturer in law, Liverpool John Moores University.

A booklet produced by Merseyside Police called *Working Shifts* includes the main findings of several years' research which support much of the advice given in this chapter. To obtain copies of the booklet, enquiries should be made to Merseyside Police, Work Scheduling Unit, 222 Mather Avenue, Allerton, Liverpool L18 9TG.

PART FOUR

ROUTINE SURVEILLANCE

10. Eyeing up the future

The importance of eyecare

Most of us would agree that eyesight is the most precious of our senses, yet many of us take our eyes for granted.

Recruits to the service will, as the general rule, have passed force eyesight tests with unaided vision and force drivers are subjected to regular 'Keystone' vision tests. (Most forces accept applicants to the Special Constabulary who wear spectacles or contact lenses, provided they achieve a Keystone standard for unaided and aided vision.)

So your eyes pass the test - all the more reason to take care of them!

This chapter will explain how best to look after our eyes at home and at work. It will also explain some of the common defects and diseases affecting eyes and sight.

Looking after your eyes

The key to looking after your eyes is to visit the optician regularly. The fact that police officers and support staff generally have good eyesight does not make them exceptions to this. Opticians still recommend that all adults have their eyes checked with them every two years.

This is important because an optician will screen for eye disease and some general health problems such as high blood pressure and diabetes.

If you have a family history of glaucoma you can get these check free of charge, and if any of your family has diabetes or glaucoma, require very strong glasses or who are registered blind or partially sighted, they also are eligible for free checks.

If you have children they should be seen at least once a year and can start to visit the optician from as early as three years old or - earlier if they have problems (eye tests are free for all school children).

Drivers' eyesight

Force drivers, as mentioned, undertake regular 'keystone' tests. If it is found that their eyesight has deteriorated, most forces will pay for them to have 'approved' spectacles or contact lenses so they may continue in their role. If eyesight for whatever reason becomes seriously impaired then the officer will be referred to the force medical officer. A decision will then be made to redeploy or medically retire the officer.

Private car drivers must be able to see a standard size number plate at 67 feet in good daylight. This is a minimum requirement - the better the driver's vision, the better this is for his safety and others. UK drivers also have a duty to inform the Driver Vehicle Licensing Agency if they suffer from any eye disease likely to affect their vision; such as glaucoma. It has been estimated that as many as 20 per cent of drivers do not reach the required vision standard.

For drivers who need to wear spectacles to meet the standard, it is a good idea to keep spare glasses in the car. Prescription sunglasses are also a good idea for summertime driving.

Eye protection

Managers are required to conduct risk assessments for police employees.

For example staff working in police garages may be at risk from activities such as drilling or grinding which can result in serious eye injury.

Prescription safety glasses or safety goggles should be worn when performing these tasks.

Officers on public order duty should be provided with NATO helmets with visors.

Safety glasses usually consist of plastic or polycarbonate lenses. These lenses are stronger than glass and do not shatter when broken. It is a good idea to wear plastic lenses rather than glass lenses for driving as they are safer in an accident. Plastic lenses are also recommended for children for the same reason.

Sportsmen and women should also consider wearing eye protection, especially when playing racquet sports. There is an ever increasing incidence of injury to eyes during sporting activities, particularly squash where the serious injuries result from the both the ball and the racquet hitting the eye.

If officers are injured 'on duty', ie playing for the force - for example suffering sight loss from a detached retina as a result of a blow to the head - then they would qualify for disability enhancement as for any other injury sustained on duty.

There is growing evidence that you should protect your eyes from strong sunlight by wearing sunglasses. Generally officers are allowed to wear sunglasses on duty, but must remove them when speaking to members of the public.

Also remember that this is particularly important when visiting hot countries or on skiing or sailing holidays where light is reflected from the snow or water into your eyes.

The sun's rays have been linked to cataracts, macular degeneration and eyelid cancer. Look for sunglasses that provide protection from UVA and UVB. These can often be obtained in your prescription if you need glasses to see.

Eyes and computers

Contrary to popular belief, there is no evidence to show that doing close work or using computers for long periods can damage your eyes.

However, because of the concentration involved, it is not uncommon for users to experience tiredness and eye strain.

In a recent survey, 41 per cent of people using a computer regularly said they had suffered from sore eyes.

When using a computer it is important to observe the following steps to get the most comfortable vision...

√ Make sure you are sitting in a comfortable position.

√ Position the screen and your documents so that you can see both easily without having to move your head a long way.

√ Adjust the angle and position of the screen so that there are no reflections from windows or overhead lights.

X Don't put the screen too close to a window.

√ Set the screen brightness to a comfortable level.

√ Look away from the screen periodically to allow your eyes to relax.

√ Remember to blink if your eyes feel dry (concentrating reduces your blink rate and can cause your eyes to dry out especially if you wear contact lenses).

√ Have an eye examination at least once every two years (you may be able to reclaim the cost). Generally the cost of approved-pattern spectacles or 'normal' contact lenses would be borne by the force.

Common myths about eyes

A true or false quiz

Q1 Cataract is a skin which grows over your eyes ?

Q2 Wearing glasses makes your eyes dependent on them ?

Q3 Short sight causes distant objects to look blurred ?

Q4 Children can grow out of squints ?

Q5 Opticians can assess general health from looking at your eyes ?

Q6 Computers are bad for your eyes ?

Q7 Sitting close to the TV will damage your child's eyes ?

Q8 Eyes cannot be transplanted ?

Answers

1 F Cataract is a misting up of the lens inside your eye.

2 F Sight defects are caused by the shape of your cornea. Glasses cannot change the shape of your cornea.

3 T Short sighted people can see close up but not far away

4 F Squints need prompt treatment to avoid further sight problems

5 T Certain diseases such as diabetes and high blood pressure can show up first in the eyes

6 F Computers do not make your eyes worse. However using a computer needs a lot of concentration and can show up small sight defects that did not cause symptoms before.

7 F Children have very strong eyes and can focus easily at very short distances.

8 T Although certain parts of the eye such as the cornea and lens can be replaced or transplanted to restore sight.

Better sight without glasses

Unfortunately, there are no herbal remedies, miracle cures or exercises which will get rid of eyesight defects. While spectacles are becoming more acceptable as frames become more fashionable, there are still alternatives for those who dislike or find wearing them inconvenient.

Contact lenses

Modern soft contact lenses are surprisingly comfortable and are available to correct long sight, short sight and astigmatism. It is even possible to get bifocal contact lenses or 'cosmetic' lenses to change the colour of your eyes.

Contact lenses can be worn to replace glasses on a regular basis. However long-term wearers should be aware that their eyes can suffer from lack of oxygen if they are constantly covered by lenses. It is advisable to always have a pair of 'back-up' glasses to hand and to give your eyes a 'break' and wear glasses for a couple of hours in the day when possible. Also contact lenses should not worn overnight.

It is very important to clean contact lenses every time you wear them to avoid irritation and eye infections. If you find this inconvenient you could try daily disposable lenses. There are a variety of packages available from options.

Laser surgery

This is currently only available to treat short sight although techniques for long sight and astigmatism are being developed. Low amounts of short sight can be treated quite reliably but the procedure works less well for higher degrees of short sight - the people who need it most. The procedure is reasonably safe but is still in its infancy. You should consult an optician or doctor for advice before going ahead with laser treatment. (Generally there is no force policy with regard to this new treatment.)

File 10.1 Anatomy and eyesight

Our eyes are very similar to a camera in structure. The clear window at the front of the eye is called the cornea. As well as allowing light to enter the eye, the cornea serves as a lens to focus light onto the retina at the back of the eye. Our eyes also have an internal lens which allows us to focus on close objects when we read.

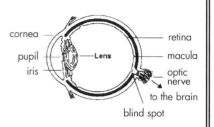

structure of the eye

Between the cornea and the lens lies the iris. This is the coloured part of the eye which is visible when we look at a person's eyes and the hole in the centre of the iris is the pupil. It is the pupil which controls the amount of light entering the eye by enlarging in poor light and becoming smaller in strong light. The pupil normally appears black but can appear white in some eye diseases such as cataract and red when the eye is lit by a bright flash of light (the cause of red eye reflections on photographs).

The lens and cornea focus light onto the retina at the back of the eye. The image projected onto the retina is actually upside down and back to front. Fortunately for us, the brain interprets this as being the right way up. The retina acts like the film in a camera. It is a layer of nerves and receptors which convert the focused image into electrical impulses that can be understood by the brain. The electrical impulses are carried to the brain along the optic nerve, which is one of the largest nerves in the body.

The cornea and lens focus the image onto the retina. The image is upside down.

Where the optic nerve leaves the eye, the retina is absent. This area is know as the blind spot. The brain normally ignores the blind spot so we do not notice a hole in our field of vision and because the blind spots for both eyes do not overlap, with both eyes open there is no actual blind area in the field of vision. To demonstrate your own blind spot, close your left eye and look at the centre of the eye in figure 2. Move towards the book, you will notice that at a distance of about 20cm from the page, the cross disappears from view. It is in your blind spot.

Demonstration of the blind spot

File 10.2 Common eyesight defects

Short sight (myopia)

In a normal eye, the cornea focuses the image of what we are looking at so that is falls on the retina. A short sighted eye focuses light in front of the retina resulting in a blurred image. This can happen when the eye is too big or if the corneal shape becomes too steep.

Short sight focuses the image in front of the retina

Short sight makes it difficult to see objects in the distance. It is corrected by using concave (diverging) spectacle or contact lenses which move the image back onto the retina. Recently, doctors have developed a technique which uses a laser to reshape the front of the cornea allowing short sight to be corrected by flattening the cornea to its ideal shape.

Long sight (hyperopia)

Long sight is caused by the cornea being too flat or the eye being too short. Consequently, the image is focused behind the retina.

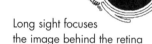

Long sight focuses the image behind the retina

Long sight can cause both near and distant objects to become blurred. It can also be a cause of headaches and eye strain particularly when reading or using a computer. It is corrected with convex (converging) spectacle or contact lenses which move the image forward onto the retina. Unfortunately, laser treatment does not yet work for long sight.

Astigmatism

Astigmatism is caused by the cornea having a slightly irregular shape. A normal cornea is spherical like a football but an astigmatic cornea is more like a rugby ball with a different curvatures at different angles. This leads to part of the image being focused in front of the retina and part of it behind.

Astigmatism focuses part of the image in front of the retina and part of it behind.

Astigmatism can cause blurring of both distant and near objects and can produce headaches and eyestrain. It is corrected using sphero-cylindrical spectacle lenses or toric contact lenses.

File 10.2 cont... Common eyesight defects

Presbyopia - the ageing process

As our eyes get older, the lens inside becomes harder and begins to lose its ability to focus near objects. This problem, known as presbyopia, affects everyone eventually but is usually first noticed between the ages of 40 and 50 years.

Presbyopia does not affect distance vision at all because the cornea is unaffected but near objects will become blurred. Presbyopia can compensated for by moving the book further away from your eyes or increasing the amount of light on the page but this is not always practical. Presbyopia will also cause eye strain and headaches when trying to read if left uncorrected.

Presbyopia is corrected using simple reading spectacles or by using bifocal or varifocal lenses. Reading spectacles can be purchased without an optician's prescription but these assume that the defect is the same in both eyes and that there is no other defect such as short sight, long sight or astigmatism. While buying the wrong reading glasses will not damage your eyes, it may lead to discomfort or blurring when reading. It is also important not to forget to have your eyes examined regularly by an optician to check for disease.

File 10.3 Common eye problems and diseases

Glaucoma

This is a particularly debilitating disease which slowly reduces the visual field to cause tunnel vision and eventually blindness. It is caused by a build up of fluid pressure within the eye causing damage to the optic nerve. Glaucoma cannot be cured but its progress can be halted using eye drops or surgery, hence the importance of detecting it at an early stage. However, glaucoma does not cause any symptoms until the very late stages so the only way of detecting early stage glaucoma is to have your eyes checked regularly.

Glaucoma affects about 1 in 200 people and is more common after the age of 40 or in people who have a family history of the condition. Certain ethnic groups - such as Afro-Caribbeans - are also more likely to develop the disease. People who have a relative with glaucoma are entitled to free eye tests and should have their eyes tested every year.

Cataract

Cataract is caused by the misting up of the lens inside the eye. This usually occurs with age but can be brought on by eye injury, certain medications and by exposure to high levels of ultraviolet light. Cataract causes dazzling in bright light and, as they become more advanced, cause blurred vision. Over half of the population over the age of 65 have some degree of cataract. In many cases it does not need treatment but more advanced cataracts are easily treated by a simple operation to remove the lens and replace it with a plastic implant lens.

Diabetes

Diabetes can affect the eye in a number of ways. Temporary blurring lasting a few days can occur if your diabetes is poorly controlled. This is due to swelling of the eye and will disappear as soon as good control is regained. Long term effects of diabetes include cataracts which may develop at a much younger age than normal, and a disease of the retina called diabetic retinopathy. Diabetic retinopathy occurs when the blood vessels in the back of the eye leak blood onto the retina. In its early stages, this will cause no symptoms and does not need treatment. More advanced retinopathy can cause permanent damage to vision and the eye and requires laser treatment. Diabetics must have their eyes checked at least once a year as a delay in treatment can cause irreversible loss of sight.

Floaters

Everyone has small clumps of cells floating in the gel inside their eyes. If these float in front of the vision, they are seen as black specs - more often seen when looking at a bright background. Floaters are usually harmless and require no treatment but they can sometimes be the first sign of more serious problems such as retinal detachment. You should see your optician if you notice a sudden increase in the number of floaters in your eyes or if you begin to see floaters for the first time.

Retinal detachment

In this condition, the retina becomes detached from the back of the eye. It can occur at any age and often affects people who have very active lifestyles or jobs. Diabetics can have a retinal detachment as a complication of diabetic retinopathy. Symptoms are often a sudden increase in floaters before the eyes coupled with flashing lights. A retinal detachment may also cause a loss of vision or a dark patch in the peripheral vision. It needs treating straight away - preferably the same day because the longer the retina stays detached the greater is the risk of serious irreversible sight loss.

11. Ear today, gone tomorrow

Keeping your sense of hearing

Our ears form an essential part of our nervous system. Moreover, where would we rest our spectacles if we had no ears?

Our ears, or more correctly the fluid in the inner ear, allow us not just to hear, but to keep our balance when standing still and when on the move. The effect of damage to the ears can be both dramatic and devastating. Deafness - for which there is often no cure - can result. It is imperative, therefore, to protect this vital sense.

Those with hearing impediments or who use hearing aids are not generally accepted as police officers. Support staff may be employed depending on the tasks to be performed. In situations in which an officer's hearing was severely impaired for any of the reasons cited later in the chapter, he or she would be referred to the force medical officer with a view to receiving a medical pension.

Deafness

Deafness is a common, but distressing symptom with numerous causes.

Noise damage deafness

Repetitive noise exposure is a serious problem and highlights the the necessity to wear ear defenders in 'at risk' environments.

Police motorcyclists and those involved with firearms training are particularly vulnerable. Health and safety risk assessments now involve regular audio metric tests for firearms officers and those who wear covert ear pieces and motor cycle helmets.

However as well as the obvious high-risk groups, it must be remembered that at one time or another most people are exposed to noise intensities sufficient to cause damage. Ear plugs or other such protection may be necessary in certain situations and should be considered as part of the ongoing risk assessments carried out as part of health and safety requirements

Remember; avoidance and protection can save your hearing. There is no known cure for noise damage deafness!

Other causes of deafness can be summarised as follows:

Trauma - Often sudden onset following a blast exposure or a head injury. May be reversible depending upon the site.

Foreign bodies - May be sudden onset following an insect flying in to the ear for example. Reversible with care and proper treatment.

Wax - This is very gradual onset of hearing loss often noticed by others as a lack of attention. Immediately reversible by syringing.

Otitis externa - boil in the ear canal - Gives slow onset of deafness with pain around the ear canal on chewing and moving the ear. Often spontaneously reversible.

Chronic otitis media - A chronic deafness and discharge from the ear made worse by swimming or head colds. Reversible by operation if necessary.

Drugs - certain drugs are the remaining common causes of deafness.

There is also the condition known as 'advancing years', which comes to us all and often causes selective deafness! The treatment for the latter is often to tell the person involved to listen more attentively!

Trauma

The eardrum forms part of the middle ear (see File 11.1 - structure of the ear - at the end of this chapter). It is by definition a thin and delicate membrane, which unfortunately leaves it susceptible to damage. A slap on the ear can lead to a high pressure wave being transmitted down the external ear canal, causing a rupture of the eardrum.

Similar eardrum trauma can occur in bomb blasts or close range gunfire where excessive pressure is exerted in the ear. The wearing of ear protectors in high risk environments - such as for a firearms officer or police mechanic - is highly advisable.

Skull fractures are another traumatic cause of hearing loss and ear damage. The ear canal has a bony portion and the delicate middle and inner ear mechanisms are encased in bone. Fractures can thus involve these areas or the small holes through which nerves pass.

Fortunately damage of this type is often reversible, although in extreme cases permanent damage may be caused.

Officers examining or administering first aid to accident victims must remember that clear fluid or watery blood coming from the ears (or the nose) is likely to indicate an underlying skull fracture. In such cases the officers must ensure that the airways are kept open and arrange for emergency transport to hospital.

Foreign bodies

Objects in ears range from insects to small sweets or candies and the patients from babies to grandparents. Whatever the object, the symptoms are usually the same. Earache, sudden deafness or a discharge (if long-standing) are the commonest.

ANY object lodged in the ear should be removed by a doctor, preferably someone with ear, nose and throat experience.

One situation in which immediate relief can be offered however, is when an insect flies into the ear. If the head is tilted so that the affected ear faces upwards, some warm water can gently be poured in, often allowing the insect to float out.

Ear wax

Ear wax is formed from secretions and dead skin from within the ear. Wax usually moves out of the ear with time and is not normally noticed. It can, however, build up into a blockage in the ear canal causing deafness and occasionally pain. There are many wax softening drops available from chemists although warm olive oil is a good alternative.

Ultimately the wax may need syringing out which involves squirting water into the ear canal. It is not as unpleasant as it sounds and relief is generally immediate. Syringing is widely available at GP surgeries and occupational health departments.

Infections of the ear

See File 11.2 at the end of the chapter.

Skin cancer

The ears are exposed to the sun nearly all the time and are often never even treated to a smear of suntan cream during the trip to Spain. They are a susceptible site for the two most common types of skin cancer. Any scabs or freckles which itch and bleed or change size, colour or shape are a cause for concern and should be looked at by a doctor. Indeed the symptoms listed above on any skin should be treated with suspicion.

Perhaps a dab of sunblock on the ears should be part of the shirt-sleeve-order uniform!

Cauliflower ear

Cauliflower ear arises when a severe bruise of the ear is left untreated and the cartilage dies. Such bruises may be as a result of contact sports or acquired in the line of duty by a blow to the side of the head. If promptly and properly drained by a needle or a small cut, the injuries need not lead to permanent scarring or swelling. Time is of the essence and officers who have been on the receiving end of such an injury should consult a doctor as soon as possible to get the best results.

Vertigo

Vertigo can be a very distressing condition. The feeling is similar to that experienced when coming off a rotating fairground ride. It is the impression of movement without actually moving. The cause of vertigo is often difficult to establish. Apart from the viral causes of vertigo (see File 11.2 - infections of the ear) a few more can be added.

Psychological causes

Psychological conditions can lead to vertigo in certain situations. Fear or panic can have profound effects on the central nervous system and can ultimately lead to hysteria. Officers should be aware of this when dealing with victims or witnesses who have suffered trauma.

Physical causes

Physical problems can also cause vertigo-type symptoms. Feeling giddy or dizzy on standing up may point to a low blood pressure or one which varies profoundly with posture (this latter is known as postural hypotension).

Menieres disease is a condition in which the fluid pressures in the inner ear are poorly controlled and cause recurrent attacks of sudden deafness, ringing noises and dizziness. Attacks may be interrupted by popping noises in the ears and can last for several hours. Unfortunately a cure for Menieres disease has not yet been found and support and sympathy are needed.

Positional vertigo is another cause of dizziness worthy of mention. Often experienced when lying down, this is due again to problems with the fluid of the inner ear. Sufferers are often awoken at night with a spinning feeling, perhaps after rolling over or changing position. As with a number of other complaints affecting the ear, the condition is poorly understood and although some drugs may offer relief, there is no known effective cure other than time.

Symptoms of vertigo, if serious, repetitive or troublesome should be referred to and discussed with a doctor. Simple reassurance is often of assistance in trying to resolve this notoriously difficult condition.

File 11.1: Structure of the ear

Our ears are made up of an outer ear, a middle ear, an inner ear and an eardrum. The outer ear includes the external structure of the ear which contributes to our individual appearance and picks up sound. It also includes the so called auditory meatus, which is basically a canal down which sounds pass.

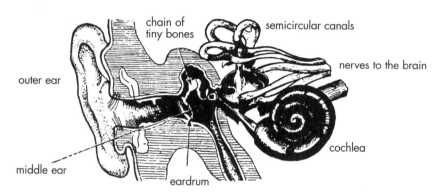

Sound is converted into movement by the eardrum and onto small bones called ossicles in the middle ear. The ossicles' movements are then used to excite small hairs in fluid filled channels within the inner ear allowing our brain to interpret different pitches and volumes. The fluid of the inner ear is also what governs balance.

The eardrum thus connects the outer ear with the middle ear keeping the outside world out. The only connection between the middle ear and the air is the eustachian tube which opens at the back of the mouth. This is how pressures can be equalised in the ear at altitude by yawning or swallowing.

File 11.2 Infections of the ear

The outer ear can be the site of fungal and bacterial infections. The fast onset swelling and pain around the opening of the ear may be due to acute otitis externa. This is basically a boil in the external ear canal which can completely fill the channel causing temporary deafness. Pain is usually made worse by chewing or moving the ear around. Paracetamol is often a sufficient painkiller in this situation. In time the boil may settle or rupture offering relief. If symptoms do persist a doctor should be able to help. Often old remedies such as glycerine and ichthamol can be used, but in persistent cases antibiotics may be deemed necessary.

File 11.2: Infections of the ear (cont...)

Longer standing odourless ear discharge or itch may be due to chronic otitis externa. This can be bacterial or fungal and is often best treated with ear drops from the doctor. The infection is more common in warmer weather and can be prevented by good ear hygiene. Any cleaning of the external ear, however, should be done with caution. The use of cotton buds, hair grips and rolled up tissue is not advisable and will actually worsen any chronic otitis externa. In particular, never try to push anything into the external opening of the ear canal as this can lead to internal damage or the introduction of infection and foreign bodies.

Viral and bacterial infections can affect the middle ear as they can the outer ear. Self-limiting, sudden onset episodes of middle ear infection (otitis media) classically occur only in young children. Adults usually experience a more chronic condition of recurrent ear discharge perhaps after swimming or during a cold. The discharge should not be foul smelling although it can be a nuisance, as can the slight deafness which accompanies the problem. Unfortunately the cure for this condition is not a simple tablet, but it requires an operation to repair a small defect in the eardrum. Treatment, however, is only needed if the discharge is excessive or if the deafness cannot be tolerated.

If the discharge from the ear is at all foul smelling it may be a different thing altogether. Sometimes a problem within the middle ear leads to a build up of skin cells around the eardrum edge. This is known as a cholesteatoma and if ignored can expand in the surrounding space destroying neighbouring skin and bone. Deafness and a smelly discharge should therefore always be attended to as quickly as possible by a doctor. Again, treatment is complex, although the operation it requires has a high success rate.

Doctors sometimes diagnose viral neuronitis or viral labyrinthitis. These names encompass a mass of middle ear symptoms such as deafness, ringing in the ear, dizziness and nausea, for which there is no definite diagnosis. It is rumoured that the word virus is derived from the Latin, *I'm not sure*! If you experience an isolated attack of vertigo, perhaps associated with a flu-like illness, it may well be due to one of these mysterious viral conditions of unknown origin.

12. Chewing it over

*Oral hygiene -
caring for your teeth*

There is undoubtedly room for a brief chapter on teeth in a police health manual. Although there is little to be said that is specifically job-related, caring for - and keeping - your own teeth is to be advocated whatever your profession!

The dental check-up

It is easy to get out of the habit of going for a six monthly dental check up. There is rarely a convenient time particularly if you're not working regular hours, and there is usually something 'better' to do. 'If your teeth feel OK what's the point and if they don't it's probably going to be expensive!'

However this does not work well as a long term strategy. Your dentist is looking for many signs of early disease involving not only tooth decay but also the gums and other oral tissues. It makes sense to catch potential problems before they become expensive ones - some simple preventive treatment may be all that is required.

Also a regular visit to the dentist often helps to put you in the right frame of mind to make a little extra effort with your teeth during the intervening months.

Most police employees would be allowed either officially or unofficially to arrange a treatment visit to the dentist in duty time, although routine checks should be arranged during off-duty periods when possible.

Diet

Sugar consumption is of great importance to the decay process. The frequency that sugar is eaten is actually more significant than the amounts. As a police officer, particularly when working shifts, it is tempting to regularly snack on high sugar foods.

Many 'convenience' foods are very high in sugar and acid, but beware, many health foods can also be damaging to the teeth - orange juice for example is high in both sugar and acid.

R Stephan plotted a curve to show the increase in acid in the mouth after eating sugar and how this relates with time and the onset of decay. This 'Stephan Curve' is often used in adverts for toothpaste and other dental products.

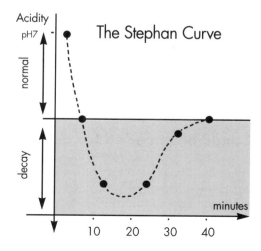

After eating a sugary food the acid level in the mouth increases to a level where decay will begin. It takes about 40 minutes for the saliva in the mouth to neutralise the acid. Therefore if someone were to be continuously snacking on sugary or acidic food and drink the acid level remains constantly high and teeth will decay.

One way of combating this is to chew sugar-free chewing gum. This stimulates an increase in saliva flow which in turn neutralises plaque acid and encourages the repair of early damage.

Smoking

Everyone knows that smoking is bad for their general health (see Chapt 5, Drugs of first choice), but the influence of cigarette smoke on the mouth and teeth is not usually considered.

Not only does smoking cause staining which is difficult for even dentists to remove but it causes damage to the oral tissues. This damage may in turn lead to disease and sometimes oral cancer. (A high alcohol intake is also associated with such problems - again see Chapt 5.)

What is dental decay?

Decay is the bacterial invasion of the tooth tissues resulting in their destruction. The oral cavity actually contains the highest number of bacteria compared with any other part of the body. However, decay cannot proceed unless certain conditions are present in the mouth.

Conditions needed for decay

Plaque is the build up of bacteria on the teeth surfaces due to poor oral hygiene. The bacteria metabolise sugars from the diet to produce plaque acid which then attacks the teeth. The more sugar a person eats, the less they brush

their teeth and the longer acidic and sugary foods affect the teeth, the greater the increase in the amount of dental decay.

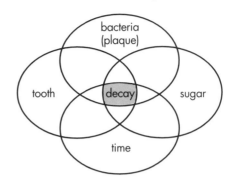

Prevention

Prevention is the key word in any dentist's vocabulary. The aim is to prevent decay occurring in the first place by education.

Brushing

The removal of plaque which causes decay is probably the most important factor influencing prevention. Teeth need to be efficiently brushed twice daily using a fluoride toothpaste. There are many, many different types of toothbrushes and toothpaste on the market and it can be confusing to know which one to buy. Dentists recommend a medium sized toothbrush with medium textured bristles.

Toothbrushing techniques

There are many advocated techniques. The most popular is a combination of two of these - the 'Bass' and the 'Roll'. This method involves small circular movements across the teeth with the bristles angled at 45 degrees to the gum margin and then rolling the brush down and away from the gums.

Approximately two minutes needs to be spent brushing your teeth. However be warned that over enthusiastic toothbrushing causes its own problems such as wearing away the teeth and gums.

Other methods of plaque removal include using dental floss, dental tape and special brushes designed to clean in around gaps between the teeth. Electric toothbrushes are very effective at cleaning teeth. They are particularly useful to motivate children and for people with disabilities.

Toothpaste

As previously mentioned, dentists advise the use of a fluoride toothpaste.

Fluoride has been shown to enter the tooth to renuteralise it at the site of early decay to actually 'heal' and strengthen the tooth. Other dental products that contain fluoride such as mouthwashes are sometimes recommended by dentists if a patient has a high rate of decay.

Gums - the foundations

There is very little point in beautiful, pearly-white teeth if the gums become diseased and no longer support them. More adults in Britain today lose their teeth due to gum disease than because of tooth decay.

Gum disease is a response to the build-up of plaque bacteria around the gum margins. It is more pronounced in people who are immuno-suppressed, on certain medications and also if they smoke. After a while the soft plaque left on the teeth hardens due to mineralisation to form calculus or tartar which has to be dentally removed.

The first stage of gum disease is gingivitis. This is inflammation of the gums causing reddening, a nasty taste and bleeding on brushing. Gingivitis is reversible but will progress if the oral hygiene is not improved.

Gingivitis progresses to periodontal disease or destruction of the gums and bone that support the teeth. This leads to pocketing of the gums which fill with bacteria, calculus and other debris and can become infected. This in turn is followed by halitosis (bad breath) and eventually loosening and loss of teeth.

If you have any specific questions or concerns visit your dentist who will be happy to discuss any aspects of treatment or prevention with you.

Lost and broken teeth

Avulsion means the complete or partial loss of one or more teeth. This is often due to trauma such as assault or accident.

Officers in such situations are unlikely to be in a position to retrieve or care for a tooth that has been completely knocked out. However, if this can be done, it may be possible to re-implant the tooth - if a dentist can be reached within the hour. Care should be taken not to touch the root of the tooth, and it should be placed in milk or held in the cheek where it can be bathed in the officer's own saliva. Arrangements should be made to get to a dentist immediately.

Officers having caps, crowns or dentures could get them damaged in public order situations, during an assault or when participating in sport etc - especially when the front teeth are involved. Force occupational health units will give advice and help in such areas and protectors such as gum shields should be considered.

Finance

Policy for reimbursing the cost of dental treatment varies, but for damage sustained while on duty the normal civil law remedies will apply and officers should seek advice from their Federation representative.

File 12.1 Teeth as living structures

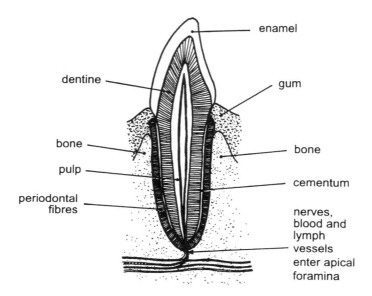

enamel

dentine

gum

bone

bone

pulp

cementum

periodontal fibres

nerves, blood and lymph vessels enter apical foramina

Teeth have their own blood and nerve supply. The outer coating is enamel which provides the hard protective shell of the tooth. The next layer is dentine which surrounds and communicates with the pulp, the nerves and blood supply at the centre of the tooth. The dentine is a much softer structure and once decay breaches the enamel it can spread rapidly through the dentine layer. If the decay reaches the pulp, the tooth will usually die and eventually an abscess may develop.

Adults have up to 32 teeth (this includes the wisdom teeth).

Wisdom teeth

Fewer and fewer adults now actually get their wisdom teeth. However if they do, there is a high chance that they may be impacted, that is, unable to erupt fully into the mouth. If this is the case, the gum overlying the teeth may become infected (pericoronitis) which is acutely painful and can cause severe swelling. A course of antibiotics will usually settle the symptoms, but it is often necessary to remove the teeth which may require referral to a specialist and a visit to hospital.

File 12.2 Repairing the damage

Once a tooth has started to decay, the dentist must remove all traces of damage leaving a hole in the tooth that has to be filled.

Traditionally, amalgam is the most commonly used filling material. Amalgam is a mixture of several metals and alloy. It is long lasting and functional. Other filling materials include gold, porcelain and white composite fillings. Composite fillings are obviously useful for front teeth and the new improved composite can also be used in the majority of back teeth.

A dentist may advise a patient to have a tooth 'crowned' or 'capped'. This may be for either functional or cosmetic reasons. A crown is often needed when a tooth has been heavily filled or has broken. Cosmetically, crowns can improve the appearance of discoloured, malshaped or malpositioned teeth. Veneers and bleaching can also be used for stained teeth.

Sometimes if decay has become very advanced or if the tooth has been damaged, the nerve of the tooth can die. This may in turn result in an abscess which may be treated in one of two ways - either by extracting the tooth or carrying out a root canal filling. A root filling (otherwise known as endodontic treatment) involves removing the dead nerve and sealing off the root canal so that bacteria cannot live inside the tooth. If bacteria are allowed to live in the nerve chamber another abscess (or infection) may develop.

If teeth are extracted due to abscesses or other reasons such as fractures, this will obviously leave a gap. Gaps can be unsightly or cause problems with eating. These gaps can be filled either using dentures or by more complicated measures such as a bridge.

File 12.3 Medical problems and medication

Certain medical problems affect the mouth. Diabetes affects a person's response to injury so problems such as gum disease would be more serious. Anaemia can appear in the mouth, often before it is discovered medically elsewhere. Other more serious illness such as leukaemia or even immuno-deficient diseases often manifest in the oral cavity. Some heart conditions may require caution before dental treatment can be carried out. Epileptics and people taking certain medications for high blood pressure can suffer from swollen gums.

13. Feet first

Podiatry - pampering your feet

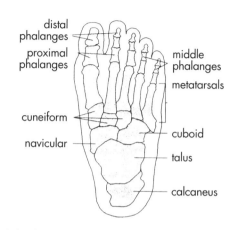

The foot is an amazingly complex piece of machinery which allows us to cope with some 8,000 to 10,000 steps per day. That amounts to approximately 2,500 miles per year - the equivalent of walking from London to Liverpool 12 times (or, for our Scottish and Welsh readers - Ayr to Inverness and Cardiff to Holyhead respectively.) In an average lifetime we can walk up to four times around the world - so how far will the beat officer walk?

To give ourselves the best chance of carrying out these quite amazing feats (pun sort of intended) in an efficient and pain-free way, it is important to look after our feet.

How the foot works

The structure of the foot consists of 26 bones forming 33 joints. One hundred and seven ligaments and 19 muscles hold it all together and allow it to move.

The bones of both feet make up approximately a quarter of the total number of bones of the body. This gives some indication of the importance of the foot (if we hadn't already realised) and the complexity of the structure.

When walking, the foot accepts the force of twice the body weight with each step. When running, this increases to a force of three to four times body weight. Consider then, that if you are 10 stone in weight, with each step the foot is accepting the force of 20 stone - and it is not doing this once a day, but 8,000 to 10,000 times a day.

It is little wonder then that the foot occasionally has problems. In fact, when you do calculations like this it makes you realise how efficient the body is as a machine.

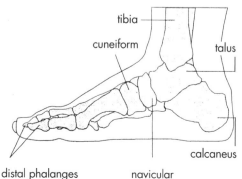

Not only does the foot have to cope with hitting the ground thousands of times in a day, but it has to be adaptable enough to allow us to walk up and down hill and on all sorts of terrain. Then, once it has adapted to the ground, it has to turn itself into a rigid lever to allow us to move forward onto the next step in an energy-efficient manner.

However, the unique engineering of the foot cannot always be perfect and things don't always function as well as they might. The fine tuning can be knocked off true by all sorts of things - from inherited features to accidents, from injury to surgery.

When things go wrong...

There are medical specialists who dedicate their professional lives to problems of the lower limb and foot - these are podiatrists. Research is constantly increasing the body of knowledge of the mechanisms of the function of the lower limb and foot. Podiatrists then take this knowledge and apply it to a variety of techniques to bring you comfort and improve the function of your feet.

In the next few pages I will be discussing some of the many problems that can affect the feet - and aim to give even the seasoned beat officer some tips on how to minimise the likelihood of suffering from these problems.

If there is one golden rule when it comes to footcare it is that if you are having problems with your feet - visit a podiatrist. In most cases it will take one visit and he or she will diagnose what the problem is, and be able to advise you accordingly. In common with other pieces of complex machinery, the more complex it is, the more there is to go wrong with it, so it is worth taking the time to get things checked out by the professionals.

Basic footcare

Feet have a pretty thankless task. We ask them to work for hours on end in hot, cramped spaces and after all of that we still don't always treat them kindly. Parallels with life in the office or patrol car are purely coincidental…

Here are a few tips to help get your feet through the day.

Treat your feet to a nice warm bath

Good daily hygiene prevents so many problems with your feet. Wash in warm soapy water, gently using a nailbrush to remove any debris around your toenails. Take this opportunity to reduce any areas of hard skin by carefully using a pumice stone or a foot file.

Take care to dry your feet thoroughly, especially between your toes. If the skin of your feet tends to be moist, rub surgical spirit on them after you have dried them with a towel. Surgical spirit has a further drying action and will remove any last traces of moisture. If your skin tends to be dry, use a moisturising cream to replace your own natural body oils.

Check daily for cuts, cracks, bruises, blister, redness and swelling

While you are getting ready to give your feet their daily dip, take a few seconds to check that everything is OK. The sooner any problems are noticed, the less chance there is of complications, such as infection, setting in. If there are any breaks in the skin, keep them clean and cover with a plaster.

Seek professional advice if you have any wounds which don't seem to be healing, and also if you notice any bruising or discoloration for which there is no reasonable cause. (If you drop a brick on your foot it is not unreasonable to expect some bruising.)

Give your shoes a day off

You have something like 250,000 sweat glands on your feet. They can produce four to six ounces (100-170grams) of sweat a day. All that sweat has to go somewhere - some goes into your socks and some into your shoes. Dry shoes are a much healthier place for feet than damp, soggy ones. It takes 24-36 hours for a pair of shoes to dry out - so have two pairs for normal wear and alternate them to give yesterday's pair a chance to dry out.

Look after your toenails

To prevent painful ingrowing toenails, do not cut them too short, and do not cut them down into the corners. The best way to cut your toenails is to use specially designed nail clippers (available at most chemists) and to cut your nails to follow the contour of the end of your toe. File any rough edges with an emery board (this goes for you too fellas!).

Get professional help

The proper diagnosis and management of small health problems can prevent them turning into big ones. A check up by a podiatrist can help you to avoid complications and keep you on your feet!

Common foot health problems

I hope that the following information will give an insight into some of the problems that feet can encounter, and what to do if your have the misfortune to experience any of them.

Sprains and strains

Ankle sprains

The term 'sprained ankle' is often used to loosely define any ankle injury. However, a true sprain involves tears in the fibres of the ligaments around the ankle. A sprain occurs when a violent twist or stretch causes the joint to move beyond the point of normal movement for that joint. The resulting excess 'stretch' placed on the ligaments causes them to tear.

Ankles can become strained in a wide range of situations. Walking or running on uneven ground, landing awkwardly from a jump, or wearing shoes inappropriate for the activity can all lead to a truly sprained ankle.

No matter how the sprain occurs, the symptoms follow the same pattern. This will usually include rapid swelling and bruising of the ankle - which may extend up the leg - stiffness in the ankle joint and pain and tenderness all around the area.

If you do have the misfortune to sprain your ankle, the quicker you can treat it the quicker it will heal. In most cases an ordinary sprain will respond well to RICE therapy:

Rest, Ice, Compression, Elevation.

RICE

Rest means get the weight off the affected foot as soon as possible, wandering around on a sprained ankle does it and you no favours at all.

Ice is applied to reduce the swelling and the pain. An ice pack or a bag of frozen peas or sweetcorn (broccoli is a bit lumpy) wrapped in a tea-towel should be applied for 15-20 minutes every two hours. Do not leave the ice pack on for any longer than 20 minutes at a time as the extreme cold may freeze the skin

Compression by means of an elastic bandage will help to reduce the swelling. Be careful that this is not too tight or it may reduce the blood supply to the area.

Elevation will also help to minimise the swelling, so get your feet up, preferably higher than the level of your heart.

It is always wise to seek professional attention if you have sprained your ankle so that the likelihood of any fracture to the bones can be eliminated. The sooner you can do this the better. I have been present in Accident and Emergence Departments to which many a person has come limping on an ankle they sprained a week ago and have been wandering around on, wondering why it is still hurting.

In most cases a sprained ankle, if treated promptly, can bear weight 24-48 hours after the injury and be fully healed within two weeks.

However, sprains do vary in severity and if the ligaments have torn away from the ankle entirely, the foot and leg will have to be encased in a cast to allow the ligaments to heal. This is usually for a period of six weeks, and on removal of the cast a regime of exercises to strengthen and mobilise the ankle will be needed.

If you find that you have a tendency to 'go over on' or frequently mildly sprain your ankle, you would be well advised to seek professional advice. In cases like this, it may be that there is a structural problem with your foot that is resulting in this weakness, and this can often be aided by insoles or orthoses to help stabilise your foot.

Achilles tendonitis

The Achilles tendon is the tough fibrous cord which attaches the calf muscles to the back of the heel. If the area around this tendon becomes inflamed and painful it is often referred to as Achilles tendonitis.

Most cases of Achilles tendonitis are caused by placing excessive stress on the tendon, by such means as:
▶ wearing high-heeled shoes;
▶ wearing boots or shoes that rub excessively in the tendon;
▶ uneven leg length;
▶ running uphill.

So watch out if you have one leg longer than the other, wear tight high heels and have to run up hill!

The symptoms of this uncomfortable condition include tenderness or pain in the back of the heel and a burning sensation in the heel that lessens with activity but returns during rest. The best way to deal with it is to avoid any of the factors which aggravate it, apply ice to the heel, and put a foam heel pad in your everyday shoes to take the pressure off the tendon.

If the symptoms persist after several days of rest and ice packs, seek professional assistance so the root cause of the problem may be accurately addressed.

Stress fractures

Stress fractures of the feet are most common in the metatarsals (see earlier illustration) and occur when the stresses placed on the bone exceed those with which it has the capacity to cope. Remember that bones are designed to cope with a lot of work but, like all of us, can crack under pressure or a dramatic increase in workload.

Such additions may be a sudden increase in your average daily mileage (either walking or running) or wearing footwear inappropriate for the activity you are undertaking, such as running on unyielding surfaces with non shock-absorbing footwear. If you add to this any exacerbating factors such as poor mechanical function of the foot and leg, then the stresses placed upon the bones of the foot are extreme and this can result in a fracture.

If you suspect that you have a stress fracture of your metatarsal(s), you will be experiencing pain and discomfort around the ball of your foot. This discomfort increases when you do any activity and the area will be tender to the touch.

Heel pain

Heel pain can also occur on the bottom of the heel, and is especially common in those occupations that require a lot of standing and walking - it is frequently referred to as 'policeman's heel'.

Medically, the condition is referred to as plantar fasciitis. The plantar fascia is a broad band of fibrous tissue which runs along the sole of the foot from the heel to the toes, and it helps to maintain the arch of your foot. If the plantar fascia becomes strained for whatever reason, this can result in pain in your heel.

If the problem is long-standing (there we go again!) it may even result in the laying down of extra bone at the point where the plantar fascia attaches to the heel bone, resulting in what is known as a heel spur.

The heel pain is often worse first thing in the morning or when you first stand up after sitting for a while. After a few steps, the pain lessens and may disappear completely until later in the day after you have been on your feet for a while.

Other causes, or contributory factors, include obesity, improperly fitted or excessively worn shoes, or a structural imbalance in the functioning of your foot which allows excessive stresses and strains to be place upon the heel.

'Policeman's heel' can often take six to 12 months to resolve and you would be wise to seek professional advice if you are experiencing this problem.

You need to seek professional attention if you are experiencing any pain in your foot, especially pain like this. As with any fracture, there is a risk of it not healing properly if left unattended, and this will result in not only a few weeks' discomfort but possible life-long problems.

If a fracture is suspected, an X-ray of your foot is pretty standard procedure. However, the fracture may not show on X-ray until a few weeks after you start to feel the pain. This is because the fractures can be so fine that they are not immediately 'visible'. A few days or weeks later, the body will be endeavouring to heal the fracture, and it is the characteristic changes that take place with healing bone that is actually picked up on X-ray. So don't despair if the X-ray does not give you an immediate answer to your pain.

Depending on the age and the severity of the fracture it will be necessary for you to rest your foot, and plaster may even be necessary.

Toenail problems

The main function of the human nail is for protection (and fingernails also help with fine manipulation).

Nails grow continually and fingernails grow faster than toenails. The rate of nail growth slows down as you get older - it can slow down by 25-30% in a normal lifetime. A toenail takes, on average, nine to 12 months to be replaced by new growth. Nails also tend to grow thicker with age, so you may notice them becoming slightly more difficult to cut.

Nails have a colour all of their own, and I am not talking about nail varnish here. The natural colour of nail is an opaque creamy white, but as it normally grows as such a thin plate

the colour of the skin will show through. As the nail becomes thicker its natural colour becomes more evident.

Not all of the nail is exposed - about a quarter of it lies beneath the nail fold. This explains why injuring the toe just behind the nail can be reflected in the nail growth.

The cuticle at the base of the nail also has a function. It provides a waterproof seal between the skin and the nailplate. If this becomes detached or 'pushed back' the seal is broken and this can allow various irritants and organisms to wash under and set up and infection or irritation.

Toenails do have their fair share of problems.

Black toe or runner's toe

This is basically bruising or a blood blister under the nail. It is a common problem and usually comes about because of injury to the toe or nail. This might be a single 'major' injury such as that caused by the heal of someone's boot - hint, it is not advisable to retaliate by kicking your assailant, unless you want to end up with double the discomfort!

However, it also may result from repetitive 'minor' trauma. The commonest form is caused by the toenail constantly stubbing against the shoe if it is too narrow or shallow. Runners often experience this problem as the foot drives into the front of the running shoes. Tennis, badminton or squash - and walking down hill - can cause the same thing to happen.

It follows that officers on the beat - or when involved in a chase - will be prime candidates for this sort of injury, and well fitting shoes should be high on their list of priorities.

The problem can be exacerbated if toenails are a bit on the long side. The front edge of the nail can catch in hosiery and, as the foot moves forward with every step, this lifts the nail.

It is painful enough if we receive a bruise anywhere on the body, but underneath the nail can be particularly uncomfortable as the normal swelling that accompanies an injury is restricted by the hard plate formed by the nail. This results in the build up of pressure underneath the nail.

If professional help can be reached with all speed, this pressure can be released by making a small hole in the nail to allow the blood to drain. However, this is only worth trying soon after the injury, otherwise the blood with have clotted. It might otherwise be necessary to remove the whole nail to ease the discomfort. This is a quick and straightforward procedure and can give great relief in a short space of time.

Please note that these are jobs for the professionals and self treatment should not be attempted as you are likely to injure yourself or cause further damage to the nail. Always seek assistance from a podiatrist, who will also be able to ascertain whether there might be an underlying fracture as well.

It is not unusual for a badly bruised nail to fall off of its own accord. If the tissues responsible for nail growth were damaged by the injury you may find that the new nail is thicker than normal. In most cases bruised nails just grow out - though this can take months.

However if you notice an area of discolouration beneath your nail which *does not* seem to be growing out - and may even be getting larger - seek immediate attention as it may be a skin tumour.

Ingrowing toenail

This is the old favourite of toenail problems - or not so favourite if you have the misfortune to experience one. Anything which causes the toenail to become embedded in the surrounding flesh will result in an ingrowing toenail.

If you are born with highly curved nails, or fan-shaped nails where the width of the nail at its tip is much broader than that at its base, you are at greater risk of getting an ingrowing toenail.

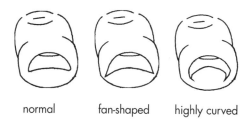

normal   fan-shaped   highly curved

They can also be caused by external factors such as ill fitting footwear. Tight shoes and hosiery squeeze the nail into the flesh, lose shoes allow the foot to slide forward and stub up against the upper which may physically drive the nail into the flesh.

Incorrect nail care may also be the culprit. If sharp corners or spikes of nail are left after nail cutting they can pierce the skin. Also if the nail is cut too short the skin at the end of the toe will roll up around it, so that when the nail grows forward it can go no where other than into the flesh.

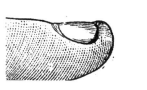

nail cut too short

nail with sharp spike

Ingrowing toenails can be extremely painful. The skin at the side of the nail becomes inflamed and it may also become infected which adds to the discomfort.

You really do need to seek professional advice if you are having problems with ingrowing toenails. Self treatment can often make things worse and increase the risk of infection. Once the skin has become perforated by the nail it cannot heal while the nail is still present.

One of the most effective ways of dealing with ingrowing toenails is to have all or part of the nail removed. I know this may sound a bit medieval, but it really is the best way to sort the problem out - and the podiatrists will use a local anaesthetic!

The tissues responsible for the nail growth will then usually be chemically destroyed so that the nail does not grow back and cause the same problems all over again. The whole thing will be over and done with very quickly - no hospital stay is required and there are no stitches involved.

Don't worry if your nail does have to be removed - its absence will not make walking difficult or painful.

What you can do to help

Careful nailcare is one of the best ways to avoid ingrowing toenails. Cut your toenails either straight across or so that they follow the contour of the end of the toe. Do not be tempted to dig down into the corners of the nail as this is asking for trouble. Also ensure that the nail is not cut too short or the skin at the end of the toe will roll up around the edges of the nail.

Avoid ill-fitting footwear as this can aggravate problems. If you are experiencing any discomfort seek professional advice.

Fungal nail infections

This is another very common problem to affect toenails. It is thought that three to five per cent of the population experience this problem, but it is quite likely that it is higher than this as the condition is painless and sufferers often do not seek medical advice.

Fungal nail infections, known as onychomycoses (on-ee-co-my-co-sees) are an infection of the nail bed which can also affect the nail itself. They are caused by various types of fungi, and can be associated with athletes' foot in which there is fungal infection of the skin.

The effect of the fungi is to cause the nail to change colour - anything from chalky white to dark brown. The nail may also become thicker and crumbly in texture. It is not uncommon for debris to build up beneath the nail and this build up can cause considerable discomfort.

What you can do to help

If you notice any changes in the colour of your nails you are best to seek professional advice so that a positive diagnosis can be made. Once a podiatrist has confirmed that nothing sinister is going on, then he or she may:

▶ advise you to use a daily routine of cleansing, filing and applying an over-the-counter preparation - usually a paint - to the affected nail;
▶ take a sample of nail for laboratory investigation to identify the particular organism causing the problem;
▶ if many nails are involved, consult with your GP and advise the prescription of tablets to treat the problem.

Even though your are receiving treatment for the nails, don't be too down-hearted if you don't see any immediate effect. Remember that it takes months for a nail to grow fully from base to tip, and although the treatment has been effective you will only see the real benefit when the nail gets chance to grow out.

What can I do to prevent the problem?

The ideal environment for these organisms is where it is warm dark and moist. So to minimise one or all of these factors is to minimise the chance of the nail infection thriving. Good foot hygiene and regular changes of footwear help to prevent these problems.

Foot odour and sweaty feet

Foot odour and sweaty feet are two very common, but none-the-less annoying conditions affecting the feet.

The 250,000 sweat glands on a pair of feet are continually producing sweat to keep the skin soft and supple - and to help with cooling - and can produce the equivalent of two egg-cupfuls per day. Some people sweat excessively due to an underlying medical condition, but usually there is no underlying problem, it is just the way the body works. However, there can be a problem associated with having sweaty feet.

The excess moisture means that the skin of your feet becomes water-logged and soft. It is less able to stand up to the rigours of everyday walking and can lead to cracking or fissuring between and under the toes, and blistering any-

where on the foot. Sweaty feet are more prone to infections, particularly fungal infections.

One of the most frequently reported problems of sweaty feet is the accompanying odour. This results when bacteria, which are present quite normally on the skin's surface, break down the sweat and old skin thus producing the chemicals responsible for the characteristic smell.

The warm, moist environment inside shoes, especially athlete' shoes, promotes the growth of the bacteria responsible for this.

What you can do to help

The best way to deal with the problems of sweaty feet is by diligent attention to hygiene. Wash your feet regularly and frequently - daily or twice daily washing in warm water using a mild soap is the best bet. Ensure that you make a point of washing in between your toes as bacteria tend to lurk in the toe spaces. Dry your feet well after bathing, as feet left soggy after washing have just the same problems as feet made soggy by sweat.

The use of products such as surgical spirit (which can easily be purchased over the counter from most chemists) and antiperspirant will also assist in keeping your feet drier and in better condition. These are best applied after washing and drying, and allowed to dry off before putting hosiery on.

Many people have used talcum powder to try and 'dry' feet out. Talcum powder has its place but its primary function is as a lubricant. It helps to reduce friction between feet and hosiery, but it does not reduce sweating. If too much is left in between toes it can even increase the likelihood of problems. A small moist pellet of talcum forms, and this actually holds moisture against the skin. The best way to use talcum is to put it on, then wipe off any excess, especially from in between the toes.

After you have made sure you have clean dry feet, the next thing to consider is clean, dry hosiery. If you have particularly sweaty feet you may have to change your hosiery twice a day.

If you wear socks, it is best to wear ones which have a high absorbency. Natural fibres such as cotton and wool always used to be the best recommendation, but some of the man-made fibres have their role to play.

Recent research and development has produced acrylic fibre socks which 'wick' away sweat. They were developed for the sports market and the best ones are of the loop-stitch design. This is where the lining of the sock is made up of hundreds of small loops of thread. Hill-walking socks tend to have this throughout the sock, whereas running socks may only have the sole and heal lined in this way - either design is OK.

The disadvantage of these socks is that they can be rather bulky, which is fine if you are in boots all day, but might not be the best thing to wear with an interview suit. If you are in a situation in which it is more appropriate to wear a thinner sock, choose the ones made from natural fibre.

The type of socks to avoid if you have sweaty feet are ones made entirely of, or with a high percentage of nylon.

The mention of nylon brings me to the subject of tights and stockings. These, by their very nature, are nearly all made from synthetic poor absorbency fibres. However, it is possible to purchase ones which incorporate a cotton sole, or, failing that, try cotton 'footsies' worn under the tights or stockings.

If you do have sweaty feet, avoid the temptation to wear footwear (other than sandals) without hosiery. The lack of hosiery to mop up the sweat means that the inside of the

shoes become very wet, and, although you may feel that 'getting the air' to your feet would help them get dryer by evaporation, the enclosed nature of full shoes does not allow this to happen.

Remember that bacteria can thrive in the moist environment of a shoe, so it is our aim to keep the inside of the shoe as dry and as clean as possible. It is far easier to throw a load of sweaty hosiery into the washing machine than to wash the inside of a shoe.

However, even with hosiery, the inside of shoes can get pretty damp. It can take between 24 and 36 hours for a pair of shoes worn for one working day to dry out. So, whenever you can, allow shoes to air out before wearing them again. Alternate between two pairs of boots or shoes.

If is is possible to wear open sandals without hosiery then do so. The recent development of the walking sandal has meant that they can be worn on pretty rough terrain. Maybe not the most appropriate while on duty but they are excellent for recreational purposes.

Athlete's foot

Athlete's foot is the common name given to fungal infections of the skin of your feet. A doctor or podiatrist may refer to it as Tinea Pedis.

A warm moist environment ideal for fungal growth can be found in areas surrounding swimming pools, showers and changing rooms - as well as in shoes.

Athlete's foot most commonly occurs in between the toes, especially between the little toe and the one next to it. If it is present, the skin between the toes becomes white and soggy and often peels. It is frequently itchy, and this irritation increases as the foot gets warmer. When the skin peels it can leave behind very red and sore skin. In some cases, small blisters, a few millimetres in diameter, form. The colour to the fluid inside the blisters ranges from colourless to brown, and again the skin become very red and tender if the skin over these blisters is broken.

The culprits are fungi which are present naturally on the skin's surface. They only start to cause problems when there is a break in the skin which allows the fungi to take hold and multiply.

If you have sweaty feet, it means that your skin is much more liable to crack and blister, and the breaks in the skin are ideal for fungal infections. Sports men and women often have sweaty feet due to physical exertion and, as such, they tend to have more problems - hence the term 'athlete's foot'.

What you can do to help

Athlete's foot is relatively easy to cure if you are diligent. Again the best person to advise you is a podiatrist, even if your are pretty certain what the problem is. Athlete's foot can look similar to some forms of eczema, psoriasis, or allergic reactions to dyes or adhesives in footwear.

What the podiatrist might do

This will depend on the severity of the problem. In the simplest instances, once a positive diagnosis has been made you will be advised on good foot hygiene. Daily washing and drying of feet and frequent hosiery changes as aforementioned will make the environment untenable for the fungal elements.

There are a whole variety of athlete's foot creams and powders on the market, and again, a podiatrist will advise you on the best to use for the particular problem. If the condition is more severe, you may have a skin scraping taken for analysis to determine exactly which fungal bug is causing the problems. In consultation with your doctor you may be prescribed prescription-only creams or tablets to eradicate the problem.

Blisters

Blisters are mainly caused when your skin is subjected to friction caused by rubbing on footwear or hosiery. The footwear or hosiery may be ill-fitting, or it may be that they fit perfectly well but that due to a mechanical problem in the functioning of your foot, one part or another is forced up against your shoe.

Once again, blisters are more common in people who have sweaty feet. The continual dampness results in loss of strength in the skin, so any stress causes it to blister easily.

What you can do to help

Whether or not you have particularly sweaty feet, it is a good idea to have a spare pair of socks (preferably clean ones) in the event of encountering flood, tidal wave or anything else that will give your feet a good soaking and so have the same weakening effect on the skin.

If you find that you regularly 'rub a blister' on one part of your foot, protect it by using a plaster or adhesive strapping over the area - let the shoe rub the plaster and not your foot. Just be careful not to put the adhesive part of the plaster onto any raw skin or it will be considerably more raw when you attempt to take it off!

Another tip to avoid blisters is to wear two pairs of thin socks rather than one of thick ones. So long as the pair worn against the skin are close fitting, the effect is that one sock slips against the other, rather than the sock rubbing against your skin.

Blisters are generally best left to resolve themselves, but if you feel you have to release the pressure from a blister, first wash your feet and then puncture the blister twice with a sterile needle, once at the top and once at the bottom. Do not be tempted to remove the skin from the blister. Once you have drained the blister, cover it with a plaster. Burst blisters, like any other break in the skin, are potential sites for the entry of infection, so not only will you have the discomfort of a blister but you will have the discomfort of an infection too.

Blisters also can result in reaction to extremes of temperature or to chemicals. It is therefore advisable to seek attention for any blisters you are not sure about.

If you do find that you regularly experience friction blisters on your feet, pay a visit to a podiatrist. It might be that the cause is due to a structural problem with your foot which is allowing excess stresses and strains on a part of your foot not designed to cope with them. If this is the case a podiatrist will probable prescribed insoles or orthoses to assist in realign-

ing some of these pressures. Orthoses are devices made specifically for your foot but sit inside your shoe.

Corns and calluses

Corns and calluses form where the skin reacts to excess forces being placed upon it by producing areas of thickened hard skin. This is an attempt to protect against those unwelcome forces.

Calluses are often pain-free, their role being protective. However, if the forces are too great for the tissues to cope with, the calluses become painful and may even form a harder type of skin tissue which is referred to as a corn. These can be extremely painful. This discomfort is the body's way of telling us that it can no longer adapt to the additional stresses and strains.

What can I do to help?

These forces I have mentioned may come from outside the foot in the form of ill-fitting footwear, or may be as a result of a problem with the internal structure of the foot. It is a relatively easy problem to sort out if footwear is the sole(!) cause. Wear footwear appropriate to your foot and the problems will be eradicated.

However, if it is an internal structural problem this can take a little bit more sorting out. As for recurring blisters, orthoses may assist in realigning the forces being carried through the foot. For the best results you would be wise to consult a podiatrist.

There are a variety of corn and callus treatments available over the counter, but I would be very wary of using any of them. They all contain acids designed to soften the skin to allow you to then remove it and get some ease.

This all sounds very well, but these acids do not distinguish between normal and hard skin. It is very easy to damage perfectly healthy tissue with these preparations, and they are only treating the symptoms, they are not getting to the cause of the problem. A podiatrist will advise on both treatment and prevention.

Verruca pedis

Warts can affect anywhere on the body, but on the foot they get referred to as verrucae - or more correctly verruca pedis (also referred to as plantar warts). They are quite a common but innocuous problem caused by a virus which is thought to enter the skin by an abrasion or cut.

Verrucae are much more common among people who go to swimming baths or gymnasiums with communal showers.

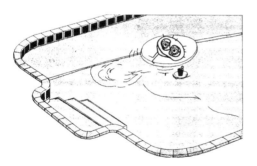

It is thought that the damp environment on the floors assist in transfer of the virus. Add to this the fact that the skin on your feet is damper than normal and as such is less resilient to cuts and scratches, then it is clear how the likelihood of contracting verrucae increases.

Most warts are harmless, even though they might be occasionally painful. They are most often uncomfortable if they occur on the weight-bearing areas of the sole, or where pinching from a shoe can occur. The type of discomfort experienced tends to be a sharp or burning pain at the site of the verrucae.

Verrucae are often mistaken for corns, but is also possible that a variety of other, less common but more serious skin lesions - such as malignant tumours - may be mistakenly identified as a wart/verruca.

Because of this potential problem of ID, it is wise to consult a podiatrist about any suspicious growth on skin change on your foot.

What do verrucae look like?

On the bottom of the feet, they tend to be hard and flat with a rough surface. This often appears to be white and soggy after bathing. They are often grey/brown in colour and in their centre there may be one or more pinpoints of black or dark brown. They can be as large as an inch in circumference, and they may grow in clusters.

If they are present on the tops of the toes or somewhere which is non-weight bearing, they appear to be much fleshier, resembling the lumpy wart that you may see on fingers.

Until they resolve themselves, verrucae can last for varying lengths of time - the average being 18 months.

What is the treatment for verrucae

There are a range of treatments available and once a podiatrist has made a positive diagnosis he or she will advise you on the best course of action for your particular case.

If the verruca is pain free and causing you no concerns - other than wanting to know what it was - the podiatrist may well recommend that no active treatment is required. Like any viral infection it has a limited life span and will eventually regress - that is to say, go of its own accord.

It is not uncommon for a previously painless verruca to become painful for approximately two weeks before regression. It is often during this painful stage that people seek treatment from the professionals!

If, however, it is decided that treatment is advisable, a podiatrist may recommend an over-the-counter preparation. These preparation are very similar to those produced for the treatment of corns and, like them, all contain acids which destroy skin tissue. These need to be applied carefully because, as mentioned previously, they are not clever enough to distinguish between verrucous tissue and normal skin.

old advertisement for a wart paint

A further cautionary note against the unguided use of these preparations is that if they are used on some of the skin conditions which mimic verrucae you will almost certainly make them worse, and in the case of a malignant tumour this could be potentially fatal.

If it is decided that more vigorous treatment is required, a podiatrist may advise cryotherapy. This is where the verrucous tissue is frozen to destroy it. The cold treatment lasts from 30 seconds to two minutes depending on the system used, and is usually performed after the podiatrist has removed the overlying hard skin with a scalpel.

This treatment may be slightly uncomfortable, especially during the thaw period, but does not last for long. The advantage is that if further applications are required it is only on a weekly or fortnightly basis as opposed to a daily one.

Chilblains

Chilblains are an abnormal reaction of blood vessels to cold.

The body's normal reaction to the cold is to cause a constriction or narrowing of those blood vessels which transport blood to and from the skin's surface. This ensures that we do not lose too much of our precious body heat. When the surrounding temperature increases, these blood vessels relax to allow blood to flow freely to and from the skin once more.

In the case of chilblains it is thought that the blood vessels which are responsible for bringing blood to the skin relax before those responsible for taking it away. This results in a congestion, a veritable circulatory traffic jam causing irritation to the skin tissues. In order to avoid this possible congestion it is always wise to warm up from cold slowly. Do not put your feet on the radiator or hot pipes - just warm them up slowly.

Chilblains often start in early winter, but may also occur in the spring if there has been a cold snap - it only takes one cold day on duty at a football match to result in a chilblains. They can affect any extremity - fingertips and earlobes are likely spots. Chilblains are however, most common the feet, especially the toes and heels and you may experience them on single or multiple sites.

The common symptoms are itching, redness and swelling. The earliest symptom may be the feeling that you have a splinter in your fingertip or toe, but there is nothing to see when you investigate. A couple of days later you may notice a slight change in the skin colour at the site, and it may also be swollen.

What you can do to help

In terms of treatment, it really falls back on the old adage 'prevention is better than cure'. Make sure that you wear warm clothing, and if at all possible avoid the cold and the damp. Wear many thin layers rather than one thick one - this allow air to get trapped in between the layers and provide further insulation.

Be careful though, if you are going to wear two or three layers of thin socks, make sure that you don't end up making your footwear too tight as this can cause a restriction in the circulation which may result in chilblains!

Anything which can affect the circulation can make you more prone to the discomforts of chilblains. Smoking can affect the circulation, both in the short term by causing narrowing in the blood vessels and by a thickening in the vessel walls. If you are a smoker, and you have problems with cold extremities, you will be doing yourself a multitude of favours by stopping.

If you do have the misfortune to experience chilblains, they usually subside in two to three weeks. However there are no hard and fast rules with chilblains. There are creams available to assist the treatment of the symptoms but really you just have to ride them out, taking the preventative steps mentioned.

As with anything foot-related it is always advisable to consult a podiatrist. What you think is a chilblain may, in fact, be something more serious and it is wise to get a positive diagnosis.

Footwear

When you consider that the entire body is supported by your feet, then shoes deserve some thought and time.

Tips for buying shoes...

▶ Buy your shoes in the afternoon rather than morning. If you have a duty in which you are on your feet for most of the day, they will have the tendency to swell slightly. If your new shoes feel comfortable when your feet are at their most tired, it might be safe to assume that they will be comfortable at all times.

▶ Footwear should be purchased and worn to match the activity it is intended for.

▶ Wear the type of hosiery you anticipate wearing with the shoes you are buying. Also try them on with any insoles or orthoses you may wear.

▶ Shoes should feel comfortable in the shop and, when trying them on, have a good walk around. Remember that you may be taking 8,000 - 10,000 steps a day so is really fair to your feet or your pocket to determine in five the comfort required?

▶ Always try on both shoes, and fit for the larger foot. If a shoe is slightly loose, any 'play' can be taken up with an insole. It is difficult, however, to make a tight shoe more roomy.

▶ Don't rely on the size of your last pair of shoes as feet alter in shape and shoemaker's sizes vary in width and depth.

Everyday footwear...

▶ The heel height should be no more than one inch. The higher the heel, the greater the pressure that is forced onto the front of the foot. This can result in the sole of your foot becoming painful and uncomfortable.

▶ The outsole of the shoe also has an influence on the safety and comfort of your footwear. Try to get shoes with shock absorbing soles.

▶ A more cushioned sole tends to be safer in terms of being non-slip as well. For non-slip effects, the material the sole is made from should be able to deform sufficiently to lock into the roughness of the floor. Nitrite rubber has been found to be the best of materials tested. The heel is the point the shoe first comes into contact with the ground. If the heel edges are rounded this increases its contact area and reduces the likelihood of slippage.

▶ Talking of slippage, with every step we take, our foot moves forward in the shoe. If the foot is allowed to travel into the front of the shoe unhindered it causes excess pressure on the toes, resulting in things like blisters, ingrowing toenails, corns and calluses. All these - as you will have gathered - are best avoided.

▶ The easiest way to 'hold' the foot is by having some form of fastening across the top of the foot in the form of laces or buckles.

However, we rarely wish to wear the same type of shoes when socialising as when we are working.

'Dress' shoes are often narrower and have a thinner sole - and ladies' shoes often have a higher heel. The features are not ideal for the ease and comfort of your feet and, while I am not suggesting that you turn up to the annual dinner dance in your trainers, I would suggest that you keep the wearing of such footwear to a minimum.

Shoe care

Having spent much time, thought and money on your new footwear, you want to get the best out of it. This is achieved by keeping shoes and boots clean and in good repair. Avoid excessive wear on heels and soles - get them repaired. If you continue to walk on worn down shoes your foot gets 'thrown' into an inappropriate alignment and this can result in stresses and strains on the foot.

The tread of your shoe should also be checked to ensure the channels are open to allow any liquid on the ground to be easily dispersed from underfoot and so minimise the chance of slipping.

Sporting shoes

Different sports activities call for specific footwear to protect the feet and ankles.

In running, foot movements occur cyclically, therefore the shoe is designed to accommodate and protect against the damaging effects of these repeated movements.

In court games such as tennis, squash and badminton, movements are more varied both in direction and speed, so footwear must have greater lateral stability. In football the ball may reach velocities of 140km/h, so the boot has to be designed with this sort of factor in mind. So for the best protection against injury, wear the footwear that has been designed for the sport.

Remember that the protective functions designed into shoes are lessened if they are worn beyond their useful life. The midsole of a shoe only last so long - the useful life on a running shoe is 350 to 550 miles. This means that if you are running 20 miles per week, you should be changing your shoes by approximately weeks 20-25 - less than every six months.

Walking

After all this concentration on foot problems you may feel that it is no longer worth going walking. Walking is wonderful exercise and has many benefits.

Walking can help to...

√ strengthen the heart and lungs and improve circulation;

√ prevent heart attacks and strokes;

√ reduce obesity and high blood pressure;

√ improve muscle tone in your feet. legs and abdomen;

√ reduce stress and tension.

All that, and beat officers are paid for it!

For general fitness, the best way to start is by walking 20 uninterrupted minutes at least three times a week. Walk at a steady pace, brisk enough to make your heart beat faster, and swing your arms freely by your sides. This not only helps with the momentum of walking, but it improves your breathing as well.

Looking after your feet means you are looking after your health.

Summary

So quite apart from being there to stop the ends of your leg from fraying, your foot is an extremely complex piece of machinery that deserves to be looked after with care.

I hope that the information I have provided will assist you in doing this, and remember that if anything does go wrong, always seek advice from the professional. One visit may save you from prolonged misery.

File 13.1 Podiatry

There is evidence of foot problems as long ago as 2,500 BC when footcare is illustrated on the wall of an Egyptian tomb. Given all the stresses a foot has to withstand in daily living it might be safe to assume that there have been foot problems while ever there have been feet - and long before there were police officers.

As is the nature of these things, if a problem does arise there is usually someone who finds they have the skills to assist in resolving that problem. The year 1593 brought first written evidence of a footcare specialist in England. From that time onwards, references to foot care and foot specialists become more frequent and , by the end of the 18th Century terms such as chiropodist, chiropedist, podologist and podiatrist were being used.

old advertisement for a foot care specialist

Chiropody (ki-ro-pod-ee) and podiatry (pod-eye-a-tree) are the two terms which have stood the test of time, and to many they mean exactly the same thing.

Others may draw a distinction between the two, in the sense that podiatry is an umbrella term which refers to:

'the specialisation in the structure and functioning of the lower limb and foot',

with chiropody (in this sense being skin and nail care) being just one aspect of a podiatrist's scope of practice.

Other areas which sit under the umbrella of podiatry include sports injuries; podopaediatrics (po-dow-peed-e-at-ricks) looking at lower limb structure and developmental problems in children; diabetes; rheumatology, and surgery. In actual fact anything which affects the lower limb and foot is of interest to a podiatrist.

To gain State Registration it is necessary to successfully complete three years at one of the recognised Schools of Podiatry. Currently all of these programmes are at degree level and many of the Schools also offer Masters degree programmes for qualified practitioners. Podiatry is also advancing in the field of surgery, with some practitioners specialising in surgery of the toes and the forefoot. The whole area of podiatry is continually developing with research into new ideas and treatments.

However podiatry is not a closed profession. That is to say anyone can call themselves a podiatrist or chiropodist whether they have had any training or not. Unless a practitioner has undergone the training described above they cannot describe themselves as State Registered, but it is still perfectly legal for them to practice. Currently there are moves to bring together the registered and non-State Registered sector to ensure that training can be standardised and regulated.

PART FIVE

STOP CHECKS

14. Checking your change

Examining your body for signs of the unusual

Changes to the body take place naturally as part of the ageing process - and also in response to lifestyle and environmental influences. Though some of the subjects in this chapter are more particularly relevant to later life, others can affect any age groups. Whatever your age, it is good practice and common sense to regularly check areas of the body which are particularly vulnerable.

Peace of mind is also important to your health, so if in any doubt seek a medical opinion. The earlier diagnosis begins the sooner treatment (if necessary in any particular case) can begin.

Dermatitis

Also see 'Controlling Over-reaction' (chapter 6)

Dermatitis, or eczema, is inflammation and irritation of the skin which develops through three stages. First, the skin feels dry and rough and can be itchy. Then the skin becomes red and inflamed and feels sore and very itchy. Finally, if left untreated, the skin begins to crack, weep or crust and is susceptible to infection.

Though it is unsightly and a nuisance to sufferers, dermatitis is not catching. People who suffered from childhood allergies such as eczema, hay fever or asthma - or have a family history of such - are prone to develop dermatitis. It can appear anywhere on the body at any time.

The condition is often caused by contact with irritants and allergens and many working days are lost because of it.

'Contact dermatitis' as it is known can appear at any time after exposure. It can easily be prevented by avoiding contact with the irritant or allergen - once the offending substance has been identified - which often requires a process of elimination.

Common irritants include

- acids or alkalis - oils (even oily rags in pockets can penetrate clothing), solvents and detergents;

- abrasive materials such as dust, fibreglass and cement - including abrasive skin cleaners.

Allergens include:

- nickel objects such as watches, fasteners and jewellery;

- fragrant substances (perfume, deodorants, after-shave and the like);

- shoe dye;

- fabric conditioners;

- some plants.

If a powerful irritant comes into contact with the skin, then wash immediately, rinse in warm running water and dry the skin gently on a clean towel or under a hand dryer.

Protective clothing can prevent dermatitis from a specific source or substance. If working with such substances, then gloves, visors or overalls should be worn when possible. Protective clothing should be clean and in good condition and worn only over clean skin.

Barrier creams can be useful to protect against irritation, but are not as effective as gloves when handling irritant materials. It is important to select the appropriate cream according to the substances handled. Using an after-work cream can protect against dryness. This is important because dry skin is more likely to develop dermatitis.

Cold weather or extreme heat, dry air and friction, all dry the skin and can result in dermatitis. Hobbies or occupations such as gardening, car maintenance, DIY or even cooking can bring the skin into contact with irritants as diverse as paint or citrus fruit. Working with the hands in water or other liquids as well as frequent use of skin cleansers such as soap or detergents, all remove oils and dry the skin which can cause or aggravate the condition.

Police protective body armour and other types of heavy clothing can cause sweating and rashes resulting in what is affectionately know as 'crotch rot'. If such rashes persist medical aid should be sought.

If small areas of 'contact dermatitis' get worse and become red, inflamed and itchy, a hydrocortisone cream may help, but this is best administered under medical advice. If dermatitis becomes widespread over the body, or becomes crusty or weepy, then you should see a doctor immediately.

'The big C' - cancer

Cancer is a fact of life. No society has ever been completely free of the disease. Although there are many positive things we can do to lower our cancer risk (see chapters 4 and 5 of Part Two 'Lifestyle'), there is always a chance that it may develop at some time in our lives.

Many common cancers can be successfully treated if detected early. That is why, after taking steps towards prevention, our next important defence against cancer is to get to know our bodies and be aware of the possible early warning signs.

However, many of us are reluctant, or fail to 'find time' to visit a doctor when we notice something suspicious. Medical experts believe that each year at least 15,000 more people with cancer in the UK could have been successfully treated if only they had seen a doctor earlier.

Cancer - the warning signs

As cells undergo changes that may result in cancer, some symptoms may be noticeable. Always remember that they are only possible symptoms of cancer and are far more likely to be the result of something much less serious.

However, to be confident this is the case, do see your doctor if you experience any of the following.

 if you have any of these symptoms:

√ a thickening or lump in the breast, testicles, or elsewhere;

√ changes in a wart or mole;

√ a nagging cough or hoarseness that goes beyond a cold or flu;

√ change in bowel or bladder habits, for example persistent constipation or diarrhoea;

√ persistent indigestion or difficulty in swallowing.

√ a sore that does not heal;

√ unusual bleeding or discharge.

Other general symptoms like unexplained weight loss, lack of energy or loss of appetite should also be taken seriously, especially if they accompany some of the more specific changes.

If you discover one or more of these physical signs, the golden rule is - don't panic, and consult a doctor. Once you have actually confronted the symptoms, you are half way to dealing with them.

A thickening or lump in the breast, testicle or anywhere else in the body

It is important to be concerned about an unaccountable lump. The majority are not cancerous, or harmful, but they should all be seen by a doctor immediately they are discovered. The sooner a cancerous lump is discovered, the higher the chances of successful treatment. Any lump or thickening, however insignificant it seems, merits prompt attention. Don't assume that harmful tumours are painful - sometimes they are, but most often they are not.

A significant change, in size or colour, of a wart or mole

Warts and moles are usually benign (non-cancerous). But if a wart or a mole that you've had for a long time changes size or colour, bleeds or weeps, or if you suddenly develop any new raised or irregular marks on the skin, see a doctor - it may be a sign of skin cancer. At this stage skin cancers can usually be treated quickly and easily and over 95% of such cancers are completely cured. The important thing is to get to your doctor right away.

A persistent, nagging cough or hoarseness

A persistent cough is the first sign of many respiratory problems, the majority of them non-cancerous. Such a cough is not normal however, and whatever the cause, you would benefit from medical attention.

A noticeable change in bowel or bladder habits that has no clear explanation

The rhythms of daily bowel and bladder function are easily disturbed. Most changes in the usual pattern are not serious or lasting and have nothing to do with cancer, or any other disease. Many people, for example, find they become constipated or have diarrhoea for a day or two if they eat certain foods, or when they travel, or when they're feeling nervous or under stress. This is perfectly normal and nothing to be concerned about. However, if there seems to be no apparent cause, or the problem doesn't clear up within a week or two, it is wise to see a doctor.

Again, this is unlikely to be a sign of cancer, but, whatever the cause, you will benefit from medical treatment.

Persistent indigestion or difficulty swallowing

Indigestion is a common problem that can be extremely uncomfortable, but it isn't usually a symptom of anything serious. You probably know which foods 'agree' with you and which don't. But if you have indigestion for several days for no apparent reason, you should see a doctor. Difficulty swallowing also has many causes, but it is none the less quite worrying and should be checked by a doctor.

A wound that does not heal as normal

Sores, cuts, bruises and scrapes take different amounts of time to heal depending on the type of wound, the age of the person, the strength of blood circulation and the condition of the skin. You probably have a good idea of how long it takes your skin to recover. If the process seems to be taking quite a lot longer than you would normally expect, that's the time to go to the doctor, just to be on the safe side.

Unusual bleeding or discharge

Not all bleeding, and certainly not all discharges, are a sign of cancer, but they do indicate that something is wrong. If continued bleeding or discharge have no obvious explanation, it is usually best to see a doctor. Women often have vaginal discharges for a variety of reasons, but the majority result from minor infections, not serious diseases. Rectal bleeding is certainly not normal (but it can be caused by several minor disorders); neither is blood in the urine or bleeding from the eyes, ears, nose or mouth. Any such continued bleeding or discharge that have no obvious explanation merit a visit to the doctor.

Any other unexplained symptoms

Tell your doctor about any other changes or unusual symptoms, however trivial they may seem. In all likelihood your doctor will be able to reassure you that your symptoms are not early signs of cancer. If the cause is not immediately apparent, further tests will probably be done in order to rule out the possibility of cancer. In the final diagnosis your problem is likely to have a far less serious cause.

Skin cancer (malignant melanoma)

The majority of melanomas develop in people aged 20 to 30 years onwards. Skin cancer is very rare before puberty, but can occur in children. It is found in both sexes, though more frequently on the legs of women and the trunk of men. People with red hair, fair complexions and a tendency to freckles are more susceptible.

There is a high incidence of melanoma among white-skinned people living in those parts of the world which experience regular excessive sunshine, for example, Australia and the west coast of the United States. Outdoor workers in these areas - including police staff - subjected to repeated episodes of sunburn are particularly vulnerable.

> Skin cancer is usually identified with changes to a mole, particularly if this is accompanied by:
>
> ▶ loss of the normal skin in the area;
>
> ▶ roughness, scaling or creasing over or around the mole;
>
> ▶ a change in the colour of the patch of skin in question;
>
> ▶ a brown 'halo' effect around the area.

if you notice any changes associated with a mole, particularly the following:

Changes in size and shape - One of the earliest suspicious changes is a alteration in the size, shape or thickness of a long-standing mole, or a brown spot which has recently developed over a period of a few months or weeks. Malignant growth may occur in all directions around a mole, or part of the mole itself may become wider or thicker or simply change its outline. Melanomas are usually characterised by having an irregular edge, a nodule area, ulceration and varying degrees of pigmentation.

Changes in colour - Another sign of cancer of the skin is that the mole usually becomes darker and patchy with some areas becoming almost black or having a purple hue. It should be noted, however, that some melanomas remain a pinkish-brown.

Bleeding from the mole - Frequent bleeding from a mole which is knocked can be a late sign of skin cancer. As tumour cells multiply, ulceration occurs and with even minor contact slight bleeding results and recurs whenever the scab is rubbed off.

Local or distant spread - The pigment produced by the melanoma may spread into the surrounding skin to produce a brown halo around the patch, or cause 'satellite nodules' (further multiple nodules) around the area in question.

The area in question is usually itchy though not particularly painful. Indeed so mild are the symptoms it is often the cosmetic disfigurement of a mole, rather than discomfort of its presence, that causes people to visit the doctor for investigation.

It should be remembered that skin pigmentation is associated with other diseases and does not signify cancer - though if in doubt you should consult a doctor as soon as your suspicions are aroused. Experience has shown that early treatment is the key to a successful cure.

Four main groupings of skin cancer

1. Superficial spreading melanomas - This is the most common type and may occur on any part of the body. It is usually thin with an irregular edge and has a variegated colour from pinkish brown to black.

2. Nodular melanomas - This type of melanoma is thick and usually protrudes above the skin, has a smooth surface and irregular outline. Tell-tale signs are that it is often ulcerated and bleeds regularly if knocked.

3. Lentigo maligna melanoma - This term is used to describe a malignant area which occurs within a larger area of skin pigmentation which commonly grows slowly on the face and neck in late adult life (60 years of age onwards). The cancerous area is thicker and generally darker in colour than the surrounding pigmented area and seldom ulcerates.

4. Acral lentiginous melanoma - This is a rare type of cancer which is usually seen as an expanding area of brown or black pigmentation on the palm, sole or beneath a nail - particularly of those of black African origin.

If untreated, malignant melanoma spreads through the lymphatic system of the body to the lymph nodes, causing enlarged lymph glands. Other symptoms, caused by secondary cancers to the liver, lungs and other vital organs, are weight loss, jaundice or shortness of breath.

Multiple skin cancers are very rare, although there may be multiple secondary nodules in the vicinity of a skin cancer.

Breast cancer

Breast cancer is one of the greatest fears of women, but it is worth noting that men too can suffer from breast cancer although this is much less common.

There can be many reasons for changes in the breast, but never hesitate to contact a doctor if you have any concerns - it is not a waste of anyone's time.

If there is a cancer present, the sooner it is reported, the more simple the treatment is likely to be. The most significant factor is that it offers greater prospects of benefit in terms of quality of life if diagnosed early.

Breast cancer is rare in women under the age of 40, though the likelihood of it developing increases with age. Women aged 50 or over are urged to take advantage of the National Health Service Breast Screening Programme which offers three yearly mammography.

This is an X-ray procedure which can detect breast changes at its earliest possible stage when treatment is usually simpler and offers the best likelihood of a cure. If you, or other female family members are over 50 and have not been invited to have a mammogram, ask a doctor to arrange one.

Before the menopause, normal breasts feel different at different times of the months. The milk producing tissue in the breasts becomes active in the days before a period starts. In some women the breasts feel tender and lumpy, especially near the armpits. After the menopause, activity in the milk producing tissue stops. Normal breasts feel soft, less firm and not lumpy.

Changes to look out for are:

√ Any change in the outline or shape of the breasts especially those noticeable from arm movements, or by lifting the breasts.

√ Discomfort or pain in one breast that is different from normal, particularly if new and persistent.

√ Any lumps, thickening or bumpy areas in one breast or armpit which seem to be different from the same part of the other breast or armpit.

√ Nipples - discharge - bleeding or moist reddish areas which don't heal easily - any change in nipple position - pulled in or pointing differently - rash on or around the nipple.

√ Puckering or dimpling of the skin over the breast.

It is important that men or women with any worries at all about breast irregularities should contact their doctor immediately.

Peace of mind is always important and, should cancer be diagnosed, remember that early detection assists treatment.

Prostate cancer

See also Pipes, Plumbing and Organs chapt 16 for a more extensive explanation of the prostate and possible problems which may occur.

The prostate is a small gland, found only in men, which plays a role in producing semen. Any inflammation or swelling of the prostate can block the bladder which can make passing urine difficult, or uncomfortable, or cause a change in bladder habits - for example a man may find he needs to urinate much more frequently than normal.

Most swellings in the prostate are not caused by cancer.

However, all men, but particularly men over the age of 50 should be aware of the possible signs and symptoms of prostate cancer. Most of these symptoms can also be caused by far less serious prostate problems, but all should be checked out by a doctor, just in case.

 Changes to look out for are:

√ frequent urination, especially at night;

√ any change in urinary habits;

√ the presence of blood in the urine;

√ painful urination;

√ continuing pain in lower back or pelvis.

The success of treatment for prostate cancer has improved steadily over the last couple of decades. Early diagnosis is of paramount importance. If diagnosed in the early stages there is a high chance that the cancer can be cured. And these days, even more advanced cases of prostate cancer respond well to treatment.

Sexually transmitted disease

We all catch infections of some kind at one time or another and Sexually Transmitted Diseases (STDs) are among them. They are not necessarily worse than the many other infections that are around such as measles or flu. What is different about them, however, is that they can cause serious and permanent damage to health if left untreated.

Some STDs can lead to damage to reproductive organs or to infertility in woman. It is therefore vitally important that all such diseases are diagnosed and treated as soon as possible.

Nowadays STDs are more properly called genito-urinary (or G-U) infections. There are at least 25 different infections, each of which can be spread during sexual contact. Just about anyone who is having sex can get an infection. Statistically of course, the more partners a person has, the greater the risk of infection.

 If you notice the following warning signs, you should go to the nearest clinic:

√ an unusual discharge;

√ sores or blisters for no explicable reason;

√ rash, irritation or lumps around the genitalia;

√ pain or burning feeling when passing urine;

√ passing urine very frequently or more often than usual;

√ pain during intercourse.

However, some people can have an infection and not notice any symptoms at all and many people with Herpes or warts virus do not get sores or lumps.

It is important for anyone who has reason to think they might have caught an infection to go for a check up as quickly as possible. That way, treatment can begin earlier when it is more effective.

There is a common infection called Non-Specific Urethritis which accounts for a great number of patients presenting at the G-U Clinics. (Urethritis is inflammation of the urethra.) Various germs may be the cause of this infection, however, a germ called Chlamydia is known to be responsible for most of these cases.

Chlamydia is one of the infections which, if left untreated, can cause a serious condition in women called Pelvic Inflammatory Disease (PID). This is one of the infections which can make women infertile. Symptoms can appear any time from a few days to six weeks after contact with an infection. Many women, however, do not experience any specific symptoms.

Other infections include Thrush, Genital Warts, Trichomoniasis (also called 'trich' or 'TV'), pubic lice (or 'crabs'), Syphilis, Hepatitis, HIV and AIDS. The latter three can also be contracted through infected blood and precautionary measures should be taken when dealing with drug users or other high risk groups *(see Staying Immune, Chapt 7).*

Again, the golden rule is that if there is the slightest suspicion that sexual contact may have been made with someone suffering from an STD you should go for a check up at a G-U clinic or see a doctor as soon as possible. Most hospitals have a genito-urinary clinic where confidentiality is assured.

High blood pressure

The terms 'high blood pressure' and 'hypertension' are two ways of saying the same thing.

Officers in particularly demanding roles should bear in mind that stress is widely quoted as being responsible for high blood pressure, particularly if there are other factors likely to increase their risk. Smoking cigarettes and being overweight are two of the major contributors.

It is a good idea to get your blood pressure checked regularly, particularly if any of the above apply to you. Most forces allow open access to their occupational health units for such purposes

Blood pressure measurements are normally taken when you are sitting quietly in the surgery, when the heart is beating at its normal rate. Casual resting blood pressure measurement can predict a patient's possible susceptibility to certain vascular diseases such as heart failure, stroke, coronary thrombosis or kidney failure. The higher the casual resting blood pressure, the greater the chances of one of these conditions appearing within a five-year time span.

Many people with high blood pressure have no symptoms at all and find it difficult to come to term with taking medication when they feel so well. There are, however, long term benefits from taking prescribed tablets regularly - treatment is a continuous business. If you stop taking prescribed tablets, your blood pressure will rise again.

So an otherwise fit officer with high blood pressure must adjust to the fact that he or she will have to go on taking tablets as a long-term treatment.

It is also a good idea to take stock of your general health. A 'sensible' lifestyle and a stress reduced schedule can do much to relieve high blood pressure. If controlled, the condition need not be too restrictive of 'normal' activities.

The following can help to relieve high blood pressure...

√ losing excess weight;

√ stopping smoking;

√ restricting alcohol intake to safe drinking levels and avoiding 'binge drinking';

√ reducing the amount of salt in the diet (especially not adding extra salt to food at the table);

√ taking regular medication prescribed for the hypertensive condition;

√ visiting the doctor regularly for blood pressure checks and discussion about levels of medication;

√ regular Yoga-type relaxation exercises.

Them bones

Exposure to the sun may be dangerous for the skin, but it is good for the bones. People who spend most of their lives indoors or who go out heavily covered seldom get enough sunlight for the production of vitamin D which is essential for bone health.

Therefore, regular weight-bearing exercises, a calcium rich diet and not smoking are important for bone health throughout life.

One of the most serious bone diseases is osteoporosis. All men and women are at risk and should take action to protect their skeleton. In particular, women should give serious consideration to hormone replacement therapy (HRT) to stop bone loss after the menopause.

In most cases osteoporosis can be effectively treated and prevented. However, the only conclusive diagnosis is to have your bone density measured. If you are concerned talk to your GP, you may be referred to a bone specialist.

Osteoporosis - those most at risk

men and women -

- who smoke heavily (or are exposed to long-term passive smoking) - this can damage bone building cells (and cause early onset of the menopause in women);

- who drink heavily - more than 21 units per week for women or 28 for men;

- with a low calcium intake - due to avoiding dairy produce or over-dieting;

- with diseases affecting the intestine, liver or thyroid;

- with a family history of osteoporosis - a parent or grandparent with a broken hip or other bone, or who had a curved spine or lost height when ageing;

- who use a high dose of corticosteroids over an extended period of time (NB - if under medical advice do not stop taking the treatment which may be essential for some other condition - but do talk to your doctor about compensating for bone loss with variations of dosage, or with vitamin supplements);

- who are disabled, and are wheel chair or bed bound - or elderly people who move around very little.

women -

- who have an early menopause (before 45 years of age) - this causes early loss of oestrogen as the ovaries stop working;

- who have an early hysterectomy (before normal menopause age of around 50) - early loss of oestrogen is likely and certain if the ovaries are removed;

- who have irregular or infrequent periods during their life - this can happen naturally or be caused by over exercising or over dieting which results in low oestrogen levels.

Waterworks

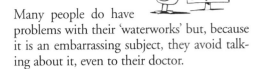

Many people do have problems with their 'waterworks' but, because it is an embarrassing subject, they avoid talking about it, even to their doctor.

This is a pity, because there are many ways in which help can be obtained. It is a more common problem than people think and something can be done to help. Too many people suffer in silence. There are several causes and nobody need be embarrassed to admit that they have a problem of this kind.

Trouble is signalled if you notice that you need to pass water more often, or you need to go very quickly with very little warning. Or it could be that you 'dribble' most of the time, or leak when you cough, laugh, sneeze or make some slight physical effort. This condition is known as stress incontinence and is a common problem experienced by women after childbirth, as well as later in life.

Fortunately, there are exercises that you can do to help strengthen the muscles which control the function of the bladder. Advice about this can be found at your local Health Centre. If you have a problem, try going to the lavatory every two hours whether you feel like it or not. That way your bladder will get used to this rhythm.

There are many ways of treating the causes of incontinence without having to undergo surgery, so don't be afraid to seek help and advice from your doctor or clinic.

Cystitis

Over half the women in this country suffer from cystitis at some time in their lives - often repeatedly. It is painful and uncomfortable and can be distressing. Symptoms include a burning sensation when passing urine, or a need to pass water more often than usual. Often, although you may feel desperate to go, there may be hardly any water to pass. Symptoms also include fever, an ache in the lower back or abdomen and cloudy urine or blood in the urine.

If cystitis is persistent or regular you should visit your doctor.

Cystitis is an inflammation inside the bladder. It can be caused by germs, allergic reactions or friction from intercourse. There is a lot you can do to relieve an attack.

To relieve a cystitis attack

√ Drinking a lot of fluid helps to flush out the germs in the bladder. Water is best but milk, orange squash, weak tea or any other bland liquid will serve the same purpose. One school of thought - backed by research - believes that drinking cranberry juice can help alleviate symptoms - but don't drink more than a litre a day!

√ Using hot water bottles helps to ease the pain in the back and abdomen.

√ Taking bicarbonate of soda (mix a teaspoonful with water or another weak liquid) acts as an antacid for the urine. (NB if you have high blood pressure or heart problems check with your doctor first, as bicarbonate of soda is a salt-based product.)

√ Taking mild painkillers if necessary.

√ Taking other preparations recommended by your pharmacist.

√ Making yourself comfortable in bed or in an armchair and relaxing.

Many women find these forms of treatment are effective after about three hours and can be repeated to advantage in three-hour cycles. If the symptoms persist for longer than a day or two then consult a doctor. In extreme cases the doctor will prescribe a course of antibiotics.

Pregnant women, and anyone who notices blood in the urine should visit a doctor irrespective of the suspicion of cystitis. The symptoms though very similar, may indicate something more serious and it is wise to have it checked out.

Men only...

See section on prostate cancer (ante)

 Men who have any urinary symptoms should go straight to their doctor.

Women only...

Menopause

Sooner or later every woman comes to the time of her life known as the menopause. All too often, it is thought of as being an illness or a sign of old age. Like pregnancy and puberty however, it is a natural stage in life that brings certain biological changes. No two women will react alike - each one will find different ways of managing the changes.

The menopause is the result of a gradual reduction in hormone levels until they are too low to bring on the release of an egg and the monthly period. It is simply a signal that a woman has come to the end of her fertile years It is by no means the end of her sexual life or the onset of old age!

It is impossible to predict when the menopause might happen. The average age for the occurrence is around 48 years of age, but the process usually occurs somewhere between the ages of 43 and 58.

Smokers tend to experience the menopause earlier than non-smokers.

In the past many women have been led to believe that the menopause is a time of misery when they will feel ill and suffer chronic depression. Happily all of this is highly unlikely to happen. The statistics reveal that almost one third of all women have a trouble-free menopause and another fifty per cent experience only slight problems. Only one in five women have problems which may necessitate them seeking medical help.

Hot flushes are the most common experience during the menopause - hot drinks or alcohol can exacerbate them. Some women wear layers of clothing so it is easier to cool off.

 If flushes of this nature become a severe problem, the doctor may prescribe HRT to regulate the condition.

However, as mentioned earlier, one serious side effect of the menopause can be osteoporosis. Fortunately, it is relatively uncommon. Unfortunately when it does occur it can lead to an increased risk of bone fractures. HRT can help and it is known that a calcium enriched diet also helps. It has also been shown that women who take part in some sort of regular exercises are less likely to develop osteoporosis.

15. You've got guts

Keeping your digestive system on track

Representation of organs concerned in digestion

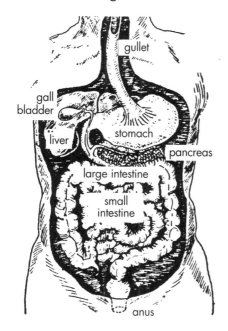

- gullet
- gall bladder
- liver
- stomach
- pancreas
- large intestine
- small intestine
- anus

Top to bottom

The human digestive system is an amazing piece of apparatus. From mouth to anus there are glands, tubes and sphincters of varying size and functions which co-ordinate their actions to yield energy, vitamins, minerals and water from what we eat.

Problems can occur from top to bottom and I will mention some of the more common and serious ones.

Lip conditions

The lips, commonly, can be a site for dry skin and infection and, rarely, for serious growths.

Particularly in winter and if out in all weathers, lips may dry out and crack, causing pain and bleeding. Protection rather than cure really is worthwhile here using moisturisers or purpose-made lip balms.

Swelling and blistering of the lips or sores at the corner of the mouth may be due to herpes. Ask your pharmacist for an effective cold sore remedy. Such infection will resolve itself, but can be cured much more rapidly if treatment is started at the very first sign of a problem.

More seriously, do not overlook the fact that lips are also sun exposed and can therefore be at risk of cancer or pre-cancer type growths.

See your Doctor if you find a sore or growth on your lips which seems reluctant to heal.

Sore mouth, tongue and lips

Mouth ulcers/infections

The common or garden mouth ulcer is known as an aphthous ulcer and the exact cause of these is unknown. They are usually small, multiple and recurrent and can be very painful.

As the ulcers resolve spontaneously in 4-15 days they do not usually require treatment, although steroid ointments, or lozenges have been tried. Local application of some 'over the counter' gels may be beneficial and advice from a pharmacist is advocated.

 or see a dentist, if an ulcer is extensive, deep or non-resolving.

Apart from ulcers (which are non-infective) there are organisms know to cause a sore mouth although they are generally quite rare.

Fungal infection with Candida Albicans (thrush) is probably one of the more common ones. The infection is opportunistic and may thrive during periods of stress or illness. It may also follow the taking of broad-spectrum antibiotics such as penicillin.

White patches on the tongue, throat and cheeks are seen which may form one large white sheet.

 Treatment for thrush is simple if a visit to the doctor is made and the cause can then also be investigated.

Sore tongue

A sore tongue can be a symptom of certain vitamin deficiencies, but these are rarely seen in fit people. More common causes are sharp teeth and hot drinks!

One curious condition is that of 'geographic tongue', where a sore smooth patch may occur from time to time, spread and then resolve. This condition is of no significance clinically and reassurance is all that is needed.

However solitary sores on the tongue which do not heal must be treated seriously. Smoking and alcohol are both risk factors for cancer of the tongue, which if caught early can be successfully treated.

 Long standing or deep sores, especially on the side of the tongue, should be investigated.

Mouth swellings, cysts and tumours

Swellings in or around the mouth are relatively rare. Blocked salivary or mucous ducts are the usual cause. A ranula is a cyst found under the tongue and often has a bluish hue. It arises by the above mechanism and is usually painless.

More painful is a blocked salivary duct or gland. The blockage may be due to stones, for instance, and manifests as a swelling (usually of the gland in the floor of the mouth) and pain after eating or smelling food. Sucking a lemon slice can be diagnostic as this classically leads to profuse salivation and thus exacerbation of the symptoms.

Unblocking a salivary gland usually requires surgery and a trip to the doctor is the ticket.

Infection can also affect salivary glands sometimes causing pus to leak into the mouth and swelling of the glands as well. The parotid gland sits in front of the ear and runs down to the angle of the jaw. It secrets saliva into the mouth at the back of the cheek by the top teeth. The Mumps virus is well known to cause both parotid glands to swell, giving the typical round face appearance.

Tumours can occur in a salivary gland - and classically the parotid gland is again the most affected - but these are extremely rare.

Painful swallowing

Painful swallowing can occur with severe sore throats and in rarer infections of the upper gullet. Ulcers or fungal infections (see earlier) can occur towards the back of the throat and even into the oesophagus, giving such symptoms.

Choking

Choking usually occurs when an object which should have been swallowed enters the windpipe causing a blockage.

Time is of the essence and prompt intervention can save lives.

Choking

what to do...

√ Encourage coughing the object out if possible.

√ Bend the subject over and slap him/her firmly between the shoulder blades with heel of the hand several times.

√ Check the mouth and remove any obvious debris with a hooked finger.

√ Repeat the backslaps.

√ Try an abdominal thrust manoeuvre: whilst standing behind the patient and gripping your fists together over the soft part of the tummy just below the rib cage.

√ Seek medical advice/help.

√ Manage any unconsciousness appropriately.

√ Continue backslaps and abdominal thrusts until help arrives, regularly checking the mouth.

'As part of the normal first aid training for officers this is one of the many life saving functions the "first on the scene" can perform.'

Food sticking

The sensation of food sticking on the way down is a less common complaint, but one which is significant.

Steadily growing tumours (cancers) of the oesophagus are the main thing to rule out in this situations although they are not the only cause. Strictures of the gullet due to injury or problems with the muscles involved can be to blame.

The most worrying history would be one of gradual onset problems of food sticking beginning with meat and solids and progressing to difficulty with sloppy foods and liquids. These symptoms, especially if accompanied by weight-loss, must be investigated by a doctor.

Oesophagus, stomach and duodenum

Problems within the gullet and stomach usually have similar manifestations. The main symptom are heartburn (dyspepsia), painful swallowing, or a sensation of food sticking on the way down (dysphagia).

Heartburn

Heartburn is a very common symptom. It is often felt in the centre of the chest but can spread to the neck and mimic angina-type pain. Bending, stooping or lying flat often precipitate the problem as do hot drinks, spicy food and alcohol.

Such pain may be due to an inflamed oesophagus or stomach or can even mask an underlying growth (the likelihood of such a serious cause for the symptoms increases with age).

Anyone suffering from long-standing heartburn (especially if over 40 years of age) should consult a doctor for investigation.

Depending upon the exact age and history of events, you will expect either to receive a trial of antacid treatment or undergo investigations such as a camera test to actually have a look inside the stomach (an endoscopy). The chances are that the symptoms will prove easily resolvable, although the long term use of antacid type medication without thorough investigation is not to be recommended.

Indigestion symptoms may be due to inflammation, a hiatus hernia, ulcers or (less commonly) cancers.

Peptic ulcers

Gastric and duodenal ulcers are classified together as peptic ulcers and are more common in men than women.

There is a higher incidence of peptic ulcers amongst professional men and executives - including police staff - probably caused by the greater stresses, strains and responsibilities they carry.

Domestic worries are another feature of peptic ulceration and there is an increased frequency of the condition among people who smoke.

The ratio of duodenal ulcers to gastric ulcers is 2:1 in the Western world. The majority of duodenal ulcers occur in people between the ages of 20 to 60 years of age, whereas gastric ulcers usually occur in people aged over 40.

 if you experience the following symptoms.

The main symptom of peptic ulceration is discomfort or pain in the upper abdomen which is felt through to the back and is often recognised as indigestion. It can vary from a vague and mild discomfort to a very severe pain which makes you lie down.

Generally if you have a gastric ulcer, eating will bring on the pain and you may find yourself avoiding food - and therefore losing weight - because eating seems to cause the pain.

Vomiting relieves the pain of gastric ulcer and you may find yourself forcing yourself to be sick after eating to relieve the symptoms.

By contrast if your ulcer is duodenal, you will have a good appetite and have a tendency to eat frequently because it relieves the pain.

If untreated peptic ulcers can perforate by eroding the wall of the stomach or duodenum. The subsequent escape of gastric acid or alkaline bile causes peritonitis which is extremely painful and potentially fatal.

Vomiting blood - peptic ulcers are the main cause of this symptom which requires urgent attention - unless it is just very small streaks following a bout of vomiting.

The bowel

The bowel incorporates both the small and large bowel. The small bowel is many feet long and is the portion of the gut from which vitamins and minerals are absorbed. The large bowel is a fraction of this length and serves to re-absorb water and form stools

Small bowel problems

Problems with the small bowel are rare, complex and often form part of a generalised illness. Crohn's disease (one of the inflammatory bowel diseases) and irritable bowel syndrome are two of the more common problems, the former fortunately being the rarer of the two.

Crohn's disease - is of unknown and probably multi-factorial cause. It often presents in younger people as abdominal pain, weight-loss and diarrhoea, although it can be more subtle. Unfortunately complete cures are not available and treatment options depend upon the extent of the disease. Mild cases may need only observation and diet changes, but very severe cases may require surgical management. Crohn's disease is not to be confused with irritable bowel syndrome (IBS), which is becoming increasingly diagnosed. Again the cause is multi-factorial, although stress has been particularly implicated.

Irritable bowel syndrome - encompasses non-specific abdominal pain, rapid gut transit times and frequency of bowel opening. It is probably due to spasm of some bowel muscle. Antispasmodics may be prescribed to good effect.

 If you do suffer from a persistent tummy ache, wind or frequent bowel motions a trip to the doctors would be worthwhile.

Large bowel problems

By far the most commonly affected portion of gut is the large bowel. The area is affected by infection and inflammation among other things, and it is in the large bowel in which nearly all bowel cancers occur.

The large bowel is short in comparison to the small bowel, but is of larger calibre. It is made up of an ascending colon on the right hand side, a transverse colon along the top and a descending colon on the left going down into the rectum. The appendix is attached to the large bowel.

Bowel cancer

Bowel cancer is the third most common cause of cancer death in the UK, after lung cancer in men and breast cancer in women. It is curable with surgery in the majority of cases if diagnosed early. The chance of contracting bowel cancer or colorectal cancer as it is properly known, increases with age - with the majority of cases occurring in the over 40s.

 if you experience any of the following symptoms.

√ an alteration in bowel habit (frequency or constipation);

√ bleeding from the back passage;

√ unexplained anaemia;

√ passing mucousy stools;

√ unexplained weight-loss.

The symptoms depend upon the site of the tumour and can often occur in other less serious conditions - in the majority of cases they will be due to something else. However, as bowel cancer is so readily treatable it should always be checked out. Even if, as will probably be the case, the symptoms are not the result of cancer, they still need investigation. A doctor may find a pre-cancerous polyp or growth which can be removed without surgery, thus preventing further problems.

The important thing to remember is that the above symptoms may have an underlying serious condition and must be checked out by a doctor who will arrange the necessary tests. A barium enema (x-ray of the bowel) or a camera test (colonoscopy) to visualise the bowel may be all that is necessary to save a life.

Inflammation

Crohn's disease - has already been mentioned in relation to the small bowel, but it can also affect the large bowel. It can lead to inflammation and ulceration of the bowel wall or abscesses around the back passage (anus). Again the disease can usually be controlled when it occurs.

Colitis - The other similar condition of the large bowel is ulcerative colitis and this too is another inflammatory bowel disease. It is confined to the colon, rectum and anus and can affect any or all of these parts.

 if you experience severe diarrhoea, often with bleeding and pain, which are the usual problems associated with colitis.

The condition does pre-dispose to bowel cancer and patients need careful follow-up.

Colitis may also be due to infection or of unknown cause. Some food poisoning leads to colitis and can give bloody diarrhoea with severe abdominal pain.

Infection and diarrhoea

As well as the above serious causes, diarrhoea may be the result of simply a fleeting infection.

Mild food poisoning often leads to vomiting or nausea and some diarrhoea (though more serious attacks can lead to bloody diarrhoea and colitis as aforementioned). Although such attacks often result in discomfort and listlessness, they rarely need medical intervention. Small children and the elderly are more likely to need admission to hospital than fit, healthy subjects.

The main problem to avoid is dehydration. Copious amounts of water should be drunk during any illness accompanied by diarrhoea or vomiting. Fruit juices, alcohol and fizzy drinks are best avoided. For symptom relief, there are many over-the-counter diarrhoea and sickness remedies available over the counter from your pharmacist.

 Food poisoning episodes should clear up in a few days, so any persistent symptoms should be mentioned to your doctor.

Constipation

At the other end of the scale there is the very common problem of constipation. It often affects young women and can be troublesome.

 Constipation in middle-age or elderly people should be thoroughly investigated, especially if it is not a long-standing problem or is accompanied by bleeding from the back passage or weight-loss.

In some, diet may be the problem. A regular intake of fruit, vegetables - and hence fibre - may be the answer. Failing this there are over-the-counter constipation remedies available (laxatives). These take the form of softeners and bulkers. A combination of both may be needed. Unfortunately some people are simply prone to blocking up once in a while.

Diverticular disease and diverticulitis

Generally a disease of the over 50s, diverticular disease implies that there are small outpouchings from the large bowel wall. The existence of these is very common, especially in the Western world due to our low fibre diets. These outpouchings are usually not noticed by the sufferer, although they can become infected or inflamed leading to what is known as diverticulitis.

 An appendicitis-type picture of symptoms can develop - with complaints of a temperature and tummy pain on the left side. Constipation is common during the episode and blood loss from the back passage can occur. As complications from diverticulitis can be serious, it is recommended that anyone with the above symptoms should consult a doctor, who may recommend admission to hospital for observation and antibiotics. Investigations such as ultra-sound scans may be necessary.

Appendicitis

Appendicitis is the commonest of all surgical emergencies. It is a myth that only the young are affected and it is a possible diagnosis in anyone with a painful tummy.

The usual story is a vague central abdominal pain slowly moving to the right, lower abdomen. The pain is usually accompanied by sickness, lack of appetite and altered bowel habit. In addition, these symptoms may be accompanied by a fever. Such symptoms must be referred to a doctor.

Appendicitis is simple to treat in the early stages and can be closely monitored in hospital. Sometimes immediate removal of the appendix is the treatment of choice, although occasionally scans may be done and the doctors may choose to wait and see what happens, or give antibiotics. Rupture of the appendix and subsequent severe internal inflammation needs to be avoided. The operation, if needed, is quick and relatively easy. The surgeons performing appendicectomies have had lots of practice due to the frequency with which the operation is performed!

The anus

Pruritus ani (itchy bottom)

Itchy bottom is a common complaint which often has no cause. Poor personal hygiene may be partly to blame as may sweating. Treatment may be as simple as keeping the area clean and dry.

 Itching in this region may also be as the result of haemorrhoids, worm infection or genital warts around the anus. Persistent symptoms or those associated with lumps or a discharge should therefore be investigated.

Haemorrhoids (piles)

Haemorrhoids can be considered as varicose veins of the back passage. They may occur to varying degrees ranging from transient and painless through to permanent and disabling.

Also called piles, they occur at all ages but are uncommon below the age of 20 years. Contrary to 'old-wives tales' they are not a result of sitting on cold walls. Rather they are the result of straining during defecation, or an abnormality in blood vessels within the abdomen. They are also common in pregnancy.

Symptoms include itchiness and mild bleeding from the anus - which is often noticed as a blood stain on the toilet paper or as a 'splash in the pan'. This is often accompanied by a palpable lump (prolapse) which occurs at the anus after going to the toilet and which may return to the rectum spontaneously or may need to be pushed back. Generally piles which only prolapse during defecation are not painful. In this way they can be distinguished from rectal cancer which causes pain when going to the toilet

When mild, haemorrhoids need no treatment.

 However, severe or troublesome haemorrhoids (particularly those which are big and pendulous and permanently prolapsed) will probably need to be resolved by surgery or injection at the doctors.

Peri-anal abscess (boil on the bottom)

The skin around the back passage is commonly affected by boils and some people are unfortunate enough to be prone to peri-anal abscesses.

 Large painful boils anywhere around the buttocks or in the cleft at the bottom of the back are probably best referred to a doctor. In minor cases a course of antibiotics may win the day, but in others surgery may be needed to ensure the resolution of troublesome abscesses.

Perianal warts

Perianal warts are found around the back passage and are caused by a virus which can be transmitted by sexual contact. Consequently they are often associated with sexually transmitted diseases such as herpes, gonorrhoea and syphilis.

They may also appear among people whose immune response has been depressed with steroids or other forms of chemotherapy. They cause irritation, discomfort and pain from rubbing and may ulcerate and become infected if not treated.

 The condition needs medical attention.

16. Pipes, plumbing and organs

Anatomy of the urogenital system

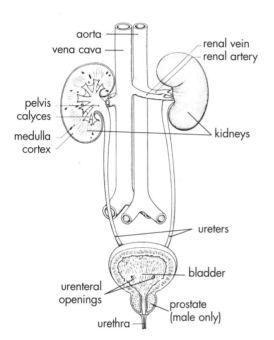

aorta
vena cava
renal vein
renal artery
pelvis
calyces
medulla
cortex
kidneys
ureters
bladder
urenteral openings
prostate (male only)
urethra

This chapter covers the kidneys, tubes, bladder and genitals and some of the more common problems are mentioned. The system as a whole is referred to as urogenital system. It involves the production and passing of urine as well as sexual function.

The kidneys produce urine and pass it down the urethra to the bladder where it is stored temporarily. Urine is then emptied via the urethra at a convenient time.

The genital organs in the male include the testes, prostate and the penis, and the female, the ovaries, uterus, cervix and vagina.

Kidneys

The renal function of the kidneys is vital to survival. The kidneys are solely responsible for the production of urine and hence the excretion of waste from the body. They govern the levels of toxic products left in the body and the amount of water lost or re-absorbed.

The amount of urine produced depends upon numerous complex regulatory issues. The concentration of chemicals in the blood, eg the amount of circulating salt, is one of the main factors.

As well as producing urine the kidneys play a part in vitamin regulation, especially vitamin D, responsible for bone growth.

Problems with the kidneys usually arise as a consequence of some other factor. This means that other diseases often have kidney function problems as a complication. High blood pressure and diabetes are two good examples.

See your Doctor

Kidney function problems will usually go unnoticed for many months or years, but can readily be detected by the commonest of blood tests at health check-ups.

Other problems can occur through direct causes such as infections or kidney stones.

Blood in the urine may be an early sign of trouble and *any* blood must be reported to your doctor for investigation.

Infection

Infection of the kidneys is called pyelonephritis and can be serious. It is usually the result of a simple waterworks infection spreading up the tubes from the bladder to the kidney. This is a good reason to get simple bladder infections treated promptly.

Symptoms usually include a very high temperature, back and loin pain and a shaky feeling. Bloody or cloudy urine may also be present. Treatment must be sought at the doctors. In bad cases, admission to hospital and a course of strong antibiotics in a drip may be needed.

Kidney stones

These are another cause of back or loin pain and their presence increases the risk of developing kidney infections. Small stones can pass down the tubes from the kidney and become bladder stones if they get that far. However, stones often become stuck on the way down causing excruciating spasms of pain called Renal Colic. If very small, these stones can pass all the way out of the body in the urine. Alternatively, they remain at various sites causing infections, blockages and pain.

There are several treatment options, some of which include no actual surgery. Stones can occasionally be broken up using special sound waves and the fragments subsequently passed.

Any loin pain or spasm-like back pains may be kidney-related and are worth mentioning to your doctor.

The bladder

The bladder is basically a muscular bag which acts as a reservoir of urine to make voluntary passage possible and convenient. It has a sensitive thin lining called the epithelium. As with most other organs the bladder can be subject to infection, inflammation and cancers. Stones can also be a problem in the bladder, as mentioned above. Again, bloody or cloudy urine may signify trouble with the bladder.

Bloody urine must be investigated. Infection is probably the most common condition affecting the bladder, but more serious things must be ruled out.

Infection

Bladder infections are more common in women than in men. This is for several reasons including a shorter urethra and the proximity of the urethral opening in women to the anus.

Personal hygiene and good fluid intake will help prevent bladder problems.

When infections do occur they usually lead to pain or passing water (dysuria), increased frequency of going to the toilet and smelly urine. Bloodiness and cloudiness may also be noticed as may a feeling of nausea or high temperature. At this stage (cystitis) infections are readily cured with antibiotics. There are several non-antibiotic cystitis remedies available from the chemist which rely on changing the acidity of the urine in the bladder. In mild infections these products can be a great help.

At the end of the day though, your doctor will be able to ensure the prompt and correct administration of an appropriate drug. Recurrent infections of the bladder should be investigated more thoroughly than simple one-off attacks.

Inflammation

Inflammation - which can cause symptoms very similar to the above - may be non-infective. Immediately following sexual intercourse there may be pain on passing water, but this is most probably transient and due to friction. Allergies and alcohol consumption can also cause bladder inflammation to a lesser degree.

Cancers

Bladder cancer is an illness of later life and is not uncommon.

Bloody urine is one of the most common symptoms, which is why any such episodes must be reported to a doctor.

Do not worry!

There are many causes for blood in the waterworks, but the doctor will probably want to be safe rather than sorry. Like bowel cancers, bladder cancers are often very easy to treat if caught early.

Investigation of urology problems will probably involve some blood tests, a simple X-ray and an ultrasound scan of the belly. More complicated investigations include X-rays involving dyes injected up the bladder pipes and a camera test to look inside called a cystoscopy.

Sex organs

Common problems for men

Impotence

Impotence is the inability to achieve or maintain a functional erection. It can be troublesome and soul destroying and is often self-perpetuating. It may be a physical or a psychological problem, but is usually curable.

A general practitioner will normally have advice on sexual dysfunction and will most certainly be able to offer advice and investigation. Urologists may deal with the more physical problem, whereas a sexual psychiatrist or psychologist may be best suited to helping psychological problems.

Help is available.

Prostate

The prostate is a small gland, about the size of a walnut, found only in men. It plays a role in producing semen, the fluid that carries sperm, but it is not essential for sexual activity, only for reproduction. The growth and function of the prostate gland is controlled by the male hormone testosterone. The prostate is wrapped around the upper part of the urethra - the tube that carries urine from the bladder to the penis. Any inflammation or swelling of the prostate can therefore block the bladder. This can make passing urine difficult, or uncomfortable, or cause a change in bladder habits - for example a man may find he needs to urinate much more frequently than normal.

 Symptoms include a delay in starting to pass water, a sensation of incomplete emptying of the bladder, a poor urine stream and an increased frequency of going to the loo. These symptoms can be a nuisance, causing disturbed sleep and compensatory changes in lifestyle. The end point of these symptoms is complete urinary obstruction i.e. the inability to pass water. Treatment of Prostate Hyperplasia (BPH) is relatively easy although it is a surgical procedure.

Prostatitis

Most swellings in the prostate are not caused by cancer.

In younger men the prostate may become inflamed due to a condition called prostatitis.

 Prostatitis can be unpleasant, but it is not serious, and can easily be treated with antibiotics. It is not cancer and does not lead to cancer.

Benign prostatic hyperplasia (BPH)

Around two million men over the age of 50 in the UK have prostate trouble. This is because in nearly all men the prostate gland becomes slowly bigger, especially after middle age.

This is usually due to another non-cancerous and easily treatable condition called Benign Prostatic Hyperplasia (BPH).

Prostate cancer

 It is important to be aware that prostate cancer causes similar symptoms to the less serious conditions aforementioned. So any noticeable change in bladder habits, or pain or difficulties experienced during urination, should always be checked by a doctor.

Around 14,000 British men develop prostate cancer annually and in recent years, there has been a clear upwards trend in the number of cases diagnosed.

This increase in numbers can be partly explained by the simple fact that men are living longer. Prostate cancer is a disease that develops most often in later life. This means that as life expectancy continues to increase, the number of men at risk of prostate cancer will also increase. These days prostate cancer is also being diagnosed more readily than in the past, causing the figures to rise.

File 16.1: Answers to the common questions asked about prostate cancer

It is important to appreciate that although prostate cancer is a growing problem, it is also a type of cancer that responds well to treatment - particularly when it is diagnosed in the early stages.

What is prostate cancer?

According to theory, prostate cancer, like all cancer, starts out as a single damaged body cell in the prostate which begins to divide at an uncontrolled rate. The resulting group of cells forms a lump - a tumour - in the prostate. Cancer cells may eventually break away from the original tumour and spread to other parts of the body. This is known as metastasis.

Are all lumps in prostate cancerous?

No. Most lumps in the prostate do not spread to other body tissues. They are caused by the non-cancerous condition benign prostatic hyperplasia, as described above. Generally this is not harmful, although it can cause discomfort and may need treatment.

Can prostate cancer be successfully treated?

Each case of prostate cancer is unique. Some very early stage prostate cancers, for example, present so little threat to health that they do not need any immediate treatment, just careful monitoring.

In general, however, a prostate cancer that does threaten health can be treated very successfully if diagnosed in the early stages.

Like all cancers, it becomes more difficult to treat in the alter stages, when it has spread to other parts of the body. Although the chances of 'curing' prostate cancer at this later stage are much reduced, effective therapists are available to control the symptoms.

What causes prostate cancer?"

As it is true of most cancers, no-one knows exactly what causes the cell damage that may lead to prostate cancer. However, scientists are currently investigating the role that genetics, hormones and aspects of lifestyle, such as eating habits, play in the development of this cancer. The following pages will discuss these factors and the influence they may have on prostate cancer risk.

Are some men more prone to prostate cancer than others?"

Yes. There are several factors that influence prostate cancer risk, but by far the most significant is a man's age. Prostate cancer is a disease that most commonly develops in later life. It very rarely affects men under the age of 50 and half of all cases are diagnosed in men over the age of 75.

However, prostate cancer can sometimes develop earlier on and the incidence in younger men has increased in recent years, which means that men of all ages should be aware of the possible warning signs.

Does prostate cancer run in families?

Studies have confirmed that if a man's father or grandfather has been affected by prostate cancer he may himself be more likely to develop the disease. This risk is higher if the affected relative is young (ie under 55) or if more than one relative has been affected. Research in the USA has also shown that black men are more likely to develop prostate cancer than white men. This increased risk is thought to be due to an inherited gene.

Far from causing anxiety, knowledge of a higher risk of prostate cancer should be seen as positive information and shared with a GP. A higher risk certainly doesn't mean that you are bound to develop prostate cancer, but it makes good sense to talk to your GP about regular screening for the disease. This will ensure that if you do have a prostate problem it will be detected early on, when the chances of successful treatment are good.

What is the link between food choices and prostate cancer?

A growing number of scientific studies suggest that, while age and genetics clearly play a role in prostate cancer risk, whether or not cancer actually develops may also be influenced by the foods we choose to eat each day. At first this may not sound like good news, but of course it is because diet is a risk factor we can control. In particular, many experts believe that eating a low fat diet, rich in fruits, vegetables and fibre, may reduce the risk of developing prostate cancer.

Are older men screened for prostate cancer, as women are for breast cancer?

At the moment there is no national screening programme for early detection of prostate cancer in the UK. Only men experiencing possible symptoms or those at higher risk, such as men who also have a family history of prostate cancer are routinely tested.

As prostate cancer is such a common disease, it may seem strange to have no screening programme in place. There are, however, sound reasons for this. Many prostate cancer specialists say that the detection methods currently available are not yet sophisticated enough to make widespread screening effective. They feel that national screening for the disease would cause a lot of needless anxiety and yet still not reduce the number of deaths from prostate cancer.

This is the subject of much discussion among doctors and health professionals and scientific trials are underway which may lead to more widespread screening in the future. In the meantime, if you are over the age of 50 and would like to be tested for prostate cancer, you can certainly ask your GP for a check up.

What are the symptoms and signs to look out for?

All men, but particularly men over the age of 50 should be aware of the possible signs and symptoms of prostate cancer. Most of these symptoms can also be caused by far less serious prostate problems, but all should be checked out by a doctor, just in case.

Be sure to visit your GP if you experience one or more of the following:

▪ frequent urination, especially at night;
▪ any change in urinary habits;
▪ the presence of blood in the urine;
▪ painful urination;
▪ continuing pain in the lower back or pelvis.

What should I do if I have any of these symptoms?

Don't panic. Remember that practically every symptom that could be a sign of prostate cancer also has a far less serious and more probable cause. But the only certain way to know what is causing the symptoms is to make an appointment to see your doctor. Whatever the problem, the sooner it is treated, the better.

What will happen when I go to the doctor?

After talking to you about your symptoms and examining you, your GP will arrange for you to have further tests if necessary, often at your local hospital. At the hospital a specialist doctor - a urologist - will usually take down your full medical history before carrying out one or more of the following tests - none of which should be painful.

Digital-rectal examination - The doctor places a gloved, lubricated finger into the back passage to feel the prostate and check for anything unusual. If a lump or hardening is found, the doctor may arrange to take a sample of cells to examine under the microscope. This is called a 'biopsy'. It is carried out under local anaesthetic and is quick and painless. It will help to assess whether a lump is cancerous or non-cancerous.

Prostate Specific Antigen (PSA) test - This is simply a blood test. PSA levels in the blood rise with age, but very high levels may also be a sign of prostate cancer.

Trans-rectal ultrasound scan - This type of scan shows a picture of the prostate. The size of the prostate can be measured any anything that looks unusual can be investigated. Other tests may also be carried out. Ask about anything that concerns you or any words or procedures that you don't understand. Don't be too alarmed if a lump or 'tumour' is found - it may be malignant (cancerous) but is more likely to be benign (non-cancerous).

How is prostate cancer treated?

The success of treatment for prostate cancer has improved steadily over the last couple of decades. If diagnosed in the early stages there is a high chance that the cancer can be cured. And these days, even more advanced cases of prostate cancer respond well to treatment. The kind of treatment a man receives depends on many different things; his age, his general health, the type of the prostate cancer, the stage of the cancer and so on. Nowadays men are also encouraged to be very much involved in decisions about their own treatment.

Occasionally, if cancer of the prostate is detected in the very earliest stages a doctor may recommend that it is not treated at all. This may sound odd, as most types of cancer are treated as soon as possible. However, unlike many other cancers, prostate cancer often develops very slowly. Sometimes it never spreads or affects a man's health. This means that it can be far better to keep an eye on the cancer through regular check-ups, than to undergo a therapy that may have side effects. Of course, if the cancer shows any signs of developing and threatening health, an active course of treatment can begin immediately.

Treatment options for prostate cancer include surgery, radiotherapy and hormone therapy. All of these may be used alone or in combination. If surgery is recommended then the prostate tumour, or the whole prostate gland may be removed. This type of surgery - known as a total prostaectomy - is relatively uncommon in the UK. Radiotherapy, which is used to shrink the cancer is more frequently used, particularly for older men.

If a cancer is more advanced then hormone therapy may be recommended. Hormone therapy works by reducing levels of the male hormone testosterone. Research scientists have discovered that, just as the growth of prostate cancer can be stimulated by testosterone, reducing levels of this hormone can shrink the cancer, help to relieve the symptoms and stop it spreading further.

All of these treatments are likely to have some side effects. Most are short term, though some can be permanent. Hormone therapy and radiotherapy, for example, cause temporary infertility and hormone therapy can cause impotence throughout the period of treatment. Removal of the prostate causes permanent infertility and sometimes, permanent impotence, although modern operating techniques make this far less likely these days.

File 16.2: The Men's Health Trust

The Men's Health Trust is a registered charity (No 1061184) set up in 1997. Its aims are to raise awareness of, encourage research into, and inform people about health complaints which only men can have. The following short article is taken from the Trust's free factsheets covering problems associated with the male organs. These factsheets also contain very useful information - including telephone helplines - about other organisations which help men with these complaints.

For further details about the Men's Health Trust, including how to obtain the factsheets, send an ordinary sized stamped addressed envelope to:The Men's Health Trust, PO Box 195, Bury St Edmunds, Suffolk IP31 3NQ.

This article is intended only o provide introductory information and should not replace medical advice or care. If you think you might be suffering from any of the following conditions you should not rely solely on the information below, but are advised promptly to seek qualified medical advice. While every care has been taken to ensure that the information in this article is correct, the trustees of The Men's Health Trust cannot accept responsibility for any errors or omissions, or for any damage or injury resulting from anyone relying on the information it contains.

Health problems relating to the penis and testicles

This short article refers to some of the health problems which men can have with what are commonly referred to as the 'private parts ' ie the penis and testicles. Medical conditions associated with the penis include Peyronie's disease, impotence, cancer of the penis, and priapism.

Most people (even including some health professionals) have never heard of Peyronie's disease, yet it almost certainly affects 100,000 or more men in the UK. One study even suggested that one per cent of men may suffer from it.

The reason for the ignorance surrounding this condition is quite simply the embarrassment likely to be caused by discussing it. Yet for many men it is an extremely distressing problem.

Peyronie's disease is the presence of fibrous plaques, like scars or hard limps, *inside* the shaft of the penis. As these lumps can't stretch, they result in the penis bending when it is erect. Some men may have a slight erection curvature which is natural, and not due to this condition; but Peyronie's disease bending can be very obvious, painful, and make intercourse difficult or impossible. Sometimes Peyronie's disease occurs in a mild form, and heals by itself within a period of up to a year or two. In others the symptoms are more severe and/or last longer.

The cause and cure of Peyronie's disease are not fully understood by doctors. There are various possible factors contributing to the condition, and more can be found out in the information contained in the Trust's Factsheet (No 1).

Impotence is not being able to gain or maintain an erection sufficient for sexual intercourse. Medical professionals sometimes call this 'erectile dysfunction' (or ED). There have been estimates that impotence affects one in 10 men over the age of 16 years - although as with all conditions of this kind, some men do not tell their GPs, and many even hide the fact from their partners - so accurate figures may be difficult to obtain.

The causes of impotence may be psychological or physiological, or sometimes a combination of both. However, as men get older, it is certainly not unusual to have problems in this area.

There are a variety of ways of coping with impotence, including psychosexual counselling, drugs, vacuum devices and, in some cases, surgery. More information can be obtained from the organisations listed in the Trust's Factsheet (No 2).

Cancer of the penis is a rare form of malignant tumour, which usually starts on the head or foreskin of the penis as a lump or ulcer. It usually grows slowly - although if it is very malignant it can spread quickly to the lymphatic glands in the groin.

Cancer of the penis can often be successfully treated if reported early, and it is important for any of the above symptoms to be reported to a doctor without delay.

Priapism is a rare complaint, suffered by only a few 100 men each year, and involves painful and prolonged erection.

Men who suspect they are suffering from this condition should seek medical advise urgently. Failure to take down the erection within four hours could lead to permanent impotence. (Men receiving injection therapy for impotence should already be aware of the increased risk of priapism.)

Common disorders of the testicle (or both testicles) in adult men include various forms of swelling, and the rarer testicular cancer. Although most forms of swelling may be harmless, incidents should always be reported to a doctor to rule out the possibility of a serious underlying medical problem.

Painless swelling includes varicocele. This is varicose veins in the scrotum (the bag that holds the testicles), sometimes called a 'bunch of grapes' in lay terms. It has been suggested that 10-20 % of men may suffer from this condition. Other forms of swelling are referred to in the Trust's Factsheet (No 3).

Testicular cancer may cause a swelling in the scrotum, and requires prompt medical treatment. Although it is still comparatively rare (about 1,500 new cases per year) this has been suggested as the most common form of cancer in young men in the UK, occurring mostly in those aged between 19 and 44. It is easily treated, and can be curable if dealt with at an early stage. It is therefore very important for men to check their testicles regularly, to detect changes which could be the early signs of developing cancer. For information see Factsheet (No 3).

PART SIX

ALTERNATIVE HEALTH CARE

17. Complementing the alternatives

An introduction to complementary medicine

In the past the medical profession viewed alternative medicine with suspicion and the practitioners of alternative medicine viewed doctors as prescribers of chemicals and users of invasive operations doing more harm than good.

A recent American movement which combines the two approaches is known as 'integrative medicine'. It encourages a burying of the hatchet in order to use the best of both worlds for the benefit of improved health. Conventional medicine now appears to be accepting the value of alternative treatments and at the same time the alternative practitioners are appreciating the need to validate their claims of effective cures by collecting and recording scientific evidence.

The opinion of the editors is that alternative medicines may help the body cope with minor ailments without resorting to non-natural remedies that may have undesirable side effects. But in the case of major ailments or possible major ailments, conventional medicine should always be the first choice.

The chapter examines everything from homeopathy to yoga and explores some of the lesser known alternative techniques.

Homeopathy and herbalism

These disciplines deal with the use of natural remedies derived from plants for the more common types of ailments. However words of warning are necessary before trying any of the following remedies.

Caution -

Only the plants that can be recognised with certainty should be used. If there is any doubt at all, seek the advice of someone more experienced in herbal medicine.

The use of any of these treatments is the sole responsibility of and at the sole discretion of the reader.

Always satisfy yourself of the credentials of the 'expert' or practitioner. Not everyone who sets themselves up in this field is actually qualified to do so. Cases for example have been cited recently of 'aromatherapists' using toxic levels of some essential oils

Having used 'the caution' it should be said that homeopathic remedies are generally less toxic than drugs bought from the chemists, and would cause less problems if children were to accidentally take them. Replicated natural remedies and pharmaceutical drugs can have unpleasant and potentially harmful side effects. There is less chance of such side effects from natural remedies. Both homeopathy and herbalism use these natural remedies which include, herbs, essential oils and honey.

Homeopathy vrs herbalism

The terms homeopathy and herbalism have different meanings and can be confusing to a person new to the world of natural remedies. While both these systems use herbs as the basis for their natural remedies, the difference lies in the way these remedies are prepared.

The herbalist uses formulae handed down from generation to generation, but also may improvise and mix different herbs together. As some medicinal herbs can be toxic, great care should be taken when venturing off the beaten track of lavender, thyme, parsley, dandelion, nettles, mint, sage, raspberry, blackberry, elder, figs etc.

The homeopathic approach is more prescribed and scientific. Medications are prepared to strict rules and usually only one remedy at a time is used. Using this strict approach allows them to use remedies containing very small quantities of poisonous herbs, which are believed to stimulate the body into curing itself.

This belief is called 'the law of similars' - that is that like is cured by like.

Therefore, a homeopathist will closely observe the symptoms of a person who is ill and will choose a remedy that will produce similar symptoms in a healthy person. An example of the 'similars' theory is quinine and malaria. In a healthy person, quinine in sufficient dosage, produces symptoms similar to those of malaria and as a result cures like with like.

When healthy people test the effects of homeopathic remedies, it is known as a 'proving'. Over many years many remedies have been 'proved' and the results documented. It is argued by homeopaths that such 'provings' are more reliable than conventional drugs testing which relies on animal experiments but which may react differently in humans.

A discipline similar to homeopathy is naturopathy. Naturopathists believe in looking at the whole person in order to cure an illness. This entails diet, exercise, fresh air, and being at peace with oneself.

Herbs

Herbs are plants of which the leaves, flowers, stems, bark, roots and juice are used for food, medicine, scent and flavour. They are drunk as teas, added to salads - and to bathwater - and used to make poultices.

Fresh herbs are the best if available (dried herbs are a substitute although these tend to be more concentrated in strength). However if you cannot identify or obtain fresh or growing herbs the next stop could be a health food or chemist's shop - though check for additives that could be counter-productive to the hoped-for remedy.

Essential oils

The concentrated essences extracted from plants such as lavender oil, wheatgerm oil, almond oil are known as 'essential oils'. They are very concentrated and can be diluted before use.

Aromatherapy is a technique in which essential oils are employed extensively. The aromatherapist will mix the essential oil with a base oil and apply through massage. Other uses include inhalation via steam for chest complaints, scenting a room with an oil burner, adding to bath water or using in a compress. Compresses can be hot or cold and are made by folding cloth, such as a cotton tea towel, and wetting it with an essential oil diluted in water, placing over a sprain or bruise and leaving to dry.

Honey, bees wax and royal jelly

Honey was the only form of sweetener readily available to ancient communities before the mass use of sugar cane and sugar beet. Honey has preservative qualities, inhibits the growth of moulds, inhibits bacteria but - of interest to those of you on diets - it is high in calories. One early use of honey was for dressing wounds. It kept out infection and protected the raw flesh until the body's healing mechanism took over.

Bees wax has some properties similar to honey, such as being antiseptic and acting as an air-proof skin barrier. The wax would allow skin moisture to pass through it when necessary. Other uses include as an addition to tablets and medicines.

Bees have provided another substance which is said to prolong and invigorate one's life - royal jelly. This substance is made by the worker bees out of pollen and bee hormones. It is fed to certain bee grubs which then develop into queens. It is these queens who go on to establish new colonies and the process is repeated *ad infinitum*.

However while some people swear by the benefits of royal jelly, other users have not noticed any change. Whether the believers actually benefit from the jelly or merely from mind over matter is debatable, but most chemists stock capsules containing quite a small percentage of royal jelly for quite a high price.

Common complaints and herbs used to cure or relieve the symptoms

Arthritis - ash

Bladder infection - horsetail

Boils - carrot, horse radish, ivy, mallow, potato

Bruises - comfrey, nettle, cowslip

Burns - nettle, carrot, mallow

Colds - basil, horseradish, marjoram, nettle, raspberry and thyme

Coughs - crab apple, garlic, horse radish, marjoram, nettle, sunflower and thyme

Cuts and grazes - cleavers, comfrey, peppermint, plantain, shepherd's purse and thyme

Indigestion - aniseed, basil, dandelion, ginger, lemon balm, peppermint, sage and thyme

Hangover - ginger

Headache - basil

Liver disorder - camomile

Menstrual problems - camomile, ginger, lemon balm, shepherd's purse

Sea sickness - ginger

Sedative - camomile, lettuce, sage and thyme

Sinusitis - thyme

Skin complaints - lotions of elder, horsetail, potato and raspberry

Sore throat - Aaron's rod, apple (crab apple), marjoram and thyme

Stings - plantain, tarragon

Temperature problems - basil, sage, willow

Urine retention - carrot, cowslip, dandelion and sunflower

Water retention - ash, asparagus, dandelion and nettle

Wounds - cleavers, coltsfoot, comfrey, horsetail and plantain.

See File 17.1 at the end of the chapter for details of the more common herbs and cures

For those who like the idea of using natural remedies and would like more detailed information, specialist homeopathic and/or herbalist publications can be found at most bookshops or libraries.

Acupuncture

This ancient Chinese therapy is based on the belief that vital energy flows around the body. This energy is called 'Chi', and must not be blocked or prevented from flowing. If a blockage occurs illness results or an organ malfunctions. To counteract the blockage, the vital life forces are stimulated into flowing again with the appropriate acupuncture treatment - the stimulation of 'acupuncture points' by fine needles.

An acupuncture point is the part of the body surface which is believed to be connected to an organ via a nerve. When the organ has problems, the patient can sometimes feel a sore part of the body surface. It is these areas that the acupuncturist stimulates with needles.

The body is covered with acupuncture points from which the Chinese have devised 12 groups. When the points of each group are joined with an imaginary line they form a meridian. For example the meridian for the heart is a line connecting nine points on the right arm from the little finger to the armpit. Stimulation of these separate points will affect the heart, but in different ways.

Nobody has come up with a scientific basis for the effectiveness of acupuncture. However, modern medicine generally accepts the efficacy of acupuncture, especially in the area of pain control. The effectiveness in relieving pain could be explained by blocking a sensory nerve message to the brain or by the fact that nerve stimulation encourages the body to make endorphins (a substance which helps control body pain).

One school of thought suggested it to be a form of hypnosis - although acupuncture seems to work with animals or while a person is anaesthetised. Another school felt that it was based on the body's electrical fields. It was found that the electrical activity at the site of an acupuncture point was quite different from the surrounding areas.

An acupuncturist diagnoses the appropriate treatment by - among other things - taking 12 pulses, six of which are in the wrist. The 'feel' of the pulse is used together with its regularity, rate and strength. This is where the skill of the experienced acupuncturist can be demonstrated. The pulse diagnosis reveals the points which need stimulating to achieve the desired result.

The needles are usually made of stainless steel for ease of sterilising and keeping sharp. There are many techniques involved in inserting the needles, but the acupuncturist generally concentrates upon the thickness of the needles, the depth of penetration, the amount the needle is moved once inserted, and the period of time the needle is left in place.

Most practitioners will only treat illness that can be reversed, such as 'nervous' ailments, headaches, menstrual, digestive and other similar problems. Conditions such as severe anaemia, kidney stones and other conditions requiring a course of antibiotics will not normally be suitable for treatment. The effectiveness of acupuncture as an analgesic (the removal of pain) has been used in operating theatres. Many such operations have taken place in China, but patients are screened as to their suitability first.

Reflexology - Closely akin to acupuncture is 'reflexology'. Here the meridians points of the foot are stimulated with the fingers or the ball of the thumb. The whole body is represented by a particular part of the foot and stimulation of the appropriate area of the foot should help to bring relief to the corresponding part of the body.

Shiatsu - an ancient Japanese therapy, uses finger pressure to help keep the body in harmony with its environment. The technique uses the acupuncture points on the whole body, but without employing the use of needles.

Massage

The much underrated massage treatment goes back in time to our earliest records. It is a treatment which has been used by many different cultures and especially by the Greeks, Romans, Chinese, Indians and Egyptians.

Massage gets some bad publicity from brothels purporting to be massage parlours but it should be pretty clear to members of police staff which are the genuine massage providers.

Massage aims to relax the muscles, improve the circulation, help the digestion, relax the mind, stimulate the lymphatic system and thereby help to eliminate waste products.

The taboo of adults touching each other, apart from in well recognised forms of social contact, makes it difficult for some people to accept the concept of massage. The professional masseur can overcome this taboo, for as in a doctor and patient relationship, a tacit approval is given to appropriate touching in these circumstances.

Partners, friends or relatives are quite capable of massaging each other and to a certain extent self massage can be effective. But the actions of

someone else's hands on the body coupled with the experience of the masseur can be therapeutic, enjoyable and relaxing.

Although there are many types of massage for different reasons, the average massage will start with gentle long strokes down the full length of the back or limbs. These will build confidence between the giver and receiver and can be used to apply oil or powder. Similar strokes will normally wind down a session of massage, but without the oil.

The in-between part can consist of one or more of the more invasive strokes, eg deeper strokes used for locating problem areas of tension.

Relieving tension

Kneading - This is working on the areas of muscles or flesh by grasping and lifting as if kneading dough. It is used on areas like the shoulders, hips and thighs to stretch and relax the tissues.

Friction - This is done by using the knuckles, finger-tips and thumbs to generate heat in the muscles. Deep direct pressure is useful for releasing tension. It can be used along the muscles of the back and shoulders. The knuckles can be used on the palms of the hands and soles of the feet to good effect.

Swedish massage - This includes slapping, clapping and hacking. Hacking is like a soft karate chop ie with the sides of the hands alternatively. Care must be taken using Swedish massage techniques as damage can be caused by becoming too enthusiastic!

Aromatherapy

Aromatherapy is a branch of massage that uses aromatic oils as a lubricant during the massage. The body and face are massaged using the essential oils extracted from plants. These are greatly diluted in the carrier oil.

The flowers, bark, fruit, leaves, stems and roots of certain plants are used, sometimes in vast quantities, to extract their essential oils. The price of oils vary depending upon the difficulties of production. For example over 200 kilos of rose petals are needed to produce one litre of rose oil compared with only 33 kilos of lavender flowers, for one litre of lavender oil.

Oils commonly used in aromatherapy...

Camomile - is used to calm the nerves and is suitable for sensitive dry skins.

Eucalyptus - has antiseptic qualities and helps to relieve bronchitis, coughs, colds and aching.

Geranium - an insect repellent, but useful for toning both dry and oily skins.

Lavender - is good for relieving headaches, insomnia, depression, acne, eczema, bronchitis, burns, colic etc.

Rosemary - is said to help the memory and thinking processes. It is also used for aches and pains associated with sport.

Sandalwood - an antiseptic oil used for dehydrated skin and acne. It has calming, sedative qualities.

To prepare oil for an aromatherapy massage, put two to three drops of essential oil to a 5ml teaspoon of carrier oil (or multiples of this quantity) and mix. Lower concentrations should be used on sensitive skin and on the face.

The Alexander technique

The Alexander technique is a method of posture training. It was devised by an Australian actor of that name, for the purpose of projecting the voice more effectively on stage.

Alexander found that a lot of people had developed bad and harmful postures, positions or movements over many years. His system required people to 'unlearn' their bad habits and replace them with more beneficial postures and movements.

All everyday postures associated with the police workplace should be examined. You may be obliged to stand on duty for long periods, spend all day in a patrol car, or sit behind a desk or in front of a computer screen. All these postures can be improved through the Alexander technique to put less strain on the body.

With practise the new postures will eventually become second nature. Back problems are relieved by this technique as are migraine, depression and neuroses.

Any officers or other police employee who would like advice on posture should ask their occupational health unit staff as a starting point.

Chiropractic and osteopathy

Chiropractic

Chiropractors use a manipulative therapy that is mainly concerned with spinal disorders. It is a drugs free treatment that relies on different types of leverage. The spinal joints are manipulated by hand to correct poor posture, to relieve pain associated with back problems and to help restore good order in the spinal and pelvic joints. In the main chiropractors deal with lower back pain, slipped discs and neck, shoulder and arm pain.

Osteopathy

Osteopathy is similar to chiropractic as it is concerned with back problems, but is not confined to manipulation of the area of the spine. An osteopath will manipulate the whole of the body to treat a problem.

Hypnosis

Hypnosis is the inducing of an altered state of consciousness. The patient voluntarily enters into a trance-like state of compliance usually experiencing deep relaxation. The hypnotist can alter a person's sensations and emotions. Medically it has been successfully used for stopping smoking; curing phobias such as spiders, dentists or heights; for asthma; insomnia; and for treating hysteria and states of anxiety. Pain, for example that experienced during a visit to the dentist or during childbirth, can be relieved by hypnosis.

Concerns about hypnosis are usually due to misconceptions. Firstly the subjects must be willing. They are aware of what is happening under hypnosis and can bring themselves out when they wish. It is not possible to remain under hypnosis or in a trance at the end of a session. The worst thing to happen would be to fall asleep and wake up naturally.

A Force doctor gives the following advise:

'As with most of these alternative treatments, it would be wise to consult your own doctor before using them. Apart from getting a medically qualified opinion, the doctor will usually know how to contact the particular alternative medicine practitioner you desire.'

Yoga

Yoga is intended to be a self-help system of health care for people of all ages. It improves physical flexibility, relieves stress and can contribute to the general well-being of those who employ the techniques.

There are eight disciplines in yoga, but the two main ones practiced in the West are the various postures and the breathing exercises. A posture has three elements - the bodily movement, the appropriate thought process and the required breathing exercise.

The more extreme physical contortions are not an essential part of yoga. There are many postures the new yoga student could achieve without undue stretching or twisting and with the help of a good book a lot of techniques can be self taught. However, to take yoga seriously a recognised class should be sought out as the more advanced postures could cause injury if not properly supervised.

A Force doctor's opinion is as follows:

'Yoga has something to offer most people and there are millions of practitioners worldwide. Not only does it provide physical benefits, but the mental 'mind over matter' control achieved by meditation. Yoga can lead to more graceful deportment, better use of the body in everyday situations, a better diet and better breathing.'

File 17.1 The more common herbs and remedies

Asparagus (Asparagus Officinatis)

Asparagus is recognised to be a medicinal plant. It has long been associated with the treatment of infection of the kidneys, urinary tract and gall bladder. It has also been used as a diuretic (something which promotes the discharge of urine) for water retention and dropsy (a disease in which watery fluid collects in cavities or tissues of the body).

The most noticeable connection between asparagus and the kidneys is the strong smelling urine of anyone who has recently eaten the vegetable. Modern day usage as a medicine is to chew tender young shoots raw or eat them cooked - either fresh or tinned - as an hors d'oeuvre to prevent water retention. When fresh tips are out of season dried asparagus' fern-like leaves can be used to make a tea. About 100 grams of leaves mashed in a litre of boiling water for 10 minutes will give the required strength. A cup a day before the main meal should help prevent water retention.

British asparagus can be found in the shops about May and June, but imports expand the season both ways. It can be established in most gardens that are reasonably warm and sheltered.

Basil (Ocimum basilicum) (USA - sweet basil)

Apart from being a well recognised culinary herb, basil is also a medicinal herb. It has been used for easing the symptoms of the common cold, fever and headaches. Migraine and headache sufferers have found that basil has a calming effect. A few leaves chewed each day are said to calm the sufferer and remove the tension that causes the problem.

Basil derives its name from the Greek *basileus* meaning King (in many kitchens it is the king of herbs). It has a warm, pungent scent which goes very well with tomatoes and is used extensively in French Provencal and Italian cooking. Dried basil can be used to good effect in soups and sauces. Basil is difficult to grow in cold climates, but can be grown indoors in a plant pot in a sunny position. Pick off the small white flowers as they show and the plant should keep producing leaves until autumn.

Blackberry (Rubur fruticosus)

The blackberry shoots are medicinal as they contain a large amount of tannin. These astringent shoots are said to be good for skin complaints and digestive problems. They can be pressure cooked (or steamed in some other way) and added to other vegetables which will make them more palatable. The mature leaves of the plant can be mashed in boiling water to produce a tea which can help with mild anaemia and debility or feebleness. About two cup fulls of crushed fresh leaves to one litre of boiling water will give the required strength. This should be left until cold and two cups can be drunk daily with a little honey to taste.

Caraway (Carum corvi)

Most people have heard of caraway seeds, which are still used in bread, sweets and cakes etc. They have a nutty toasted flavour and are used to make caraway seed-cake. They are also used to flavour sausage, goulash and cabbage dishes in Austria and Germany.

Medicinal use includes relieving stomach disorders and as an aid to digesting one's food. The seeds can be bought at most health food shops and the plant can be cultivated in the garden from seeds sown indoors in early spring. Caraway leaves can be used to flavour sandwiches and the root was ground and mixed with pastry to make a nourishing cake

If picking leaves from the wild caraway, great care must be taken not to mistake the plant for hemlock which has a similar appearance and is very poisonous.

Catmint (Nepeta Cataria x faassenii)
(USA - Catnip)

This plant is now normally found in a flower bed. Originally catmint was used as a calming agent, to relieve stomach cramps and as a constituent in remedies for colds and coughs as it is known to lower ones temperature by encouraging the eater to perspire. A drink can be made by using a cup of dried leaves to half a litre of boiling water. This should be left for 10 minutes and then sweetened with honey to taste. This tea can be used to ease stomach cramps and should leave the drinker with a general feeling of wellbeing. (As the name implies cats are attracted by its smell and appear to find it soothing!)

Camomile (Matricaria chamornilla, matricaria recutita)
(USA - Bowman, camomile)

'The camomile lawn' of book and film fame helped to revive this herb which has been in use since ancient Greek and Roman times. It is a hardy perennial and there are small and large varieties. This plant prefers a sunny position in ordinary soil. It does not tolerate areas of bad drainage in winter. All species can be raised from seeds sown in spring. Flower heads should be cut regularly to encourage side shoots. It is the dried flower heads that are used to make camomile tea. They can be purchased at most health food shops it you can't grow your own.

To make camomile tea, a tablespoonful of dried flowers should be brewed in a cupful of boiling water. The liquid should be strained off the flowers after ten minutes and is considered to help soothe menstruation pains and relieve kidney and liver disorders. It is also used in hair lotions and shampoos and as an additive to bath water (mash and strain into a jug before pouring into the bath to prevent plumbing pipe blockages!).

Comfrey (Symphytum officinale)

Comfrey grows wild along hedgerows and being a tall plant of around one metre, can hold its own amongst the grasses and smaller hedgerow plants. Its flowers range from blue to red to white. Its leaves, which if picked when young can be eaten raw with salads.

This herb can be grown from seed but care should be taken to keep it at the back of the garden because it needs a lot of space.

The leaves have been used to cover cuts and bruises and appear to promote healing. The root can be dried, cleaned and peeled and then ground to a powder and taken internally or externally. Internal use includes to relieve stomach ulcer symptoms and promote the healing of broken bones. Two tablespoons of the powdered root are heated to boiling point in one litre of water and then allowed to cool. This can be taken three times a day for three days, but care should be taken as it may act to purge the bowels. Externally a cloth soaked in the above mixture could be applied to an area of gout and a paste made from crushed roots is considered to reduce pain, swelling and discolouration of bruises.

Daisy (Bellis perennis)

To most people with lawns, daisies are considered a problem rather than a medicinal herb. The leaves can be eaten raw in a salad, or lightly cooked. Over the years the daisy has been said to relieve liver and spleen conditions, migraine, pleurisy and pneumonia.

Dandelion (Taraxacum officinale)
(USA - blowball, common dandelion, lions tooth, peasant's clock)

As a food the young leaves contain vitamin C and B and many minerals. The young leaves can be eaten raw with salad.

The medicinal qualities of dandelion centre around its diuretic properties. The plant was a treatment for dropsy (water retention in the body), liver ailments, kidney problems and urinary tract disorders. It has been used as a treatment to relieve gout pains and other conditions caused by an excess of uric acid. More recently a tea made of the dried plant is taken for general lethargy and to aid poor digestion.

To make a dandelion tea you need a cupful of the dried plant (the whole plant should be dried and chopped) which is left overnight in a litre of cold water. It should then be brought to the boil and left to cool. Strain off and drink a cupful at breakfast time. If it is taken later in the day it may result in extra urination during the night.

Dog rose (Rosa canina)

These are usually a single flowered wild rose and can be found both in hedgerows or domestic gardens. The plant has little medicinal qualities apart from the high concentration of vitamin C found in the soft outer cases of the rose hip. The outer cases when soft and ripe, can be removed and made into a puree. This puree can be made into jam, jelly or syrup providing a good natural source of vitamin C.

Elder (Sambucus nigra) (USA - Does not occur, but the sweet elder (Sambucus canadensis) does)

Elder easily seeds and is largely propagated by birds and other animals eating the fruit and distributing the seeds via their droppings. Grown both in gardens and wild in hedgerows this tree provides an abundance of both culinary and medicinal uses.

The elderberry makes wonderful wine, as does the elderflower. A word of caution is necessary when picking the berries as unripe ones contain a poison. Eaten raw, the berries are said to have a laxative effect. The dried elder flowers can be mashed in boiling water to produce a tea. This is said to be effective in promoting sweating and thereby reducing temperatures and for relieving the symptoms of nasal catarrh.

The young shoots of the tree can be boiled and are said to act as a decongestant for long-standing coughs.

Garlic (Allium sativum)

Apart from its extensive use in cooking, garlic contains vitamins, C, A and B, as well as minerals including calcium, iron and sulphur. It has been used for ridding children of worms and as a constituent of an Irish cough medicine.

Ginger (Zingibar officinale)

Although powdered ginger has been used in cooking in the West for many years, the ginger root has become more popular, perhaps as the Chinese and Indian influence has swept through Europe and the USA.

The medicinal qualities, include:

- calming effect on the stomach;
- An aid to digestion;
- A relief of gastric imbalance and flatulence;
- A way of calming the balance organs and thereby reducing the effects of sea sickness or other travel sickness;
- to reduce the effects of a hangover and nausea via a 'ginger tea';
- a remedy for dyspepsia (indigestion) via a strong 'ginger tea' which can be sweetened with a little honey;
- as a method of relieving period pains in cold weather via a very strong 'ginger tea'.

Lemon Balm (Melissa officinalis)

This plant is like mint in its growing habits. It has an invasive root system and if it is allowed to seed, lemon balm is unleashed! As with mint it should be planted in something to confine the root system, such as an old bucket with the bottom taken out.

A lemon flavour can be imported to culinary dishes with this herb and medicinally it has many uses. It is said to be good for the digestion; for nervous indigestion; for insomnia caused by heartburn; for colic (severe griping pains in the belly); and as a way of relieving pre-menstrual tension.

Balm tea can be made by mashing two cup fulls of the fresh flowering tips in a litre of boiling water. After standing for 10 minutes, the strained liquid can be drunk like a cup of tea.

This plant grows profusely in summer and to ensure enough balm for winter the leaves can be dried and stored. They can be dried in the sun or an oven and then kept in an airtight container.

Marjoram (Origanum vulgare) (USA - Sweet marjoram)

This pizza herb which is called oregano in Italy (and, rigani in Greece), has three common varieties. Pot marjoram will grow vigorously as the mint family and is a perennial. Sweet marjoram does not like cold weather and would probably not survive a British Winter. Wild marjoram which grows best in warmer climates such as Italy and Greece is the one used for pizzas. In the kitchen it has many flavouring uses such as for butter, omelettes and salad dressing.

The wild marjoram or oregano is the most valuable from the medicinal viewpoint. Like thyme, wild marjoram contains, thymol, the active aromatic oil which is so good for chest complaints. Thymol has an antiseptic effect, whether inhaled via the steam from the mashed herb or drunk as a tea. It has been found to be effective for relieving the symptoms of a head cold or a sore throat. The tea can be made by infusing two tablespoons of dried marjoram flower heads in one pint of boiling water. After standing for 10 minutes, honey and lemon juice can be added and the strained drink used while hot.

Nettle (Urtica disca)

This plant is the scourge of both adults and children for whom it lies in wait ready to release its formic acid onto legs and hands. Formic acid is also used by ants as you may have already discovered when picnicking or turning over on a sun bed and trapping an unsuspecting insect. The resulting irritating lumps can be soothed by rubbing the area with a crushed dock leaf or even crushed nettles.

As a food, nettles contain vitamin C and iron and other minerals and trace elements. Boiled young nettles make an interesting, healthy vegetable alternative and will no doubt cost nothing.

As a medicine, nettles have been used to relieve rheumatic pains by stinging the painful areas. Bee stings have also been used, although these practices are questionable requiring more research. As a tea, prepared by boiling the seeds and stems in a small quantity of water for 10 minutes, nettles can help relieve coughs and colds and has a diuretic and astringent effect. Over the years they have been used for treating chickenpox, gout and bruising. A soothing external treatment for mild burns can be made from mashing a tablespoon of dried nettle leaves in a cup of boiling water. When cool this should be dabbed onto the burnt area with cotton wool or a tissue. The utmost hygiene must be observed - only use freshly made lotion and the cotton wool must be clean.

Peppermint (Mentha x piperita)

This relative of the common garden mint is a vigorous grower and if necessary can easily be propagated from root cuttings. Combined with garden mint, peppermint makes a beautiful mint sauce to accompany lamb.

The herbalist has long known of the digestive qualities of peppermint. After dinner mints are a modern day example, but if indigestion is a problem the sufferer could be better off without the sugar of the after dinner mints. A dessert spoonful of peppermint leaves in half a litre of boiling water and strained after 10 minutes, will soothe away indigestion, especially when caused by over eating. As with any of these herbal remedies, if the symptoms persist, a doctor's advice should be sought. Cuts and grazes can be dressed with crushed peppermint leaves as the menthol and tannin content are disinfectants and help cool the injury and reduce the pain.

Sage (Salvia officinalis)

Sage is known as a healing herb, its name being derived from the Latin *salvere*, (to save). Its culinary usage is probably its most popular property. It is excellent for flavouring stuffings for poultry and pork. Butchers use it for flavouring sausage.

Over the years sage has been used for reducing temperature, for infertility and as a sedative. However, used in excess it can have an adverse effect on the central nervous system.

Tarragon (Artensusia dracunculus)

There are two varieties. One is a vigorous plant growing up to one and a half metres tall, but with not much flavour and it is known as the Russian Tarragon. The other, French tarragon, is full of flavour and is smaller, but requires plenty of sunshine. Tarragon is an essential ingredient of the French sauce *Barnaise*. It is also used in egg dishes, with veal and poultry dishes and along with other herbs in mixed herb dishes. A sprig of tarragon can be added to white wine vinegar to give the tarragon flavour to salad dressings etc.

Historically, tarragon has been used to soothe snake bites and scorpion stings. Today it is said to be soothing for wasp stings and mouth ulcers.

Thyme (Thymus vulgaris)

A walk through the hills of Provence in the South of France evokes the smell of thyme on a hot dry day. One of the main ingredients of herbs de Provence, thyme has a strong, warm resinous flavour and can be used in many dishes. It combines well with sage for poultry and pork stuffing; it is essential in a salad dressing; a must for casseroles and stews and puts life into various stocks.

As a medicinal herb it has been used as an antiseptic; an antibiotic; to relieve flatulence and indigestion; for coughs and colds; and externally in a lotion for dabbing on small cuts and grazes.

A thyme tea can be made by mashing one tablespoon of dried thyme in a cup of nearly boiling water. The preparation for inhaling is made a little stronger ie two tablespoons of dried thyme in half a litre of boiling water. The vapour should ease blocked sinuses etc. and the liquid can be used as a gargle.

Policing Your Health, first ed 1999 (UK)£10 (USA)$20
Stewart Calligan and Allan Charlesworth (eds)
is published by the New Police Bookshop (East Yorkshire)

Other titles from the same publisher...

The Custody Officer's Companion (UK)£16.50
revised second ed 1998, Stewart Calligan and Paul Harper

To order the above NPB (East Yorkshire) titles

please write with cheques payable to
The New Police Bookshop (East Yorkshire)
PO Box 124, Goole DN14 7FH

by the same author
Points to Prove, Stewart Calligan (Police Review Publishing)
Taking Statements, Stewart Calligan (Police Review Publishing)

Titles available from the New Police Bookshop (Surrey)...

Crime Patrol: to recognise and arrest criminals
first ed 1998, Mike McBride

Investigative Interviewing Explained
first ed 1999, Brian Ord and Gary Shaw

The Child Protection Investigator's Companion
second ed 1999, Kevin Smith

The Special Constables' Manual
revised second ed 1999, Tom Barron

The Human Factor: a guide to handling police informants
first ed 1999, Tim Roberts

Agricultural Vehicles on the Road: a guide to the legislation
first ed 1999, Andrew McMahon

Police Powers: an operational guide
first ed 1999, Alan Greaves and David Pickover

To order any NPB(Surrey) titles please write, fax, phone or e-mail

Brookland Mailing Services, Unit 4, Parkway Trading Estate
St Werburghs Road, St Werburghs, Bristol BS2 9PG
Tel 0117 9555 215 Fax 0117 9541 485
Email npb@brookservices.demon.co.uk

Please make cheques payable to the New Police Bookshop (Surrey)